the
four words
for
home

the four words for *home*

A memoir of two families

ANGIE CHUANG

WILLOW BOOKS
Detroit, Michigan

The Four Words for Home: A Memoir of Two Families

Cover photograph: Stephanie Yao Long
Author photograph: Corrine Duchesne
Cover design: Lynne Perri

ISBN 978-0-9897357-4-2

LCCN 2014933617

Willow Books, a Division of Aquarius Press
PO Box 23096
Detroit, MI 48223
www.WillowLit.net

To the two generations of women before me—my grandmother, Wai Po Hsiu Mei Chung, and my mother, Ling-shin Chen.

Because of you, I am.

Listen to the singing of the reed,
To melodies of plaintive separations:
"Many have cried of my despairing songs
As they cut me from my roots.
A listener I need,
One with a broken heart,
To whom I'll sing my songs.
He who from his roots is parted
Forever longs for reuniting,
For that which still must return."

—Jâlal al-Din Rumi,
From *Masnavi-e-Maanavi*

The names and some identifying details of Afghan and Afghan American family members, and those closely associated with them, have been changed for the family's protection.

Shirzai Family

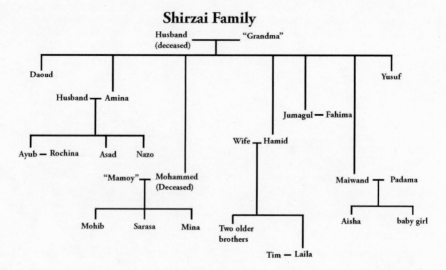

This family tree includes only family members mentioned in the book.

Prologue:
Six Syllables

In Kabul, we napped every afternoon, a two-hour siesta that made up for rising before dawn with the mosque loudspeaker's first call to prayer. As with most things in Afghanistan, naps were easy to enter, difficult to get out of. The soft breathing of the women beside me kept time, as their headscarves lay neatly folded next to them and their black hair tumbled over their pillows. Late-afternoon light filtered through gauzy curtains. The slide into sleep was liquid, unknowable.

Waking was another matter. The women tried to rouse me gently: A soft nudge on the shoulder. My name murmured in Pashto-accented English, as if through cotton batting. The nap never felt right, like I had gotten either too little or too much sleep. A dizzying chemical taste reminded me that I was on malaria pills. I always forgot where I was. Was I really in Afghanistan? Or at home?

Where was *home*, exactly?

It was 2004, about three years after I first met the Shirzai family in Portland, Oregon. They were Afghan immigrants who had brought me to stay with their relatives in Kabul. My deepening relationship with them had been, in many ways, easy to get into—the outcome of my newspaper editor's post-9/11 assignment to find a human face for Afghanistan. The Shirzais's invitation to travel to their birthplace two years later was an affirmation of my evolving role: first, as journalist; then, as friend and confidante; and finally, as good as family.

Two days before I left for Afghanistan, my mother called me, in tears, to tell me she was divorcing my father. It was a final acknowledgement that my parents' American Dream, which had begun in Taiwan decades ago, had buckled under the weight of my father's undiagnosed mental illness. I was only too eager to do what I always did when a family conflict arose— detach myself and run. This time, to another country, another family.

I felt safe and nurtured among the Shirzais's female relatives in the family's compound-style house. These women had treated me like a sister since the moment I had arrived. We cooked together, stayed up late talking, and laughed until we couldn't catch our breath.

But outside the home's walls, the city was hard on the senses and psyche, a swirl of dust, diesel residue, odors from the open sewers. Amputee landmine victims and dirt-caked, sickly children begged for *bakhshesh*; widows in filthy blue burqas silently extended hands out from under the veils. High school-aged boys, giddy with post-Taliban freedom, harassed women in the streets: *Marry me, Beautiful. Please marry me.* Even the catcalls still had fundamentalist overtones. Being out and about felt dangerous; although the Shirzai family treated me as one of them, I was still an outsider.

The disorientation of waking from Lariam-riddled naps, in a place that felt startlingly unfamiliar all over again, made me wonder what I was doing in Afghanistan, with the Shirzais. I wanted to be more than an interloper, more than an escapee from a fractured family. And why could I not, just once, wake from a nap and know where I was?

Then one day, I did.

It was a voice, not one of the women's, that brought me out of sleep that afternoon. It was faraway, male, chant-like in cadence. It got louder, then softer, then louder again. He sang the same six syllables over and over again. What was he singing? Why had I not noticed this voice before?

I had forgotten to wonder where I was. It didn't matter now. The women stirred, looked at me quizzically through sleepy eyes. Somewhere between quietly getting up, wrapping my headscarf around my head, finding my shoes in the pile outside the bedroom, tiptoeing across the courtyard, and cracking the courtyard door open to sneak a peek, the thought, *Oh, right, I'm in Kabul,* flickered across my consciousness. The voice grew louder. He was coming around the corner. In time with the chanting, cart wheels squeaked and strained. Something made a whipping sound, like sails in the wind.

Then, licks of blue, gold, fuchsia, and white teased the dusty sky and dun landscape like flames. And he was on our street. A pushcart full of fabrics—billowing from poles, folded in neat rows, nearly engulfing the wiry man behind it all.

"*Chador au chadori . . . Chador au chadori.*"

He was selling *chador*, headscarves, and *chadori*, burqas. On each corner of the cart, a post held a *chadori*, striated by dozens and dozens of tiny pleats, billowing in saffron, snow white, and dusky blue, the most commonly worn shade. The veils filled with hot Kabul air to assume the ambiguous forms of their future wearers. I studied the oval mesh face-screens at the tops of each one, as opaque and inscrutable as they were when actual women were behind them. The borders of the screens were embroidered with repeating floral patterns, works of delicate craftsmanship. Then the wind picked up, and the hanging ghost-women evaporated as the veils became flags, horizontal in the breeze.

"*Chador au chadori . . .*"

The walnut-skinned man wore a white prayer cap. His baritone was languid, his R's liquid, and the rising and falling notes of his tune so familiar. Had I heard him before, in my sleep? As he approached, I slipped behind the front door; a scarf and veil salesman surely would expect female modesty. But just after he passed, one more look.

"*Chador au chadori . . .*"

As he disappeared from sight, the voice faded. I *had* heard the tune before. My grandparents lived in Taoyuan, a mid-sized city in Taiwan's north. It was near my mother's birthplace and the city where my father had grown up. I had visited this area intermittently since I was two years old. I had been born in San Francisco, but Taiwan, more than I realized at that time, was part of who I was: the damp, tropical air; people speaking Mandarin with accents like my parents'; bitter scents of Chinese greens and ferric wafting from organ meats at the outdoor market.

For as long as I can remember, every morning in Taoyuan the same chant rang out over and over, carried by a tinny amplifier, often muffled by rainfall. The voice was female, and I can't say if it belonged to the same woman for all those years. But the words and the tune were always the same:

"*Man to bau, man to bau . . . Man to bau, man to bau . . .*"

The woman pushed a cart full of *man to*, steamed rolls, and *bau*, stuffed breads, around the perimeter of the outdoor market. Her deep voice rose and dipped, stretching out the round vowels. The chant faded and grew as she made her way around the neighborhood. I saw her once, in a conical straw hat and with a weathered face the color of weak Oolong tea. Her cart was packed with round, stacking stainless-steel containers full of those creamy white rolls, each as big as a fist. The steaming dough trailed milky-sweet clouds in her wake.

"Man to bau, man to bau . . . "

"Chador au chadori . . . "

The six-syllable, rising-and-falling cadences of her cry and his chant were echoes of each other. Different languages, different products; same song, same notes. Was it just that these two countries, in their varying trajectories toward modernity, still had economies that supported chanting, cart-pushing street vendors? Perhaps.

But to me, those six syllables were about one thing: home. As my childhood home was divided by my parents' impending divorce, I finally felt at home in Kabul. I could link the scarf-and-veil salesman's chant with something familiar, something essential to who I was, to the family and culture that defined me. Taoyuan, Taiwan, was not my home, had never been, any more than Kabul, Afghanistan, was. I wouldn't have called Portland, Oregon, home either, though I lived there at the time, and the San Francisco Bay Area might have been the closest, but I always had hesitated to claim it as my own.

In that moment of connection, I could hear both street vendors so clearly in my head they could have both been just outside the door. In my remaining time in Kabul, I heard the scarf and veil salesman a few more times, always upon waking from my nap. Once, I peered out the front door to get another glimpse of him; other times, I just languished, half asleep. I never again woke up feeling dislocated in Kabul.

I returned to the United States knowing I had to mine that connection—to know where Kabul and Taoyuan, the Shirzais and my own family, intersected. As the Shirzais themselves struggled to resolve dissonances between homeland and home, Afghanistan and America, I faced my own ragged edges as the daughter of immigrants and the inheritor of my Chinese family's American journey. In telling these two stories, of the Shirzais and the Chuangs, I came to better understand Afghanistan, America, myself—and my own limitations as a storyteller, friend, and daughter.

I came to see that home was not a place on the map. It was a state of being, of connecting. I ultimately had to get as far away from home as I could in order to truly find it, reflected in a family who opened their lives, their hearts, and all of their homes—in America and Afghanistan—to me.

Part One:

Kor / House

Everyone in the city lived in a compound, a yard surrounded by walls that divided the world into a public and a private realm . . . Those who came from the West didn't even know our private universe existed, or that life inside it was warm and sweet. And in a way, we Afghans didn't know we had this realm either, because we didn't know it was possible not to have it.

—Tamim Ansary, *West of Kabul, East of New York*

1.
Leaving

The phone rang, that insistent electronic bleat of the last generation of cordless land phones. I was sitting on my bed amidst a pile of supplies: two large headscarves (on loan from the Shirzais); *Crosslines Field Guide to Conflict Zones*; spiral-bound reporter's notebooks; remedies and preventative medicine for every imaginable malady, including four sheets of blister-packed anti-malarial pills, one for each week.

I climbed over the carefully constructed nest, over the rugged roller bag-backpack combo on the floor, over folded stacks of *shalwar kameez* outfits.

My hand hovered over the receiver. It bleated once more. I knew before I wrested it from its cradle that it would be my mother calling about my father. And I knew that she would be crying.

Silence followed my hello. A moist, labored breath.

"Mom," I said. My stomach lurched. Was I dreading what was coming? Or was this a side effect of the anti-malarial Lariam I had started taking a week ago? Among its side effects were dry mouth, dizziness, vivid dreams, and a "sense of impending doom." I had the first three, but the last was difficult to untangle from the fact that I was about to board a plane to Kabul, Afghanistan. And that my family, a few hundred miles away in my birthplace, the San Francisco Bay Area, was about to fall apart.

"I didn't want to tell you before your trip because I don't want you to worry," she said. Her voice caught on a sharp place in her throat.

I felt a stab in my gut: selfishness. I didn't want any encumberments before I left for Afghanistan, didn't want anything to distract my focus.

"I'm going to file for divorce," she said. "I'm seeing a lawyer tomorrow. It's real this time. I just can't do this anymore."

Looking back, when I picture myself taking that phone call, I see myself in the same dusky pink shalwar *kameez* I wore two days later in Baku, Azerbaijan, where Stephanie Yao, my photojournalist travel companion, and I overnighted before taking our final flight into Kabul. I had first put it on in our mosquito-infested, communist-era hotel room, feeling self-conscious as one does when wearing a costume.

I know I did not take the phone call in *shalwar kameez*. It was a hot May day in Portland, Oregon, where I lived in a sectioned-off apartment within a turn-of-the-century house with no air conditioning. I must have been wearing shorts, savoring the last opportunity to be immodestly bare-legged. Yet, I can only see myself picking up the phone in that pink cotton outfit and sitting on the bed, among all the supplies, crossing my legs in the baggy pants with the tunic draped over them, cradling the phone between my chin and shoulder.

My memory has revised the scene, written in a wardrobe change to reflect how that moment stays with me: my leaving for Afghanistan inseparable from my mother leaving my father.

The phone call came forty-eight hours before my flight was to leave the airport in Portland. I was numb with Lariam and relief—relief that my mother might find some kind of peace from my father's long-undiagnosed mental illness, for which he had refused treatment of any kind. And relief that for the next month I would be in one of the last places on Earth in mid-2004 that still had minimal cellphone and internet access. And that I would be with the Shirzai family, who had started as subjects of a simple post-9/11 reporting project and had become a surrogate family for me. Their unity in the face of upheaval in their country, and embrace of me as one of their own, was the antithesis, the antidote, to all that felt impossible and fractured with my own family.

I wore the *shalwar kameez* on my way to, and in, Afghanistan because they had asked me to do so, for the sake of safety and other people's comfort with me. Once in Afghanistan, I felt not only safe and less conspicuous in the outfit, but also accepted by the Shirzais, *one of them*. I was donning a costume for the reason most people do: To temporarily become someone, something, I was not. I was morphing from a member of my family into a member of theirs. At that moment, I could not have been happier to undergo the transformation. To escape.

༭

When I was two, before my younger brother Kelley was born, I stuck my head through the bars of a chair at a fast-food restaurant and could not get it back out. I cried, and the more I cried and thrashed, my parents told me, the more my head swelled up and became even more impossible to dislodge. Mom, Dad, the restaurant employees, then the manager, all gave it their best shot, while I shrieked and then, becoming exhausted, just whimpered. The manager wondered out loud if he should call the fire department.

I have no memory of this incident, but both Mom and Dad love to tell me the story. Mom as evidence of my fearlessness; Dad as evidence of my mischievousness. Dad always ended the story the same way: "And then, right when the manager started talking about a fireman cutting the seat back off of your neck, 'Pop!' out your head came. Like you were so scared by the idea that you mustered the strength to pull your own head out." When I freed myself, everyone in the restaurant applauded.

My mother knew, from before I could remember, that I would go through my life acting first, asking questions later. As I grew up, I was not foolish nor even reckless, most of the time. I just had an innate trust that I could get myself out of whatever mess I might find myself in, if push came to shove. "I've always trusted you," Mom always told me as an adult. "You've never been afraid to take leaps of faith, and figure things out as you went along. The best thing I could do was get out of your way." Mom presented herself as a more timid, cautious type, more like my younger brother, Kelley, who never had mishaps like the chair incident.

Even so, as I packed my bags in Portland, I had wondered why Mom didn't worry more about the month I was about to spend in Afghanistan, with a family she had never met. Yes, she was preoccupied with her own problems, but her friends were saying things to her like, "Afghanistan! And you're letting your daughter go?"

But, thirty-four years earlier, my mom, Ling-shin, had silenced her own cautious impulses and took the ultimate leap of faith: She married my father, Tien-Yuh, a man she barely knew save a few dozen letters exchanged between Taiwan and Berkeley while he was at graduate school, and a handful of formal dates. As soon as she married him, by Chinese tradition, she officially left her own family, the Chens, and became a member of the Chuang family. Ling-shin would also have to leave Taiwan for the first time in her life, and cross the Pacific to a place where she did not know the language, where her bachelor's degree in sociology would be useless to her. Tien-Yuh had made the journey years earlier, on a graduate scholarship at the University of California at Berkeley. He had gone with a purpose, a promise of a degree, a teaching assistantship, and a career in civil engineering, at a time when the United States desperately needed more engineers. Mom had nothing but a new family which, in America, amounted to one person: my father.

Even when things were good with Dad, Mom never liked her wedding photos. Like many brides in Taiwan at that time, her face was covered with pancake makeup meant to lighten her skin, and she was wearing a long-sleeved lace dress, an ornate veil, her black hair finger-combed in stylized wisps over her forehead. She looks beautiful, impossibly young, and a little ghostly. "So fussy," said Mom, who had always preferred simple clothes and minimal makeup. "I didn't choose any of that. I never wanted to wear all that makeup."

Now, if she went through with the divorce, she would be taking on a third identity, one that virtually did not exist in the Chinese American immigrant community: That of a divorcee, starting her life over on her own.

After all, Mom knew something about leaps of faith, and about beginning journeys in clothes that were not her own.

➴

We traversed twelve and a half time zones, on three different airlines, with an overnight in Baku, Azerbaijan, to get to Kabul. Stephanie and I focused on the immediate trials before us: the hungry mosquitoes in our dank Azeri hotel room, which smelled of mildew and feet no matter how wide we opened the windows; Lariam side effects and jet lag, at times indistinguishable; the need to bribe airport officials to accept our overweight luggage, sagging with gifts that Shirzai family members had asked us to deliver. Better to dwell on those than to acknowledge our larger fears of the unknown journey before us. Two of the Afghan American family members, Daoud and his niece Laila, had gone a few weeks before and were awaiting our arrival. Despite more than thirty hours on planes and in airports, I felt less like we were finally going to Afghanistan than that we were hovering in some kind of parallel universe populated by a new brand of cargo-pants-wearing aid workers and defense contractors, virtually all male. They sat around the Baku airport's waiting area for Flight 85 on Azerbaijan Air, one of two airlines that made commercial flights into Kabul at the time, with a jaded aura. They spoke of underground expat bars in Kabul's New City district, Azeri beer, and Azeri women. We were barely two and a half years into this war, and already the phrase "back in the 'Stan" was rolling off these men's tongues so easily, in American, British, and Australian accents, that I thought they were saying "back in 'Nam" the first time I heard it. They eyed Stephanie and me in our shalwar kameez, playing my travel Scrabble set, wondering what our business in the 'Stan was.

But the cargo-pants crowd, and Baku's byzantine post-Soviet aura, mattered little to me now. I wouldn't feel like I was truly Afghanistan-bound until I saw the mountains.

As we finally jostled on board Flight 85, I dashed for a window seat (there were no assigned seats), making sure it was clear of the wing. Stephanie took the side opposite mine. The engines roared to life and rattled the aging Tupelov jet's flimsy hull. Soon, I would see the Hindu Kush.

The Hindu Kush were a 600-mile spinal ridge that soared as high as 19,000 feet, separating Afghanistan from Pakistan, South Asia from Eurasia. So many stories about Afghanistan, from Alexander the Great's invasion, to the great Soviet empire's military failure, to the Shirzai family's own exile and return, began and ended with this foreboding fortress of granite and ice. The Khyber Pass served as Afghanistan's physical and symbolic gateway. The mountains stood as an ever-present backdrop to Afghanistan, visible in the distance from almost anywhere in Kabul, reminding us that despite the rubble and devastation in the foreground, that this was an unconquerable land.

No matter where in the country they lived, Afghans looked to the

Hindu Kush as a point of reference, an anchor to their identities. Not only were they mountain people, but they also were people of the most rugged, unforgiving geology in the world. Even the mountains themselves were created by an act of violence: 55 million years ago, India was an island east of Africa. It smashed into Asia, the brute geological force lifting up the edge of tectonic plates, creating the Himalayas and the Hindu Kush, as well as the Tibetan Plateau. The unsteady coexistence of these plates also made Afghanistan one of the most earthquake-prone regions in the world—as if the country were destined for upheaval.

For Afghans, it was a love-hate relationship, equal parts reverence and fear. "When the war is over, I want to read Persian poetry and go somewhere where there are no damn mountains," Ahmed Shah Massoud famously said during the civil war years of the 1990s. The rakish *mujahideen* commander was the Lion of Panjshir, a reference to the valley that nestled along the western flank of the Hindu Kush. It was there that Massoud set up his base and demonstrated a brand of mountain guerilla warfare that had been credited with defeating the far-better-armed Soviets. Massoud proved that Soviet military might, their tanks and helicopters, their disproportionate numbers, meant nothing in the Hindu Kush, whose contours and quirks he and his men had learned like the body of a lover. It was this familiarity, this mastery of their own terrain, that over the years reduced the Soviet machine to defeat, as its men froze in the winter, expired from dehydration in the summer, and contracted debilitating illnesses from the harsh conditions. Even so, countless Afghan refugees fleeing one war after another had died in those mountains as well, in ill-equipped, overloaded vehicles careening off icy mountain passes or breaking down and leaving passengers without provisions. Many had even tried to cross by foot, and met fates similar to the Soviet soldiers.

I wondered, if Massoud had not died in those mountains on September 9, 2001, in an assassination that strangely presaged the attacks in the United States two days later, had he lived to see the overthrow of the Taliban, what he would make of the expats flooding into Kabul to help, make a buck, or seek adventure, remaking themselves in his swashbuckling image. On Flight 85, I had barely noticed that a man had sat down in the aisle seat of my row, leaving an empty seat between us. Unlike the cargo-pants crowd, he had gray hair and a dapper air in his cream-colored linen suit. "First time to Kabul?" he said, with a patrician Virginia accent. By the way he leaned back in his seat, unconcerned with the view I was so determined to catch, I suspected he had done this even more than the cargo-pants guys. He was the manager of a U.S. aviation company that operated flights for contractors and NGOs. He had come back from "a few days of R&R" in Baku, he said. "There are two things you can do there that you can't in Kabul: drink and look at women." I made small talk, but kept turning back toward the window, checking the view.

"We've got about thirty minutes before you see them," he said, reading my mind. "You'll know."

He was right. Not long after, the atmosphere in the cabin shifted. Men who had been joking or napping sat up straight and began peering out the windows in anticipation. The plane was so old, the window glass was so thin, we had views of the land below us that felt shockingly real and close compared to those through the distorted submarine portholes of modern commercial airliners. The undulating brown land suddenly gave way to jagged slate-gray peaks, as if the massive, knife-edged ridges had broken through the earth. Rivers of ice snaked and branched a network of veins down their sides. The mountains seemed to go on forever. I inhaled sharply. The plane was, for the first time since takeoff, dead silent. Even the lone, sour-faced flight attendant had paused. The edges of the peaks were so sharp I couldn't help imagining the plane crashing, split open like an egg as we joined the millennia-old list of the Hindu Kush's victims. We would all die in a fiery explosion as the fuel tank broke, or else perish on impact, bodies and parts of bodies frozen in the snow.

Some say the world will end in fire / Some say in ice.

Virginia Gentleman broke my grisly reverie: "You know, they're putting bounties on foreigners. Anyone who's desperate can sell you out. As head of an American company, the price on my head is seven thousand dollars."

"An American woman journalist . . . I'm not sure what that's going for, but probably more than me." Irritated by his warning, I yanked my *chador* out of my backpack, wrapped it around my head, trying to appear more practiced at it than I was, and said, "Thanks." I looked out the window for Kabul.

A lower, rolling set of dun mountains opened in twin bowls to reveal

haphazard brown sprawls of buildings. We descended past a graveyard of
bombed- and burned-out helicopters, jeeps, and tanks, a rusting monument
to the vanquished Soviet military. The old jet bounced a couple times on
the runway, rattling my teeth and nerves. As the ground finally felt solid
under the airplane's wheels, I exhaled and looked at Stephanie, who had
been carrying on what I guessed was a similar conversation with a younger
man in camouflage pants (they were an anachronistic dark-green jungle
camo). She and I made eye contact. My heart was pounding. *Finally here*,
I mouthed. Even if I were somehow going to die the minute I stepped out
of the airplane, I could at least say now that I'd been in Afghanistan. The
airport was a squat concrete building with submarine-like windows. The
"Ariana graveyard" of blown-up planes belonging to Afghanistan's national
airline, the result of the October 2001 U.S. bombing at the start of the
invasion, was no longer evident. Virginia Gentleman told me the Afghan
government had cleaned up the hulls of the airliners for a recent state visit.

"Good luck," he said, and shook my hand. I stepped off the stairway
and onto the tarmac. The sky was expansive, waiting, the air hot and dusty.
It smelled ancient and alive. I was here.

Before I left for Afghanistan, even before my mother called with her
news, I knew this: Malaria pills did not agree with me. The large, chalky
white Lariam tablets I had to start taking before my trip made my insides
ripple and knotted my stomach into a hard pit. They made one hour of
uneasy slumber feel like five, waking me many times during the night.
Another Lariam side effect on the long list, in addition to the paranoia,
hallucinations, sense of doom, and the terrible sleep: May cause emotional
detachment.

I wondered if my normal state was indistinguishable from the side
effect. Some feelings simply take hold *like* drug side effects: a reflexive
reaction, lingering with chemical stubbornness.

I had wanted and feared my parents' divorce for many years now,
frustrated that my mother had told me a year and a half before that she was
going to do it, and then didn't go through with it. Back then, too, she waited
until right before I was about to leave on a reporting trip to Vietnam. By

the time I returned, she had changed her mind. I was too exhausted and raw from my trip to do anything other than tell her, "I support any decision you make."

It was a cop-out, giving her permission to leave my ill, recalcitrant father without saying, Yes, you should leave him. It was easier to murmur platitudes on the phone and then bolt onto a plane, relieved to feel the push of the jet engines hurtling me away from it all.

On that afternoon before I left for Afghanistan, sitting on the bed in the pink *shalwar kameez*—or not—starting at the repeating abstract patterns embroidered into the tunic, I said to Mom what I always said:

"You know I support whatever decision you make."

"I know," she said, her voice less teary, more flat. We were following a script we had written with our previous conversations. "I'm not going to tell Dad until after I see the lawyer. But I will."

"You do what feels right." I studied the sound of my own voice, familiar yet odd, an alto that got lower and throatier when I was tired. Sometimes, when I was a child, I answered the phone and the person on the other end thought I was my younger brother, Kelley. I had been relieved when his voice changed. "Mom, you're not going to hear much from me in the next few weeks. Are you going to be OK?"

"Yes, yes, please don't think about it too much," Mom said. "This is something I just have to do. You have a good trip. Be careful."

"I want you to be happy," I said.

A long pause. "I haven't," she said, voice like dry twigs snapping, "I haven't been happy in a very long time."

I tried to remember Mom's smile, so much like my own. We had always resembled each other, always had the same big-toothed, broad smile—so much so that dentists wanted to remove four of my permanent teeth in the back when I was young because they feared my large front teeth were overcrowding them. I had refused, settling for braces and, later, wisdom teeth removal, instead. Mom used to smile like that on the many family roadtrips we took when Dad was well, busying herself with a cooler full of food at her feet, popping pieces of fruit or bites of sandwich into Dad's mouth as he drove. She smiled like that when we used to visit Taiwan, at her parents' house, when my grandmother would cook for two days before we arrived, a feast to welcome her firstborn back. But lately, she merely forced herself into a tight-lipped grin when she was trying to be polite, and never at home.

"You will be. Someday," I said, wanting to believe my own words, wanting my eyes not to sting, glad she could not see me forming tears. I did not like to cry, never had.

But at that moment, I wanted nothing more than to be far away, completely unreachable, in another land with another family.

⌘

Kabul International Airport had old linoleum flooring, no air conditioning, and free-standing metal barriers that barely separated those of us just getting off the flight from the loud chaos in the terminal. If the Hindu Kush were Afghanistan's proverbial gateway, then this last passage was rather battered and flimsy, watched over by some cranky-looking uniformed men.

Stephanie and I stood near the end of the passport control line, in *shalwar kameez* and tentatively wrapped *chador*. Seeing that we were the only women in line, an olive-drab uniformed man approached us and beckoned us to cut to the front. Members of the Back-in-the-'Stan crowd grumbled in English as I slid our passports under the window.

The man behind the bulletproof glass had a tan complexion and a trimmed beard. His tight-lipped expression stretched into a horizontal line. He looked down at the passports, with our photos in western clothes and uncovered hair. In mine, my unruly thick black mane drapes over my shoulders and takes up substantial background space as I smile broadly at the camera, showing teeth. When traveling, I usually flashed the same grin at passport-control officers, as if to say, *See? It's really me.* I didn't dare do that now, instead, pressing my lips together, mirroring our expressionless officer. He looked up at us, in shalwar kameez and headscarves, and did a double take. He melodramatically flipped the passports to gawk at the navy-blue covers, with their gold-embossed eagle logo and "UNITED STATES OF AMERICA" in block letters.

"You're *American*?"

Blood thudded behind my eardrums He seemed to be feigning surprise, being ironic. But what if he wasn't?

I nodded apologetically. "Sorry. That's what the passport says."

The passport-control man guffawed to himself, shaking his head in disbelief. "Sucker," I heard one of the Cargo Pants mutter behind us. *Don't turn around and glare.* I focused on the man on the other side of the window, the pressure of my lips against each other, the horizontal line.

He stamped the passports, wood and rubber echoing hard against the cracked marble table that had seen better days, and he shoved the booklets back. I grabbed them, too quickly, passed Stephanie's to her, and tucked mine away. *Let's not take those out again, until we leave, I wanted to say to her.*

We walked past the metal barriers to the terminal, and another olive-drab-clad man extended his arm to show us the way. He was scrawny and had a disarming smile. He said, in English and more loudly than I would have liked him to, "Welcome, Americans. You are welcome to my country." A compensation for his colleague's surliness. He pressed his right palm to his heart a couple times and half-bowed. I struggled to not smile back too hard. I could have just as easily laughed or cried at that moment.

"*Tashakur,*" I said. Thank you. And I instinctively pressed my right hand to my heart, obscured by the voluminous fabric of my scarf.

From the staid passport-control area, the terminal bloomed forth in chaos. There were more local men in *shalwar kameez* than arriving passengers, and by the time Stephanie and I entered the area, all of the baggage from Flight 85 appeared to have been claimed: That is, the bags were grouped in piles, each one closely guarded by a small group of men. How unprepared I was, with my developed-world expectation that I would get off a plane anywhere in the world and that my bags would be waiting, seemingly untouched, for me. This, more than the passport-control man, more than Virginia Gentleman's warning, brought a stab of panic to my chest. Was this where it began to fall apart?

Stephanie's bags and mine, large ones, were clustered in a heap, being watched over by three men. How had they known we were traveling together? As soon as I got close enough to the bags to check the tags, two of the men took off with the bags at a brisk jog, shouting in accented English, "Taxi! Taxi this way!" as they headed toward the door. A jangling in my nerves warned of danger, but like the child that goes barreling into the busy street after his runaway ball, I chased them. Stephanie followed, reluctantly. "No, no taxi!" I called after them. My entry into Kabul was on the heels of a man absconding with my suitcase into an unmarked car.

As I exited the airport's double doors, the hot wind blew through on my hair as my scarf blew off and sagged around my shoulders. *Not a minute in Kabul and I'm already exposing my hair, losing my luggage.* I swept the *chador* back on the way the Shirzai women in Portland had shown me, reminded myself to breathe in order to calm my pounding heart, and jogged to the car where the man had already thrown our bags in the trunk. His partner was holding the door open for us. They could have taken off with our bags, or forced us into the cars as kidnapping victims. *Just get the luggage back*, I thought, as I faux-calmly marched over and lifted the unwieldy bags out of the trunk. Then men looked at each other mutely, raising their eyebrows. Then, discomforted by the sight of a woman handling heavy luggage, they shrugged their shoulders and helped me. I handed the ringleader a five-dollar bill to make him go away. He did, and then each of the other men wanted cash too. "Share with him!" I barked and pointed, in spite of myself. They glared, more from shock than anger. I felt naked. Stephanie touched my elbow, telling me to get back to the terminal. We were two American women standing alone in front of the Kabul Airport, loaded down with luggage.

Stephanie turned around to march back into the airport, and I followed a few steps behind, watching her tense motions. She thought I had been too forceful with the luggage men. I had put us both in danger. I started crafting an apology in my head. But then her posture lost its tension, she stopped in her tracks and started jumping up and down, waving madly.

"Laila! Laila!"

"Angie! Stephanie!" She was in *shalwar kameez* and *chador* too, unlike the jeans and T-shirt we had last seen her in before she had left Portland ahead of us. And still, with her stylish glasses and distinctly erect carriage, she stood out from other Afghans around her. I had never been so happy to see her. We had been spotted by the only human being in this crowd who would have recognized us: Laila Shirzai.

2.
Origins

My father, Tien-Yuh Chuang, and Daoud Shirzai, his family's patriarch, were born within two years of each other, during World War II. Geographically, they were a world apart, but in many ways they traveled on parallel trajectories. They both grew up poor —can't-afford-shoes poor, watched-half-my-siblings-die-young poor—in Fujian, China, and rural Ghazni, Afghanistan. My father was one of nine, the fifth, surviving children out of sixteen born to his mother. Daoud was also one of nine, the eldest, out of fourteen born to his mother. They both made life-changing moves when they were boys, Tien-Yuh with his family to Taiwan where his father sought better job opportunities for himself and his children, and Daoud to Kabul for boarding school, as part of an education equity program for rural children. Through education, both men found their way out of poverty and, eventually, to the United States for doctorates. Prized for their smarts, they were both the first in their families to make the journey to America. They were both in graduate school in the San Francisco Bay Area in the tumultuous 1960s, and both found scholarships and work as a result of the post-Eisenhower, post-Sputnik hunger for talented foreign engineers, scientists, and educators. These were the years of the Interstate Highway System and the Space Race, of the Peace Corps and peace protests. The world was expanding and becoming global —the American Dream suddenly opened up to countries, particularly those in East and South Asia, which had never been included in the United States' early visions of the Melting Pot.

Another thing my father and Daoud shared was the relentless burden of being the first in their family to cross key thresholds: the first to gain a college education, the first to go to America, the first to raise the second generation in the Land of Opportunity. Even as other family members made their way to the United States, even as the next generation thrived in ways their parents never dreamed for themselves, The First Son to America was always held up to the highest standard of success and responsibility. That took the form of money wired home, of reports of his accomplishments as a professional, as well as a patriarch—not just to his children, but to all those who followed him.

In their own ways, both men sacrificed under this burden. Daoud never married nor had his own children, focusing his energies on raising six of his nieces and nephews in the United States. My father struggled in his engineering career, plateauing when tensions between white and the newer Asian immigrant engineers came to a head. He abruptly quit a cushy job at a government lab and proclaimed he would start over in real estate. He did, but also succumbed to a decades-long illness that looked a lot like bipolar disorder, but for which he always refused diagnosis or treatment.

Despite these parallels, at the time I was traveling to Afghanistan, and my mother was divorcing my father, I only saw the differences between Daoud and my father. They seemed like opposites: Daoud was public, eloquent and glib in his professorial sport coats, at his endless post-9/11 speaking engagements—his self-deprecating humility belying his love for ritual and showmanship. My father, pre-illness, was fiercely private, a man of few words who had never quite mastered English, though his way of expressing itself had its own Chinese-accented cleverness. He actively resisted wearing suits and ties, as he did most trappings of formality.

Before his illness took over, my father's love for and pride in me was demonstrated not in words, but by his fixation on shaping me as an independent, capable daughter; he taught me to ride a bike, swim, use tools, drive stick shift, perform basic maintenance on a car. He praised me for my intellect, for doing well in school, for being resourceful, by simply saying, You're just like your dad. In my young mind, it was the best compliment.

But at the time of the divorce, when my father was descending into another depression, spending his days inside one room of my childhood home, watching television or playing games on his laptop computer,

I couldn't conjure up those warm memories. Meanwhile, Daoud was ascendant, gaining prominence as he became a local, then national, voice for Afghanistan's precarious post-Taliban future. I chose to align myself with an upward trajectory, first latching onto Daoud as a journalistic source and then, as what he was to all the Shirzais: a patriarch.

అ

"We're looking for someone," my editor at the newspaper in Portland had said, chewing on the end of his pen, "to put a human face on the country we're about to bomb."

That was how it had begun. It was simple, at first. Daoud Shirzai was the only local Afghan immigrant willing to speak out, undeterred by the fact that local mosques were being attacked with hate mail and graffiti, or the bumper sticker that read, "Weather Forecast for Afghanistan: 13,500 degrees Fahrenheit," over a mushroom cloud. While others whom I called begged me not to publish their names or photos, fearing that their houses would be vandalized or their children tormented in school, Professor Daoud Shirzai was giving public lectures with titles like, "Where is Afghanistan?"

Professor Shirzai of Mt. Tabor College, a well-regarded liberal arts school on the edge of the city, had sounded guarded, impatient when I had first called. But he was willing to talk, tell me a little about his family's story. He had raised six nieces and nephews in Portland but was not married and did not have children of his own. His family had suffered greatly in the Soviet takeover and war; he had lost a younger brother, father of three of the children he had raised. They all went to Mt. Tabor, many had graduated, and the youngest of the six, Laila, was starting her senior year.

But he avoided specifics about his family, preferring instead to fill me in on the United States' long and muddled involvement with Afghanistan. I, in turn, steered him away from history, trying to ask more about his family. But Daoud's reluctance felt like a wall between us, and I searched and searched for a door.

"Don't make it too focused on me," he said as I pressed. "I don't want this to get maudlin. It's about Afghanistan, not about me."

"I think it's important to tell your family's story, to help people understand," I said, trying not to plead.

"Why?" he said. "I want them to understand that bombing a country that has already been bombed to the ground will do nothing to curb terrorism.

"So, why me? Why us?"

I had been called on in class by the professor. I cleared my throat, took a breath, and spoke the first words that tumbled to mind.

"Because family is the most universal story there is," I said. "I'm writing for people who don't go to your lectures, who might not care what happens to Afghanistan. But you left behind one family, now in mortal danger, and raised another here. People relate to that. And maybe that will make them care about Afghanistan."

A pause. Blood coursing through my veins.

A sigh, on his part. "OK."

I felt victorious. The line went silent again.

"My adopted country is waging war on my country of origin," he said. "It's a very difficult position to be in."

⁊

Between country of origin and adopted country, which one is home?

In Pashto, "home" is not a single word, but four. There is *kor*, a word that means "house," *watan*, which means "country," still another, *mena*, that means "birthplace," and *tatobay*, a fourth that means "homeland." In a land that had endured invaders, occupations, war, and the displacement of its people, many times over, the idea of home had evolved as elusive, fractured, and dissonant.

In Mandarin, "home," *jia*, is synonymous with "family." In the single character, the radical representing a roof lies over the character for *zhu*, pig. Chinese families kept pigs in their courtyards, hence the association with home. The character itself is a swooping set of nine strokes, curving and long like willow branches, evoking the idea of all things—sustenance and wealth, which a pig in ancient China represented—contained under one roof. In the typical compact flexibility of the Chinese language, *jia* could be modified by adding single words, so that *guo jia*, "nation home," was synonymous with country, and *jia ren*, "home people," was synonymous with family members. Reversing the phrase *jia ren*, "home people," to *ren jia*, meant "people outside the home," or simply, "others." Unlike in Pashto, the Mandarin home coalesced, made no distinctions: Home was where the family was, and country was where the family was from. Period. Everything else outside the courtyard wall was "other." My parents' friends from Taiwan, even after becoming U.S. citizens, living in the country for decades, raising thoroughly American children, still referred to visiting Taiwan as *hui jia*, or returning home.

My father was unusual among his friends. He deliberately referred to the United States, our ranch house at the end of a suburban San Francisco Bay Area cul-de-sac, as *jia*, home. He liked to boast he was a "banana, with yellow skin on the outside and a white brain on the inside." He bragged that he loved hamburgers as much, maybe more, than he loved rice, noodles, or other Chinese staples. During his first days in the United States, while living in a dormitory in the first year of graduate school at UC-Berkeley, he only knew how to order a hamburger in the dining hall. He ate hamburgers for lunch and dinner for three weeks straight. "I am American as apple pie and hamburgers," he used to crow during his upbeat (or manic, in some cases) times.

What was behind this aggressive desire to assimilate, to reinvent home while all his compatriots were longing for it? I never knew, but as I watched him decline mentally, I couldn't help wondering what demons or burdens from Taiwan he had wanted to escape. My father had always had a bit of the lone wolf lurking in him, eager to lash out against what others did, even since he was young in Taiwan. Whether being bipolar made him not a team player, or that not being a team player brought on the underemployment and solitude that allowed mental illness to thrive, was a chicken or egg question.

While my father aggressively reinvented *jia*, home, for himself in America, Daoud, curiously, never used that word in English at all. Neither Afghanistan nor America was "home" to him. He preferred formalities like "country of origin."

ॐ

As I first encountered the Shirzais, beginning with Daoud, I felt as if I were slowly being let through a series of doors, past layer after layer of protective walls—at the center of which lay the true family behind the professor's public face.

Entering an Afghan home, whether a modern compound in Kabul or a mud-brick house in a village, is like peeling an onion. Guests first enter through an outer wall that shields its inhabitants from onlookers. The door in the outer wall leads into an open-air courtyard, in which the guests are inside the compound, but still outside of the house. Male guests are then ushered into the most-accessible room from the courtyard, usually the formal sitting room for men. The innermost rooms, which are not visible from the courtyard, are reserved for the women. This positioning allowed the females protection from prying eyes. Full-length curtains hung in the entryways, for added privacy.

Purdah, the Hindu and Islamic term for keeping women hidden from men through separation and veiling, comes from the Hindi word for "curtain." In the 1950s, then-Prime Minister Mohammad Daoud Khan had abolished *purdah* in Afghanistan in an effort to modernize, and the communists, though they later assassinated him, kept the ban in the spirit of Soviet male-female equality. In the 1990s, the *mujahideen*—anti-Soviet resistance fighters who waged civil war—brought it back. After that, the Taliban enforced *purdah* in its most extreme form. Nevertheless, some version of it was almost always practiced. Entering an Afghan room, through the curtain, literally lifted a veil into another, inner world.

"Everyone in the city lived in a compound, a yard surrounded by walls that divided the world into a public and a private realm," author and Afghan American Tamim Ansary recalled in his post-9/11 memoir, *West of Kabul, East of New York*. "Visitors never really knew us, because they never saw the hidden world inside our compounds. Those who came from the West didn't even know our private universe existed, or that life inside it was warm and sweet. And in a way, we Afghans didn't know we had this realm either, because we didn't know it was possible not to have it."

Afghan home design reflected a society which was fiercely protective of its own, distrustful of outsiders—out of necessity, as the often-invaded but never-conquered nation had learned. But at the same time, the famed Afghan hospitality dictated that once you were let in past the walls, you were a guest and would be fiercely embraced, provided for, and protected, as one of the family. This was particularly true of the Pashtun ethnic group, to which the Shirzais proudly belonged, and which operated by a tribal code of *Pashtunwali.*

Ironically, this was the code that compelled the leadership of the Taliban, Afghanistan's ruling regime, to protect Osama bin Laden, the exiled son of a Saudi construction magnate, after the September 11 attacks. Bin Laden was not one of them, but the Taliban considered him their guest. And a guest, once invited into the home, was to be shown the utmost hospitality and protected at all costs. If not for Pashtunwali, the United States' longest war may not have ever started.

On the phone with Daoud, I had made it past the outer wall. Next, I asked to accompany him to one of the many lectures he was giving on Afghanistan. He had a meeting at Portland State University, which was right next to my office, before the lecture at a left-leaning church across town. He said he'd give me a ride there from the university. Stephanie—who had been assigned to team up with me on this "human face" story—agreed to meet me at the church.

When I arrived, five minutes late, Daoud was standing in front of the building he'd asked me to meet him at, looking at his watch. He was a smaller man than I had imagined from the resonant voice on the phone. The authority he projected and my sheepishness about being late—few people in Portland were that punctual—caused me to hesitate. "Daoud Shirzai," he said in greeting, extending his hand and motioning with his head as if to say, *Let's go*, at the same time. In time, I'd get used to his brusqueness. We walked together to the parking garage. He was professorial and rumpled at the same time, in a navy blue blazer, light blue shirt, patterned burgundy tie and khaki pants. They were neither outdated nor fashionable, and later, his nieces and nephews would joke to me that "Uncle Daoud has only one outfit." I pictured the Inspector Gadget cartoons of my youth, in which the cyborg Sherlock Holmes-esque hero would open his closet with rows of identical tan trenchcoats and say, comically, "I wonder what I should wear today?"

Daoud walked quickly, his build compact and square-bodied, fit. He had told me he was fifty-eight over the phone. (Later, one of those same nieces would say, "Uncle Daoud has been fifty-eight for three years now!" In truth, few of the Shirzais were born in hospitals and rural Afghans rarely tracked birthdates, so there was room for poetic license.) His sweep of side-parted hair bore not a hint of gray, and his brown face was tired, but relatively unlined. He had a strong, furrowed brow and eyes so dark they looked black.

He strode through the parking garage, stopping at a bright red Volvo sedan. Turbo. He didn't seem like a red-car kind of guy.

"Ooh, don't get into a car with Uncle Daoud. He's a scary driver." That was another one of the "Uncle Daoud jokes" the nieces and nephews would tell me later. These observations weren't really jokes at all, but ways in which they affectionately made fun of him. "His mind is always on a million other things, and he drives *fast*."

I, of course, didn't realize this until we were in the car, whipping out of the garage exit and onto Southwest Broadway, tires squealing.

"How long have you had this car?" I said. "It . . . handles well."

He shrugged his shoulders. "One of my nephews chose it for me a couple years ago," he said, accelerating through a yellow light turning red. "I know nothing about cars."

When we arrived at the church, it was packed. The minister, a tall, enthusiastic man in a polo shirt and jeans, gave Daoud a bear hug when he walked in. Daoud accepted the warmth of the greeting, pumping the reverend's hand a couple times in a handshake as he pulled away. As I followed him into the makeshift green room, he pulled out a yellow note pad and started to flip through pages of longhand notes written in precise printed script, tilted at a slight forward angle like warriors marching into battle. "Do you still work at the homeless shelter here?" I asked. I had done some research and found an article from a few years ago, about how he took a part-time job as the church shelter's morning janitor and sent the money home to his family in Afghanistan. The story had painted a picture of a solitary man sweeping and scrubbing in the dawn hours with the nobility of a Benedictine monk.

He raised his head and turned to me, surprised. "Oh. You read that. I had stopped over the summer because I was traveling, and meant to come back in the fall. But then, well, I've had other things on my mind of late."

He went back to studying his notes. I thought about the article. Something about his monastic humility—cleaning toilets, scouring shower stalls, telling the homeless children to stay in school—felt like more than just charity. It felt like self-imposed penitence. But for what?

As he approached the lectern to speak, I found a folding chair in the audience of a couple hundred. On the side of the room, Stephanie was poised with a camera. I waved at her. As Daoud started to speak, it became clear that the notes he had reviewed were unnecessary. He never looked down. He began with a history of Afghanistan, just like he started our phone conversation, but drew the audience in with details like, "My younger sister Amina, who is illiterate because she never had the educational opportunities that girls here take for granted, lives near the Kabul Airport, which has been identified as a target for bombing. It is people like her who will suffer if we invade, not Osama bin Laden and Al Qaeda." He had the booming, deliberate voice of a skilled public speaker. His hands gestured emphatically as he scanned the crowd, letting his dark-eyed gaze settle upon certain individuals now and then. They sat up straighter, like they were about to be called on.

When I found him after the speech, his face slack with exhaustion, I introduced him to Stephanie. "Did you get my good side?" he said. She flashed her winning smile, made all the more endearing by her wispy, pixie-like haircut. I, on the other hand, always struggled with my long, thick hair that tried to go in too many directions at once, like my own frenetic nature. We were both Chinese American, a year apart in age. But she had a naturally demure way about her, something I lacked completely. I felt a pang of envy. Why hadn't I been privy to this charming, joking Daoud?

He turned to me: "What next?"

Your family, I thought, but hesitated. "What do you suggest?" I said.

"OK, here, write this down," he said, and started reciting a phone number from memory. I scrambled to find a blank page in my notebook.

"My brother Maiwand. He'd like to speak to you."

I suppressed a smile. Maiwand was the second youngest of the three Shirzai brothers who had settled in Portland. The door in the next wall was opening.

3.
Brothers

Daoud had six younger brothers: two who followed him to Portland, two still in Afghanistan, one who was killed during the Soviet War, and one who died in childhood in the village.

I had one brother, Kelley, three years my junior, and we were as different as two people could be. I was as extroverted as he was introverted. I was audacious, occasionally a little reckless; Kelley was careful. I was messy, constantly being yelled at to clean my room and make my bed as a child; he was organized, never a speck of dust in his room, his painstakingly constructed model cars in neat rows to rival a showroom's. I looked like my mother, with a roundish face, flat nose, long neck, and easy, toothy smile. Kelley looked like my father, with his angular features, thick, stern-looking eyebrows, and wiry frame. Yet when it came to personalities, my brother's conformist, more timid nature mirrored my mother's, while my tendencies toward chaos and rebellion made me more like my father. There is a childhood photo of Kelley and me, at about four and seven, on one of our first trips to the Sierra Nevadas to experience snow. We're in our winter coats, mine red and his green, and we're sitting in a huge snowdrift somewhere near Reno. I am covered with snow, white blobs sticking to my coat, blotchy with darker wet spots, bits of snow in my hair. I am holding up my hands; one has a soppy mitten, and the other is bare and flushed red from cold. Kelley sits next to me, pristine and dry, his two clean mittened hands folded on his lap.

That is how we always were. As an adult, I criss-crossed the country, and then the globe, for jobs and assignments. He only left the Bay Area once, for medical school, and only because he didn't get into equivalent or better ones close to home. Kelley became a surgeon. I became a reporter. It was amazing we shared DNA at all.

Yet, when we were young, we developed the coded language of brothers and sisters, inventing games and imaginary worlds, with rules that only made sense to us. We each collected stuffed animals and created for them elaborate personalities, occupations, dwellings, and a town in which they all coexisted. When Mom asked us to sort and fold all of Dad's just-washed dress socks, each navy blue or black pair bearing a slightly different yet maddeningly similar pattern, Kelley and I invented a game we called "War." Quite simply, we would draw a line in the carpet and time ourselves for two minutes, hurling as many socks as we could at each other. When the timer sounded, each of us was responsible for the socks in our territory. The game always ended with a truce, as we each had to cross enemy lines and work together to match up the last stray socks with their mates. Another favorite activity was pretending-fighting, complete with pillow-punching, door-slamming, and descriptive exclamations like, "Ow! You socked me in the eye!" or "Ohh! I'm bleeding!" The goal was to see how far we had to escalate until Mom or Dad barreled into the room, alarmed and angry, to break it up. We'd fall over into peals of laughter and the irate parent would be flummoxed, unable to punish us for our performance.

Always, no matter how we eventually drifted apart, we shared one common bond: We were both silent witnesses to my parents' slowly disintegrating marriage and my father's decline. Growing up in the Bay Area Chinese immigrant community, where family problems were not to be openly shared, not even with relatives outside the nuclear family, we became the sole keepers of the secret that my parents' American Dream was not what it appeared to be.

An exchanged glance, a look away. I was eight and Kelley five the first time we began to share that terrible knowledge, the first time the idea of our parents getting divorced felt plausible. I was in the third grade, and some of my white friends at school had divorced parents, shuttling between separate homes. They seemed grim, embarrassed. But at Chinese School, which Kelley and I attended for three hours every Saturday morning, I received reassurance from one of my older Chinese girlfriends: Chinese parents don't divorce, she insisted.

For as long as I could remember, my father's demeanor had no middle ground. He could be delightfully upbeat, full of compliments, or silent and simmering with rage, ready to snap at the smallest perceived slight. I can't remember a time when Kelley and I didn't instinctively tiptoe around him. When my father was unhappy, he picked fights, baiting the nearest person into provoking his anger. Like the time he had asked me to get him a Phillips-head screwdriver and I, at eight years old, had told him I didn't know what that was. "Don't argue, just listen!" he barked. I stared at the vast array of screwdrivers in the garage, my stomach in knots, and picked a yellow one that said "Stanley" on it, thinking at least that was a man's name too. He spent the rest of the day berating me about not being helpful enough around the house. "Useless," he muttered in English, the word stinging.

Yet at other times, his effusive praise had made me feel like I could burst with pride. As with the screwdriver, his attention to me was often filtered through wanting to make me capable and handy, like he was. He taught me from a young age to help him with home repairs, to know how to jump-start a car, use a hammer, a drill, and, of course, tell a Phillips from a flathead screwdriver. Sometimes, I wondered if he had wished I were a son, but as if reading my mind, he made it clear that wasn't the case.

"You are the best daughter a dad could want," he had said, when I had received the top ranking in my Chinese School class in the first grade. "How could I have been so lucky to get a child as smart and wonderful as you? You know, when Mom was pregnant with you, I wanted it to be a girl."

Still, I began to wonder about my Chinese School friend's assurances. One evening, my parents, Kelley, and I took one of our regular trips from our suburban home to San Francisco, to eat at one of those Chinese restaurants with grimy linoleum floors and sheets of butcher paper all over the walls. The papers listed dishes in black-markered Chinese characters that were not on the "American" menu. The argument had begun long before we had gotten into the car. Late that afternoon, before we went to the restaurant, I started hearing loud voices in the garage, where Dad had been tinkering with the family cars, as he often did. I wondered if he had asked my mother to get a Phillips screwdriver as well. Mom stormed out of there, her footsteps loud as I heard her pull pots and pans out of the cabinet with loud clangs. Then he stomped into the kitchen.

"What the hell are you cooking for? We're going out tonight," he yelled in Mandarin.

"No," Mom said, her voice tight and shaky. "I don't feel like going out anymore."

"I said we're going out and we're going out," my father's voice boomed.

Normally, I loved the drive from the East Bay to San Francisco, careening through the rolling Berkeley Hills, Kelley and I trying to hold our breath through the entire Caldecott Tunnel, then the excitement of passing through the toll plaza for the Bay Bridge. And the Bay Bridge itself, a magical structure, the upper level on the way there, a multi-phased, seemingly endless thrill ride. Past industrial Oakland, where the rows of container cranes along the harbor, like mechanical dinosaurs at attention, were said to have inspired George Lucas's four-legged AT-AT Walkers in *The Empire Strikes Back*. Then through the tunnel at Treasure Island—*They really named an island that! Would they find the treasure someday?*—and emerging into the magic of the suspension bridge's thick steel cables and soaring towers, like the string art we did in school, on a grand scale. And of course, the San Francisco skyline, from the pointy Transamerica pyramid to the Bank of America building above it all to the defiant white nub of Coit Tower jutting out from the surrounding trees. And all around us, the Bay itself, sometimes calm and azure, sometimes murky and roiling.

On this evening, there was a blanket of steely fog across the bridge, denying us a decent view of the skyline, and the water, barely visible, looked to be gray-green, swirling like a cauldron. The drive to the restaurant was painfully tense, and felt like it went on forever. My parents barely spoke, and Dad took his anger out on the accelerator.

"Don't tailgate. It's hard to see the cars in front of us in the fog," Mom muttered, gripping the handle above the passenger-side window of our Oldsmobile station wagon. Unlike his Chinese American friends, who favored Japanese cars, my father insisted on buying American—part of his "apple pie and hamburgers" persona.

"If you want to drive this car, you go ahead," Dad spat back, knowing my mom didn't like to drive in the city. Later, when I learned to drive, he would insist that I became comfortable driving everywhere, even on San Francisco's steepest hills, with a stick shift.

Mom and Dad were silent in the restaurant, he making a big show of eating lots of food and she picking at hers. Kelley and I did what we always did when they argued—we became very, very quiet and pretended it wasn't happening. But this time felt different.

"Why aren't you eating?" Dad asked.

"I told you I didn't want to eat out," she said, putting her chopsticks down. Like many Chinese couples, I never once heard them address each other by their first names, "Tien-Yuh" or "Ling," which were seen as too direct, too formal. Even Kelley and I had Chinese nicknames that my parents used well into adulthood. He was "Kai Kai," I was "Xiao (little) Fan," both based on our Chinese names of I-Kai and I-Fan, respectively. If anything, they called each other "Dad" and "Mom" in Mandarin, Ba ba and Ma ma, but only when they were feeling somewhat affectionate toward each other. At the restaurant, they were not using any form of address at all, just loaded questions and accusations. "But you always get your way, don't you?" she added.

"What do you mean by that? I'm treating the family to a dinner out. I just drove for forty-five minutes through the fog, I'm using my hard-earned money to give us a nice meal," he said, sounding so spiteful I didn't dare look at him. I stared at my rice, thinking about how Mom used to tell me every uneaten grain of rice would turn into a pock mark on my face. By now, I knew that wasn't true. "And now I'm doing something wrong?"

"Never mind," she mumbled. I could hear tears in her voice. She poked at her food with her chopsticks and looked at the wall.

"Why do you have to be like this?" he said, his voice rising.

"Like what? Like what?" she yelled back. "Why is it never your fault? OK, then, you're perfect, and everyone else is wrong. Who acts like this, just yelling and getting mad at people for no reason? This isn't normal."

I would learn in time that the quickest way to provoke my father's rage was to suggest that he was not normal, to hint at some kind of mental illness or deficiency, what he regarded, with contempt, as "crazy." In fact, the Mandarin word for "sickness of the mind and spirit," i.e., mental illness, was synonymous with "crazy."

"You want a divorce?" my father thundered. "Is that what you want? If that's what you want, just say it!" My mom wiped her eyes with the pink cloth napkin. I had never seen them like this. Sure, they fought, but at home, or in the car, but never, ever in public. And they never spoke of "divorce" in front of us. The word in Chinese is *li hun*, or "leave marriage." The Chinese notion of saving face—of maintaining a dignified public exterior, and never airing dirty laundry outside of the immediate family—meant that for a husband and wife to fight in public at a Chinese restaurant (where arguing in Mandarin provided no buffer from the other patrons), it had to be serious.

Once, just once, I looked over at Kelley. Still chubby-cheeked at five, he turned to me with wide eyes, pleading. For what, I didn't know. Did he want me to comfort him? To stop the argument? To give some guidance by example of what to do, other than stare into space and pretend it wasn't happening?

I couldn't. Our shared glance was like fire, burning at my insides, melting the icy protective shell I had cultivated with mantras like *Chinese parents don't divorce*. When Kelley and I looked at each other, what was happening became real. After a split second, I looked away from him—a move that could have been instinctive if it were not for the lingering weight of the guilt that followed my averted eyes. I had abandoned him when he had pleaded with me. I stubbornly stared at the lazy fan making its rounds against the backdrop of the dirty, grease-splattered ceiling. I studied it for what seemed like hours, squishing my eyes, on the verge of tears, until the fan blurred and appeared to be leaving dark streaks as it swept past. I counted fifty-two spatters of grease on the ceiling. In time, when I had kept at this long enough, willing myself not to see or hear my family, my parents had stopped talking and we were getting ready to drive home, in silence. I still didn't make eye contact with Kelley, not even when we got back to the car and Dad drove us back into the East Bay.

The fog had lifted and the night was a soft violet with a near-full moon. I usually loved how the yellow glow of the lights on the lower deck of the Bay Bridge made our return trips from the city feel ethereal. Usually sleepy and content from a big meal, I would drift halfway to sleep, look up at the underside of the upper deck, and study the patterns in the steelwork. I liked to imagine the right-angled supports were upside-down seats in a huge ship, or a movie theater. Mom would lean her cheek against the passenger side window and fall asleep. Dad would look at me and whisper, "Shh, Mom's asleep," even though I hadn't been talking.

This trip home was not like that. Everyone was awake and silent. The word *li hun*, divorce, hung in the still air. When we got to the Caldecott Tunnel, neither Kelley nor I challenged each other to hold our breath. We got home, went our separate ways. I was relieved to shut the door to my bedroom. I did not sleep much that night. I imagined the upside-down seats of the Bay Bridge at night whooshing over my head, seeking their usual soothing effect. But I kept thinking back to Mom's tears, the pink napkin, and Kelley's desperate eyes. I had turned away from both of them. I had failed them. It felt like a precedent, like I was locked into this state: *May cause emotional detachment.*

I had set my course. It would cost me, all of us, too much to turn back now and acknowledge what had just happened. Because acknowledging it would mean that our family would someday break; denying it still provided the possibility that we would be the same as before. Kelley would have to endure this on his own, as would I.

We never spoke of it. And that was how I learned to look away. I was eight years old.

❧

After Daoud gave me his younger brother's phone number, Maiwand did not call me back for about a week. He finally asked to meet the day after the United States started bombing Afghanistan. He suggested we meet at a Starbucks on the ground floor of a downtown office building. When I found him there in line, he was fingering a newspaper on a display with aerial infrared photos of bomb-damaged Ariana Airlines planes at Kabul International Airport. The headline: AMERICA STRIKES BACK.

"Disgusting," he muttered to himself, and dropped the paper like it was toxic. Then he turned around and found me, the newspaper reporter, ready to greet him.

"Thanks for meeting with me," I said sheepishly, as we shook hands. Maiwand nodded.

"They're *commercial* airplanes," he muttered as he turned to the barista to order. "Venti coffee, please. Extra hot. With room."

Maiwand's intimate knowledge of Starbucks lingo suddenly put me at ease. It was to him what a red, turbo-charged car was to Daoud, these quirky anomalies that gave me footholds onto their personalities. Maiwand looked a bit like his older brother, with a similar compact build and black eyes. He was forty, and had married an Afghan woman from Pakistan a few years ago and just become a father to a baby girl four months ago. He had a thick mop of wavy black hair that had been tamed into a professional-enough hairstyle, accentuated by the Portland business-casual uniform: light blue button-up shirt, khakis, brown Timberlands that looked office-acceptable but could go for a hike. I wanted to feel comfortable with him. But the raw edge of his anger rested between his thick brows, knitted in concentration as he sipped his giant cup of coffee. A piano player in the building lobby was offering up gentle classical music against the trickle of fountains. Had United States had just started a war? We settled on some couches overlooking the lobby.

"What do you want to know?" he said, wary.

Slowly, I asked questions, easy ones at first, then harder ones, and Maiwand described his youth in the village and then Kabul. He and the youngest brother, Yusuf, also in Portland, were the closest in age. They played together, stole apples together, were each other's shadows as eldest brother Daoud was already out in the world making his name, sending back toys, books, and clothing to them. Maiwand was attending the Kabul Polytechnic University when the communist coup started.

"And then my older brother Mohammed was lost," he said. "And everything changed."

"He was lost," I tested out this odd phrasing in my own mouth.

"That's what we say," Maiwand said. "His body was never found. He was taken by Soviets and Afghans working for the KGB, put in prison, and a year later they handed his wife his clothes, his wedding ring, and watch and told her to stop looking for him."

In Afghan culture, he explained, when a death is unconfirmed and there is no body, everyone says that person is "lost" until both parents die. "My mother is still alive. She still says her son disappeared."

"Daoud doesn't say that," I said. Could I push him a bit on this? Somehow, the khakis, Timberlands, and Starbucks cup made me feel like I could.

"No. But that's Daoud," he said. "You can bet he says 'lost' in front of our dear mother."

Calm washed over me. He had decided to trust me. I was being let in through the next door of the family compound. I asked about how he and Daoud raised the six nephews and nieces in Portland, including Mohammed's children.

"It was a sacrifice. I would have never married so late," he said, the tightness dissipating from his brow, replaced by something new. Regret? Melancholy? Tenderness? "I would have never waited so late to start a family."

Soon, I was asking to see his daughter's picture, and the first real smile broke out across his face. It was a toothy, almost giddy, smile. He pulled out a day planner he had been carrying, and in a pocket on the inside flap of the front cover, there were two photos of a plump-faced infant in the hospital, with a mass of black hair much like his own, only baby-fine. Unlike most squinty-eyed newborn pictures, in this one her eyes were wide open, chocolate brown, already with a luxurious fringe of black lashes.

"She's beautiful," I said, really meaning it.

Her name was Aisha Diwa. Her middle name meant "light." "She changed everything," he said. "Not just for me. I mean, I became a different person, a softer person. But I think she's good for the whole family."

He paused, not sure if he wanted to say more. Tell me more, I wanted to whisper, but was afraid to break the spell that had transformed Maiwand before my eyes.

"You know, in Islam, the *adhan*, or call to prayer, is said into a newborn's right ear after birth, sometimes before the umbilical cord is cut," he said. "And when Aisha was born, the whole family came together in the hospital for that—for the first Shirzai born in America."

The family in Portland had become a somewhat unnatural, if tight-knit, product of untimely death and war, he said. It had been a long time since new life was breathed into it.

"She's the only one who doesn't know this bombing is going on, the only one who has a chance to grow up knowing only a peaceful Afghanistan," he said. "And we, we needed to see that this is how life happens—how family happens."

He looked back down at Aisha's photo. "She's much bigger now. You should see her."

"I would love to, and to meet your wife," I said.

"We get the whole family together for dinner on Sundays. This Sunday should be interesting," he said, explaining that they needed to make a call to Pakistan to check on news about relatives in Kabul near some of the bombing sites. Phone lines and internet had been cut off after the invasion started. "You're welcome to join us. If you're free."

If I'm free? I was the guest whom they had let in past the courtyard wall, invited into the home—and finally, allowed to peer through the curtain between public and private, what Tamim Ansary described as "the hidden world inside our compounds." Now, as war began in their homeland, the Shirzais were letting me in. Maybe they trusted me, maybe they needed a witness to their pain and worry, maybe they just needed to share something with someone other than lectures about their country and war. But I was not stepping into their hidden world to learn more about Afghanistan, or even to share in their news from Pakistan and Kabul. I needed to see, as Maiwand put it, "how family happens."

And the bonds that held them together within the walls of their home were all that was certain, unchanging.

4.

The First and the Last

That first Sunday dinner at the Shirzais was, like so many things in their family, a series of rituals. By the time I went, I had also met other members separately: The youngest brother, Yusuf, lanky and artistic, exuding a hippie vibe despite his day job as a software engineer; Mohib, Sarasa, and Mina, the three children of Mohammed who were half of the six raised by the uncles—it was important to Daoud that I meet Mohammed's children first. Now, I was about to meet the other three of the nieces and nephews: Laila, the youngest of the six, and her two older brothers, children of one of Daoud's other brothers. By now, only Laila and Mina were still living in the house with Maiwand, his wife, and daughter. But nearly everyone would be coming from their respective places nearby for tonight's weekly meeting.

My throat was dry and tight as I hesitated before the doorbell. I was, finally, entering into the inner sanctum. Now what? Would they sit around awkwardly and wait for me to ask questions? Would I feel at ease? What was the next test?

From the moment Maiwand opened the door, to the seamless flow of Mina and Laila's hospitality, seating me around an L-shape sectional in the family room, keeping my glass cup of amber-colored cardamom-scented tea full at all times, making sure every family member who was there shook my hand, I was enveloped into a flow.

The unlocked front door swung open. Everyone stopped talking and stood up.

Daoud strolled in, his stride heavy, face slack, and professorial uniform rumpled. He paused at the threshold of the family room, took a breath, and straightened his posture as he walked in, hand extended toward Maiwand. The rest had placed themselves in a receiving line. Mohib, Daoud and Maiwand's nephew, motioned for me to stand in it as well, so I took a place at the far end, opposite Maiwand. Daoud shook every family member's hand, saying, interchangeably, "*Salaam aleikum*" and "How are you?" When he got to Maiwand's wife, who was holding baby Aisha, Daoud shook the mother's hand and rumpled the baby's feathery black Kewpie-doll hair. Daoud's greeting routine was a deliberate revision of Afghan gender protocol. I'd later learn that, in Afghanistan and even in many Afghan immigrant families, men and women never shook hands with each other. When he got to me at the end of the line, he didn't hesitate as he clasped my hand. "*Salaam aleikum*, Angie."

Everyone sat down. Daoud remained standing. "What's the word from Peshawar?" The family had been waiting for phone calls from relatives in the Pakistani border city who might know news from Afghanistan, to which all communication had been cut off since the start of the bombing. But there had been no news that day, Maiwand said. Unblinking, Daoud continued asking questions, scanning the room like he did during a lecture: "So what's the latest on the bomb damage?" "Is the Northern Alliance attacking?" "What do you think will happen to Afghanistan in a week?"

Before he had arrived, the living room had been a cacophony of separate conversations.

But now, as each of the nieces and nephews sat up straighter as Daoud's eyes fell on them, I understood. As with my first phone interview, and his lecture audiences, Professor Shirzai had a way of making them want to pass muster with him. But here, the didactic, professorial demeanor was a diversion. His voice spoke the words but his eyes were far away, his mind on his sister and her family in Kabul, near the bombing, and his brother, who was traveling the dangerous border region to Pakistan, where phones lines were working, so that he could deliver the long-awaited news from Kabul.

Fragrant steam from big plates with stewed chicken and eggplant, piles of basmati rice, and crispy pieces of puffy flatbread, wafted around the family members casually camped around the coffee table. Talk of the war continued. I was interested in what they had to say, but more so, in their rapport, the sense of shared purpose, shared blood, in this room among so many, all talking at once, but never interrupting. Dinners at my house growing up were always quiet, because we were wary of setting off my father if he had come home from work in a bad mood. It had almost always been the four of us; extended family had dispersed around the country and rarely came together. And since my father's latest depression, going my childhood home for visits were consumed with an awful silence, us tiptoeing around his stagnant presence in the downstairs master bedroom, hardly moving or talking, Mom grim and exhausted, sleeping upstairs in our old rooms, still with their Pac-Man and Miss Piggy comforters my brother and I had chosen ourselves.

No wonder the warmth of the Shirzais's food and their bonds felt irresistibly novel and nourishing to me. I wanted so much to be a part of something that felt easy, inviting, yet larger than myself. Something that felt like family.

When fresh pots of tea and trays of after-dinner snacks appeared on the coffee table, Daoud yawned, wrapped a cookie in a napkin, and stood up. "So, everyone is OK so far?"

"So far," said Laila, the youngest niece at age twenty. Curled up in the corner of the sectional couch in track pants, she had been quiet since Daoud arrived. She and Daoud exchanged a look. Recognition? Knowing? Something passed between them in that instant. Daoud nodded and said his farewells much as he had greeted everyone. They stood up in line and he shook everyone's hand, ending with mine again. "*Khudai paaman*, Angie," he said, and headed out the door.

As everyone retreated back to their separate conversations, I sought out Laila, whom I had just met earlier that evening, looking for her petite frame and casual outfit among her more formally dressed cousins. They had described her as a goody-goody, the youngest one who followed all of her uncles' rules and still lived in Maiwand's house while the others had moved out. She wore small, fashionable glasses, which seemed to fit her image as the studious, obedient one in the family.

"I think this is a bit different for me than the rest of my family because I was so young when I left Afghanistan for Pakistan," she said, measuring her words. She was born right before the Soviet War started, the same year her cousins'—Mohib, Sarasa, and Mina's—father was killed by the communists. "So I've visited Afghanistan, but I don't remember it the way my cousins do, and certainly not like my uncles do."

Was she explaining why she didn't participate in the family conversation about Afghanistan? Or apologizing for not having a deeper connection to her birthplace as it was being bombed?

"Do you want to go back?" I asked, not sure if that was the right question.

Something came alive in her big eyes, something I had not seen in her all night. "Yes," she said. "More than just about anything. September 11, this war, just makes me realize how much I need to be a part of Afghanistan. Or have it be a part of me."

I wanted to ask her about Daoud, to understand that glint of recognition that passed between them, but family members started leaving, and my conversation with Laila was sidetracked. Before this dinner, Mohib and Mina had reached out to me first, and their gregariousness had made it easy to get to know them. Laila had been easy to overlook, the youngest, the goody-goody, the quiet one in a boisterous family. There was something guarded about her, that made her a bit of a cipher. Laila's reticence, her relationship with Daoud, the light in her eyes when talking about going to Afghanistan—these things made me want to know her even more.

As I got ready to leave, Maiwand motioned to a small color photograph hanging near the threshold of the family room, where we had eaten dinner. The silver department-store frame gave me a window into another universe: a village of sunbleached adobe, the same color as the dun earth, against a wide sky—deep blue, unadulterated by trees or telephone poles.

"Shinzmaray. Our village," Maiwand had said. "Daoud and I were born in this house. Our father built and ran the mosque next door. They're still standing today."

The family's village was a tiny warren of mud-brick buildings, comprised of no more than a few hundred people, in the Ghazni province southwest of Kabul. Though it had been heavily bombed by the Soviets, the Shirzais's home and the mosque there had escaped unscathed. Shinzmaray, like most of rural Afghanistan, to this day did not have running water or electricity. The village was completely alien to the Kabul cityscapes I had seen on the news, as well as to Maiwand's comfortable American home.

Something essential about the family lay between those three worlds: Shinzmaray, Kabul, and Portland. I wanted to climb into the frame and feel the dry brown earth below my feet.

Maiwand watched me stare into the photo.

"You should go with us," he said. He smiled, as if he weren't sure whether I'd think he was crazy.

"I should," I replied, keeping my voice steady and quiet. I wanted to shout, "Yes!" As I was being let in through the walls of the compound, feeling the trust between me, Daoud, and Maiwand grow, I had started letting myself think of what had seemed impossible: I could go to Afghanistan with them. The idea had started developing hard edges earlier that evening, as I had really started to feel like a member of the family. Hearing Maiwand articulate it seemed too good to be true.

By the time I was talking to Maiwand about the photo, Laila had excused herself to go upstairs and get ready for bed. But right after I said, "I should," and before Maiwand got my coat out of the closet, I glanced upward and saw Laila at the top of the stairs. She had been watching, listening intently. She had seen me grinning to myself after Maiwand had turned away. I blushed. She had an inscrutable half-smile on her face. I shook Maiwand's hand in parting, thanked him, and stepped out the door into the cold, damp autumn night. I turned back one last time, and Laila's eyes met mine. At that moment, I knew it: We would go someday. She and I. Though we had just met that night, our fates felt inextricably tied.

༄

As 2001 came to a close, the war, and the rebuilding of Afghanistan, limped along. Two weeks after September 11, Hamid Karzai, a dapper Pashtun from an aristocratic Kandahari family, had literally ridden into town, through Pakistan and over the Khyber Pass, on the back of a friend's motorcycle. He was appointed the post-Taliban interim leader in December 2001 in Bonn, Germany, at a conference that established the structure of the new Afghan government.

As the first post-Taliban leader of the reborn nation, Karzai became known for his flashy trademark outfit which blended elements of Afghanistan's various ethnic groups. Gucci's Tom Ford proclaimed Karzai "the chicest man on the planet." His *karakul* hat, a close-fitting, angular topper made from the just-barely-fleecy hide of a fetal lamb, became a fashion statement on Manhattan streets. Unimpressed, Daoud nicknamed Karzai "the Gucci Afghan."

As the new democratic government took shape in fits and starts, Daoud got the call in the winter of 2002, asking him to work for the new Minister of Higher Education. Despite his skepticism of Karzai and the cabinet, Daoud trusted the Minister, also an expatriate Afghan. He had to do it. He feared not getting the call more than anything. So Daoud took a leave from teaching and prepared for a nine-week stint in the spring. It would be his first extended stay in his birthplace in more than thirty years.

Since that first Sunday family dinner last fall, I had thought I might be done with my reporting on the Shirzais and began accepting social invitations from them, eager to drop the reporter mantle with them. When Maiwand asked me back for another Sunday evening, I again found myself easily absorbed into the family's rituals. Daoud encouraged me, in his own understated way, to make visits to his long, narrow office at Mt. Tabor College to discuss what was happening in Afghanistan and his plans to return and help with the rebuilding. I could see the Ministry appointment was something he'd been waiting for—his words conveyed cynicism for the red tape and corruption in the new government, but light in his eyes and spring in his step told me of newfound hope and purpose. It was the same light I had seen in Laila's eyes at that first Sunday dinner, when she spoke of returning to Afghanistan.

Laila had continued to remain more elusive than her cousins. Mina and Mohib routinely invited me to lunches or dinners on their own, amused that their uncles' new "friend" was closer to them in age and culture. I did see Laila regularly in Daoud's office. She was a senior now, and in her hours between classes, she came to help Daoud with emails and other tasks that confounded her technology-averse uncle. Now that he was getting ready to go to Afghanistan, her help was needed more than ever. I watched them together in his small office. They didn't speak much but worked around each other in that narrow space without getting in each other's way. Occasionally, she read an email out loud to him. "A student wants to know when she's getting her paper back," Laila said. "Tell her as soon as I solve all of Afghanistan's problems, I'll get to grading her paper," he fired back. "So that'll be about 2025. Hope she doesn't mind waiting." They both chuckled. I smiled too, but they hardly noticed me once they got into their work groove.

When I was close to Laila's age, I had worked for my father's then-budding real estate and mortgage business for a summer back from college. He was in that precarious and precious transition between depression and mania, when he was both productive and tolerable to be around, often pleasant. He stationed me in his home office he had built out of a basement he finished and renovated largely by himself. He'd sit in one of those backless "posture" chairs that used two slated cushions to support the sitter's knees and buttocks, in a position that was ultimately so uncomfortable, it's no surprise the contraptions eventually disappeared. I'd be on a rolling desk chair, sliding across the large plastic floormat he had laid in the workspace so I could help him edit letters and documents on one computer, check the Multiple Listing Service on a separate computer, and grab curling paper off the fax machine. Soon, I knew the business and his deals-in-progress well enough that he had me drafting letters from scratch, handing them off to him to proofread them and sign his name. I enjoyed this role, writing in my father's official, and sometimes officious, voice, only with better grammar.

As we became easy and relaxed in our workflow, I would sometimes intentionally write a trick sentence into a letter just to see if Dad was paying attention when he proofed. Once, on a buyer-seller dispute over whether the appliances conveyed with the house, my father asked me to write a stern letter informing the buyers they were told from the beginning that the appliances were not included in the sale price. "*However,*" I wrote toward the end of the letter, "*You may keep the toilets. Though I believe you are full of crap, let us flush the past behind us and plunge into a better relationship in the future,*" stifling my giggles as I typed these lines and hit "print." My father laughed and laughed when he found those sentences and then chided me, "What if we accidentally had sent it that way?" Which made him laugh harder. For weeks after that, he would repeat those lines. "Full of crap, flush the past!" he would guffaw. I felt a great weight being lifted from me, replaced by warmth. My father and I actually had an inside joke for the first time in as long as I could remember.

Most of all, Dad thrived on having me as witness to his homegrown business, insisting that I accompany him on errands—my only official role always turned out to be chauffer, driving his new "realtor car," a BMW 535, to various title companies, banks, clients' homes and offices. But he wanted to mutually show us all off to each other. I had grown so tired of my father's depression, been so relieved to leave the pall his stillness left over our house by going away to college, that returning that summer to find my vibrant, productive father whom I could spend time with (if even only doing menial office tasks), I was thrilled to be his secretary-assistant. Maybe if I helped him enough this time around, business would be so good that there would be no inevitable depression to follow.

But by the time I was watching Laila and Daoud in his office, those memories of my father were far away. I felt a pang of envy at Laila and Daoud's unspoken connection, because I no longer had that with my father. But I also wanted both of their attention, my growing friendships with each of them, and the Shirzai family entire, becoming increasingly important as my relationship with my own family felt broken, painful, and cold—all that was the opposite of the Shirzais. At that time, as the post-9/11 economic crash had slowed Dad's real estate business down, he was sliding into another depression—the one that would finally lead my mother to divorce him a couple years later. I hated calling home and hearing the catch in Mom's voice as she spoke in code about Dad ("Business is not so good. He's home watching TV a lot."). By then, we knew what was coming, and I wanted to be as far away from it as possible. Work had been very busy after the terrorist attacks, and I used the vague idea that I was always at work to avoid calling home as often as I normally would. The truth was, I was spending a lot of time with the Shirzais, but I didn't explain to Mom that it wasn't exactly work anymore.

Once, as Laila and I left Daoud's office at the same time, we walked through the lush, tree-lined campus of the college to the parking lot as she told me a story about Daoud. When all six of them first arrived in Oregon, they were all middle- and high-school aged, completely culture-shocked after spending most of their childhoods in the Afghan refugee schools of Peshawar. Laila, the youngest, was twelve. Thanks to the legacy of British colonialism in Pakistan, they had learned some English. But Daoud wanted their entry to American public school to be as seamless as possible. He decided that the girls could go without chador and wear western clothes to school. Against school administrators' advice, he enrolled them at grade level in mainstream English classes, bypassing the English as a Second Language track. He hired an English tutor to come to the house after school. Laila recalled Daoud sat them in front of the nightly six o'clock news to watch anchor Peter Jennings. "Peter Jennings speaks the most correct English, with the best pronunciation," Daoud told them. "I want you to watch carefully, study how his mouth moves, and emulate him."

I wondered if Daoud knew Peter Jennings was Canadian, and probably had to erase traces of his own accent as well. I was about to point this out, but Laila continued.

"So none of us speak with an accent. All of us went to college, all here, on time, not missing a year," she said. "Everyone has graduated, except me. I'm the last one. Daoud says when I graduate this June, his work is done."

"Just in time for him to take on the new Afghan government," I said.

She nodded, taking my remark more seriously than I meant it. For all that they teased Uncle Daoud about his fashion sense or driving, there was such reverence for him beneath it all. And Laila's was the most palpable. And why not? He had been the first Shirzai to have set foot on American soil. She, in effect, had been the last. When he had decided to bring the three children—Mohib, Sarasa, and Mina—of his slain brother to Portland, he said he could take three more. The family in Peshawar spoke of which boys to send. But Daoud insisted he wanted equal numbers of boys and girls. Afghan refugee girls had even fewer opportunities in Pakistan than boys, he argued. "Let's save three girls and three boys," he had said. He had used that verb, "save." Because two of the three girls were already Mohammed's daughters, the family didn't protest. That left room for one more girl—Laila, along with her two older brothers.

With that decision, Daoud and Laila became the bookends to the Shirzais's patchwork family in Portland. The oldest and the youngest; the first and the last.

                          ❧

By the time Laila graduated from Mt. Tabor College with her bachelor's degree, Daoud had gone to and returned from Afghanistan. He was sobered by the state of the country, and spoke of the endless work to be done. He was already planning a longer-term trip back to do more work with the Ministry. As for Laila's graduation, the college's policy of giving each student four tickets for undergraduate commencement ceremonies could hardly make it a family event. So a few went, but as had been the case with the other nieces and nephews, everyone focused on the real celebration afterward.

"You're coming to the party at Maiwand's, right?" Laila asked me casually, as if I should already have known he hosted a barbecue after every graduation ceremony.

"Party? Of course," I said quickly, pleased. I was no longer an afterthought, or any kind of additional thought, for the Shirzais. I was a given, the ultimate kind of belonging. The idea of a family party was tantalizingly novel to me as well. When was the last time my family had celebrated anything? Or had a reason to celebrate?

I arrived at the house that afternoon, and found an array of family members and guests, the latter an orbit of neighbors, Mt. Tabor colleagues, and Laila's female friends from high school and college. I came to realize many in this orbit were young people who felt estranged from their own families in some way, whether as children of divorce and in conflict with their parents. Was I one of them? At that time, I didn't include myself in their ranks. I came to them as a journalist, I told myself, not wanting to acknowledge how much my desire to flee my own family drove me toward the Shirzais.

Nearly every family member was there. Mohib, Sarasa, and Mina were in the family room with the younger people. Mohib was flirting with his cousin Laila's friends, and his sister Mina was trying to ignore him. Their middle sister Sarasa, I learned after not seeing her at those first Sunday dinners, had not spoken to her uncles in years as a result of an old but deep conflict over house rules and a forbidden boyfriend—depending on whom was telling the story, she was either kicked out of Maiwand's house or she moved out. Sarasa was dutifully avoiding them, and they her. Laila's two brothers were in the backyard with the men, who were watching Maiwand tend to the Afghan kebab on the grill and talking politics. Baby Aisha had just passed her first birthday, and was walking unsteadily on the wooden deck. Yusuf sat nearby, swinging a long arm out to catch her when she swayed.

Even at Sunday dinners after that first one, I had rarely seen the entire family together. Laila's graduation brought them here. But one person was still missing.

I waved to Maiwand at the grill, and stepped inside to greet Laila, in a new pale blue shalwar kameez. Unlike her cousins and aunts, Laila was neither a hugger nor a cheek-kisser, so I never quite knew how to greet her. But she quickly draped a thin arm over me, and leaned in, not dislodging the matching filmy blue scarf over her shoulders. Her straight black hair, often in a ponytail, was loose around her shoulders today.

"Is Daoud still at the ceremony?" I asked.

She laughed. He never goes to commencement, she told me, not even when the nieces and nephews are graduating. "He thinks it's silly and doesn't want to wear one of those professor's outfits," she said, referring to robes and hoods of academic regalia. "He calls it a 'monkey suit.' He'll be here. He's always late. I'm sure it's because he likes to make an entrance."

When he did make his entrance, just as Maiwand's wife and Mina were putting the kebab on paper plates, the nieces and nephews converged in the family room. He greeted each one of them, shaking their hands, saying "*Salaam aleikum*" and "How are you?" as he always did. At the end, he got to Laila.

"Well, here we have the graduate," he said, shaking her hand. "*Salaam*, Laila. Congratulations."

"Thank you," she said, smiling, her cheeks pink.

"So, now that you have this degree, how do you plan to become rich and famous?" he said, uncharacteristically sunny.

"Well, let me work on finding a job first," she said.

"Very well then," he said. "And how do you plan to help the country?"

By country, he meant *watan*, a word in Pashto the Shirzais repeated so often it was one of the first I learned, after hello and goodbye. *Watan*, one of the four words for home, meant one's own country—it meant Afghanistan. Daoud had asked this question of every family member when they graduated.

And everyone always had an answer. If being a Shirzai meant anything, it meant having a plan to help the country. Now that Daoud was part of the new government, their plans and ideas became more tangible, more urgent. And they all had plans and ideas. His nephew Mohib, who worked as a hospital administrator, talked about becoming a doctor and opening a clinic there. Uncle Yusuf was applying for non-profit status to make official his efforts to renovate schools in the family's village. Uncle Maiwand thought his engineering expertise could to be used to help Kabul's shattered infrastructure.

"I'd like to get my master's in education and teach English in Afghanistan," Laila said.

"Good," Daoud said. He hoped Laila would eventually enroll in the education master's program at Mt. Tabor in which he taught. "They need you there. There are not enough female teachers."

That light in her eyes, the one I saw that first Sunday dinner I asked her about going back to Afghanistan, was back, shining behind her glasses. Were her eyes moist, even? She blinked; they were dry. Maybe I had imagined it. If this were a Hollywood movie, or a white American family, Daoud and Laila would have embraced in that moment, and Daoud would have proclaimed, eyes shining with tears, "The youngest of the six has graduated. My work is done."

But instead, Laila nodded at Daoud and after a long silence, he nodded back, rocked onto his heels, and clasped his hands together. "Well, is it time to eat?"

Plates of kebab were passed around. I found Daoud in a corner of the family room, polishing off his plate. Wanting a bit more reflection from him, I asked him how he felt about the last of the six finishing college.

"Well, I think they all knew that getting a bachelor's degree was a minimum," he said. "I adopted them until they turned eighteen, so their lives are their own now, to do what they wish with them. I hope they don't forget those they left behind in Afghanistan."

"I doubt they will," I said. It would be hard to in this family. But unspoken were the distractions, many which were present before us: Mohib's flirting, Maiwand's new family, and Sarasa's old fight with the uncles. Not to mention Laila's friends gathered at this party, and the ease and comfort of life here.

Daoud left early, as usual, shaking all the nieces and nephew's hands, and the party continued. As Laila was opening her presents in front of the younger women, the house phone rang, and she jumped up. Mina and Laila's friends looked at each other. We found Laila in the kitchen, pacing back and forth, a finger in her free ear to block out the noise of the party, and a different kind of spark in her eyes. She spoke in a hushed voice.

I looked at Mina. "It's Tim," she whispered, "calling to congratulate her."

"Who's Tim?"

"You don't know who Tim is?" one of the friends asked, incredulous.

"Shh," Mina waved a slender arm at the friend, as if fanning smoke away from a detector. "Ask Laila to tell you later. When the uncles aren't here."

⊱

Later that summer, when Laila was interning at city hall, she asked me to meet her for lunch in a park between our two offices. I wanted to ask her about Tim, wanted her to trust me with her secret. But she had other ideas.

Daoud, who was back in Kabul then, had decided take a sabbatical next spring and return there for the entire semester. The Afghan Ministry of Higher Education was giving him a longer-term position. He and Laila had exchanged emails last week, after he was granted his sabbatical. He wanted her to join him during that time—her city job would have ended by then. Maybe she could do some teaching, like she had told him she wanted to. And there was more: He had asked her if I might want to go along with her, maybe do some reporting on the Ministry and higher-education rebuilding efforts in Afghanistan. Or perhaps I just wanted to understand their country better, to see firsthand what they talked about all the time. Laila could be my interpreter and, as a woman, she could accompany me in the gender-segregated culture.

"Really?" I said. "Daoud wants me to go to Afghanistan?"

I wanted to go, more than just about anything. And I couldn't help being proud that Daoud himself had requested my presence. I knew he was thinking the media coverage might do Afghanistan some good, especially as the world's attentions were turning to Iraq. I had to go. I had passed all of Daoud's tests, made it past all the walls. Now the inner sanctum, the ultimate place of belonging, was Afghanistan.

"Yes, he wants you to go," Laila said. "He thinks we should stay in Kabul and then go to Shinzmaray if it's safe enough."

And at that moment, sitting on the brick steps of the city park, eating burritos from a streetside food cart, the silver-framed picture of the village —the promise that Maiwand's "You should go with us," and Laila's glance, had held—became a reality to me. It was as if Daoud had asked me, "And how do you plan to help the country?"

Like all the nieces and nephews, I had a ready answer.

In those first couple of years after 9/11, I was simply in the Shirzai family's orbit, observing, slowly unfurling their stories as each layer revealed greater complexity. It was impossible not to admire Daoud, to want to please him, to be flattered and proud when he included me in something as simple as his handshake-greeting ritual—or something as profound as traveling to Afghanistan. But it took longer for me to realize that to truly understand the Shirzais was to get to know Laila. She was pulled by two irrevocable forces: On the one side, family, country, and culture. On the other, the mysterious phone call, and a whispered name: Tim. How she ultimately navigated this dichotomy would alter the course of not only her own life, but also of the Shirzai family entire. For she was the youngest. Daoud had, in fact, chosen to save her. She was the last, just as he was the first. And history tells us that the last, not the first, will be the one who carries the past and writes the future.

All the while, as I became Laila's friend, and later her confidante and accomplice, I was too consumed by her dilemmas and her importance to the Shirzais to see the obvious: My father had been my family's first in the United States. And I was the first born in the United States. We were, like Daoud and Laila, bookends to a generation of migration. How would I write my family's future?

I never asked myself this question. I was too busy trying to become subsumed into the Shirzais, to flee to Afghanistan as the inevitable collapse of my nuclear family approached. I wasn't concerned with writing my family's future because I couldn't see that we had one.

Part Two:

Mena / Birthplace

No matter where I turn my head
In village or in desert
Deep silence has engulfed the dead
And they have left no message

Which way they disappeared, God knows,
And what has them befallen,
For I can find no news of those
Who from cliff have fallen

My heart is broken by the thought
That there are those with knowledge.
If so, O blessed ones! you ought
To share with me for solace

From here where do you go to stay?
What kind of dwelling is it?

—Rahman Baba, "Quo vadis?"

5.
The Women

We stood before the bright blue wooden door, a single spot of color against the long, white compound wall and the dun, rubble-strewn city of Kabul. For all the imagined walls surrounding the Shirzais when I first got to know them, this was the first time I was faced with an actual compound wall.

"This is it," Laila said.

On the other side of the wall, I would soon meet two women, Daoud's sister Amina and their mother, whom I had been hearing about for three years. The women had survived in Afghanistan through the Soviet War, the civil war, the Taliban, and the current U.S. invasion while their sons and brothers fled to America. They were illiterate and had never gone to school. They were the ones who stayed.

Daoud had purchased this house before the Soviet War, soon after taking his first university teaching job in Portland. He had originally intended to return one day and live there. But then Mohammed was taken. Guilty by association with his brother and the United States, Daoud knew he could not come back. His sister had taken over the house.

Laila's grandmother and Aunt Amina, the younger sister whom Daoud had referred to in his post-9/11 lectures, were waiting for us in the women's sitting room. What would I say to these women, I wondered? Even with Laila interpreting, could we ever understand each other?

At the airport, when Stephanie and I had first spotted Laila, I had been surprised at how different she looked wearing a cream-colored headscarf on over her head, something she had never done in Portland. Apparently, she had the same reaction to us in our *chador* and *shalwar kameez*.

"Oh my gosh, look at you guys," Laila had said, as she looked us up and down. "You look like Afghans!"

Only after she had hugged each of us fiercely did I realize that here, unlike in Portland, there had been no hesitation around our greeting.

Our driver, a gaunt, bearded man had rushed up to collect our bags. Impatient with our grinning and gawking, he threw the luggage into the trunk of the blue Volga sedan. Afghans don't lollygag, particularly not in high-density places where car bombs can go off. A second man with a long, gray beard and eyes the color and luminosity of topazes stood serenely by the passenger side, waiting to greet us. In stark white *shalwar kameez* and a *kufi* skull cap, this was Hamid, Laila's father. He was Daoud's brother who had stayed behind, and traversed the treacherous Khyber Pass roads from Peshawar to Kabul and the village to keep an eye on all the family members, while his brothers raised three of his five children in America. Laila and her two brothers had spent so much time away from him, with Daoud and Maiwand as surrogate fathers, that they referred to Hamid as ka ka, or "uncle." If that ever bothered Hamid, I never detected it.

"*Salaam aleikum*," I said to him.

"Hello. How are you?" he said in crisp English. I took Hamid's outstretched hand. Most Afghan men would not shake a woman's hand or speak such precise English, but his time as an English teacher and his understanding of American ways set him apart.

Hamid motioned for the three of us to get into the backseat. As I sunk into the vinyl upholstery, I sighed. A warm, drowsy sensation had pooled over me as my adrenalin receded. From that moment on, I had placed my life into the Shirzais's hands. I was their guest.

But now, standing before the women's sitting room at the family compound, I was Laila's grandmother's guest first and foremost. She was the oldest surviving Shirzai, having lost her husband in the 1990s; as a matriarch, her job would be to welcome female guests, like me and Stephanie, to the home.

Grandma, as I came to call her, rose slowly from a cushion, a dark, squat shape behind a filmy curtain hanging before the entrance.

Laila parted the curtain and Grandma came toward us. I had practiced the traditional women's greeting with Laila's older female relatives in America: the embrace, the left-right-left cheek kisses, and a rapid-fire series of Pashto greetings. Still, I worried I might mess it up, as I sometimes did, going right instead of left and awkwardly almost kissing the other woman on the lips.

I practically stumbled into Grandma's outstretched arms, and she engulfed me in an iron embrace, hugging me with more force than any of Laila's American relatives ever had. Her tight hug relieved my lungs of air. Her grip was cushioned, though, by the black fabric of her large chador and a voluminous traditional Afghan dress. How did a woman who had appeared so frail when she was getting up have so much strength? She placed a soft hand on each side of my face and regarded me at arm's length, her glittering black eyes attempting to focus on me as if to say, *So you are the one they've been talking about.* I desperately wanted her approval. Her hands firmly guided my head from side to side, training wheels for the kissing, as she pressed her lips into my cheeks.

"*Salaam aleikum! Tsenga ye? Jora ye? Stere me se!*" she said. Peace be with you! How are you? How is your health? May you not be tired! I repeated the words back to her as best I could, trying to roll my "r" on *Stere*, "tired," just right.

The octogenarian before me had lost five of her fourteen children to disease or accidents when they were small. Then Mohammed was taken. Then the wars, the Taliban, and, now, the Americans. Who was I to tell her not to be tired?

Behind Grandma, Amina approached. Tall and solid, she embraced and kissed us with more formality, her eyes not smiling even as her mouth did. Her pale blue dress and white chador set off her brown complexion, the same as Daoud's. She motioned for us to sit next to her on the long floor cushion. Grandma reached over for extra pillows and handed them to Laila, gesturing for her to place them behind our backs. Then she settled down into her own nest of cushions, all of them a deep red to match the overlapping *bakara* rugs, with their repeating medallion patterns, that covered the floor. I saw, then, how these two matriarchs, full skirts over their crossed legs, firm pillows behind their backs, held court in this sitting room. None of the men of the household—not Daoud, not Amina's husband, nor any of Amina's sons—were anywhere to be found. Hamid had slipped away as soon as he delivered us to the door. Now Stephanie and I were women being welcomed into the women's side of the home.

The gauzy white curtain parted and in walked a young woman, preceded by a large silver tray. On it, she balanced a teapot, cups, puffy flatbread and plates of food. The smells of the yeasty bread, the savory coins of eggplant glistening with dollops of yogurt, the cardamom in the tea reached me. They felt like a salve to the assaultive odors of our trip from the airport through Kabul, our driver's Volga windows open for lack of air conditioning. The city's medieval-style open sewers and cesspools, the thick diesel pollution, and the unrelenting dust from unpaved roads combined to form its own stew. Not to mention the dankness of our Baku hotel room and the cocktail of hangovers, Old Spice, and pheromones that had emanated from the cargo-pants crowd, still too-recent memories. The aromas now being set before us were so welcoming, so pleasing, I wanted to bathe in them.

"This is my cousin, Rochina," Laila said. Rochina had recently married into the family, as the new wife of one of Amina's five sons.

Only then did I really notice the bearer of the tray. She was close to our age, with sultry brown eyes and heart-shaped face, wrapped in a cream-colored *chador*. Rochina set the tray down, embraced both Stephanie and me in turn, with the three cheek kisses and series of greetings. As a new daughter-in-law, she was expected to do a larger share of the cooking and housework, as well as be the key provider of hospitality for guests.

She motioned for us to eat and drink.

The warm tea washed over my dust-parched tongue and throat. Since starting Lariam, I rarely didn't feel dry-mouthed and thirsty. The endless tea drinking in Afghanistan would prove to be a boon to me. The salt and grease of Rochina's eggplant, dampened by the cool yogurt, reached my growling stomach. I wanted to hug her again in gratitude. Grandma and Amina took their cups of tea, and Rochina sat down with her own, across from us.

"Are you tired?" she asked in English, with an ease that reflected her education in Pakistan. Unlike young women who had stayed in Afghanistan, Rochina had not had her schooling interrupted by either war or the Taliban. "Have some more tea. Would you like more food? Is this food OK?"

When we finished, Grandma beckoned to me and Stephanie. She put on a pair of thick glasses that covered half her face and pulled something out of the folds of her scarf, like a magician. It was a tiny black crayon, pointed at one end.

"She does this to everyone," Laila said. "She wants to put kohl on your eyes to beautify you. Just don't let her poke your eye out."

Grandma firmly propped my face with one soft but strong hand, and trained the point of the crayon straight toward my left eye with the other. Laila instructed me to blink down on the tip as her grandmother drew it across my inner eyelids. Seeing the results, the matriarch threw up her hands and made a soft sound of delight. In this world of women, familiarity occurred through actions, not words. This instant intimacy was hospitality and, more subtly, a way of keeping us in line. Absorbed into the intricate social order of the household, we would be far less likely to disrupt it.

Chuckling, Rochina slipped back into the kitchen with the tray, and Amina disappeared into another part of the house. It was just the three of us and Grandma now.

I sat down next to Grandma as she began to talk. Laila sat on her other side, facing me, so she could interpret from Pashto. Grandma began to speak of Shinzmaray. She was only in Kabul because Daoud was there, she explained. She preferred the village to the city. It's peaceful there, she said—but it was not always that way.

"They used to throw many bombs and missiles in the village," Grandma said of the Soviets. "One day, from seven in the morning to seven at night, the planes kept circling and bombing." She gestured with her hands, sticking her thumb and pinky finger out like wings. "I can't hear well because of the bombs." Laila had instructed us to lean close to her good ear and shout.

"The bombs," she said, inhaling sharply, "dropped on people's crops and tractors. Their livelihoods were destroyed. Before the war started, people had so much land. Horses couldn't go from one end to the other. But now, the land has been destroyed. People hardly get by."

Now with her glasses on, Grandma studied me and Stephanie again.

"Are you sisters?" she asked, to which we smiled and shook our heads. "Are you married? How old are you? Where are your families?"

Stephanie and I answered the questions. Laila mumbled in English,

"I'm going to tell her you guys are twenty-five, not thirty, because otherwise you'll get an earful about not being married yet."

"Twenty-five?" Grandma said. "Why aren't you married yet? And Laila too. You should tell her to get married too."

Laila rolled her eyes. I couldn't help thinking about Tim. Laila had finally told me about him, back in Portland. They had met her freshman year at Mt. Tabor, nearly six years ago. He was from Colorado, had blond hair, and was definitely neither Afghan nor Muslim. None of the uncles knew about him. How could she ever explain him to her grandmother?

As Grandma continued to espouse the virtues of marriage, Laila stopped translating and whispered, "Change the subject."

"OK," I turned to Grandma and leaned into her good ear. "I'd like to show you what I do for a living."

Only twenty percent of Afghan women were literate, and nearly all of those who could read had grown up in urban areas. How many times in her life, if ever, had Grandma picked up a newspaper? Would she be able to comprehend what a journalist did? I pulled out a newspaper from 2001 with my first article about the Shirzais, the one with the most photos. Before I had a chance to say anything, she made an exclamation of delight at her son Daoud's photo on the front page, giving a university lecture. She kissed the newsprint image, making a smacking sound. I flipped the paper to the reverse side for her, where there were photos of Maiwand and baby Aisha (she gave each a kiss as well)—and an old, black-and-white family photo of Mohammed and his three children. Grandma's smile fell. She extended a finger toward the newsprint, caressing her late son's slim face, and then each of the children's.

Mohammed wore thick, horn-rimmed glasses and an argyle sweater. His dark side-swept hair was carefully combed. His children, all under the age six, piled on top of him as he reclined on a bed. He had been taken later that year.

"Mohib, Sarasa, Mina. Their father was taken. And now they are all the way in America," she said. Laila's voice grew quiet as she translated. "The war broke so many families."

I felt a tug of regret. I looked over at Laila. "Should I not have shown her that photo?" I whispered. "It's OK," Laila whispered back. "It's good, actually."

Grandma blinked hard behind her thick lens. She folded back the sides of the newspaper and kissed Mohammed's image. She smoothed the paper down on her knee and let her son and grandchildren gaze up at her. She removed her glasses. The late afternoon sun through the sitting room window caught the wetness in her eyes and made her round face glow. She smiled and gripped my hand fiercely. Laila was silent. I squeezed back, and swallowed all that I had planned to tell her about the newspaper—and my job. She already had shown me more about both than I could have possibly imagined.

6.

The Lost

My earliest memories of my father: His thick, horn-rimmed glasses. Brylcreemed hair—I remember the oily smell of the pomade, his black plastic combs on the bathroom counter with the same scent. An array of pens in his shirt pocket. And a feeling of equal parts admiration and fear. From as early as I could remember, I knew I had to tread carefully around my father, because of what we later called his "temper," occasional fits of irrational rage or foul moods like that night at the restaurant. In between those, he performed Herculean feats in my young eyes. Anytime something in the house needed repair—a vacuum cleaner, a sink, a light fixture—he was there with his endless supply of tools, taking things apart, climbing up ladders, soldering wires until it worked again. He ran tirelessly beside my blue bike with the white banana seat, not letting go until I had my balance. He drove for what seemed like endless hours on long family roadtrips—Yellowstone, Yosemite, the Grand Canyon. He loved national parks, which, to an immigrant from a small island, embodied the very limitlessness of America.

When I was eight going on nine, several months after that tense night at the restaurant, Dad had taken us along on a business trip to Florida for an engineering conference. We had stayed on through the Fourth of July weekend, driving a rental car down the length of the state. For five days we had traveled from Disney World in Orlando to the beaches of Miami to Key West, where all four of us—Dad, Mom, Kelley, and I—posed for a snapshot in front of a sign proclaiming that we were at the southernmost point in the United States. We were supposed to drive back up to Miami by the end of the week, drop off our rental car, and leave on a Pan Am flight on Friday, July 9.

But billboards and local television along the way had relentlessly advertised Shamu and Sea World in Orlando, which we had skipped in favor of Disney World. As I watched the friendly-looking killer whale jump up to grab fish from his trainer's hand, and slide up onto a ramp, wagging his tail as members of the audience petted his large, slick head, I knew I had to go. I enlisted Kelley, five at the time, into the effort and soon we were whining a daily mantra, "We want to go to Seeeea World! We want to see Shamuuu!"

Uncharacteristically, my father relented. "It wouldn't hurt to stay through the weekend," he said to Mom. Kelley and I looked at each other in disbelief, the two of us now complicit in happiness. *Did Dad just say what I think he said?* I feared if I uttered a word I might break the spell. Kelley kept his silence too. From the phone in our Miami hotel room, Dad extended our car rental and changed our outbound flight from Miami to another Pan Am flight a couple days later from Orlando. We drove from Miami to Orlando on the day of our originally scheduled flight, and spent the night there. The next morning, Kelley and I were extra quiet as we got ready.

"Are we really going to see Shamu?" my brother whispered to me.

I took a deep breath, to muster the courage to finally ask Mom and Dad.

But they were staring at the television news, murmuring to each other. Images of emergency crews among charred, smoking wreckage—almost unrecognizable as an airplane, were it not for the blue and white Pan Am logo discernible on a broken piece of the tail—filled the screen. Diagrams of a plane taking off used giant red arrows to show how wind shear had forced the aircraft back down to the ground, into houses. There were no survivors on board. A baby girl was found alive under all the rubble of the homes, protected from the flames by a mattress that had fallen over her crib. The flight had originated from Miami.

"Miami—we were supposed to be on that flight," I heard my dad say to my mom in Mandarin. "We're very lucky."

I stared at the television. I wasn't thinking about Shamu anymore.

"What about the baby?" I asked desperately. I pictured a lone, intact crib in the middle of the charred wreckage, an infant in a pink footie pajamas, squalling. "Who will take care of her?"

My parents looked at me, surprised I was listening.

"We're very lucky," my mom repeated, eyes intent on me. That was all they said. My brother stayed quiet, too young to understand.

"Shamu saved us," I whispered to him. "But I don't know what's going to happen to that baby."

We did go to Sea World that day, and Shamu did everything the ads promised: He jumped up and caught a fish from his trainer's hand as she stood on a tall platform. He swam up close to one side of his pool, splashing us with a cascade of water. And though I waved my hand as high in the air as I could, I was not chosen to stand on the side of the pool and receive a kiss on the cheek from Shamu, his rubbery-looking whale lips pressed against the volunteer's cheek as she flinched and wrinkled her nose.

I had a hard knot in my stomach when our Pan Am flight took off from Orlando the next day. But my parents acted as if nothing were amiss, so I just gripped the armrests tight, after reading the emergency-procedures card five times, and didn't say anything. We never brought up the crash again. But I grew up with the thought in the back of my head that I had narrowly missed being killed in a plane crash. It felt like more a curiosity, evidence of the capriciousness of fate, than a true brush with death. Over time, I recalled few details except for that we had left from Orlando instead of Miami, that the plane had crashed into houses on the ground just after take-off, that a wind shear had been blamed, and that a single baby on the ground survived.

Later, as I was preparing to write about this experience, I talked to each of my then-divorced parents and to Kelley. Dad looked back at me, puzzled, and said, "What? I don't remember that." And then, ever practical, "I can't imagine I would book a flight that stopped so many times en route to San Francisco in the first place." My mother shook her head: "I don't remember that. Ask your father. He would know."

"Are you *sure*?" I asked each of them again, and then again a couple days later. "But I remember it so clearly. You said we were lucky."

"Well, we were lucky then," Mom said, emphasizing "then." And we both knew she wasn't talking about the plane crash. I didn't press any further.

"No way," my brother, by then in his mid-thirties, said when I told him. "That's freaky. I know I was only five then, but don't you think we would have talked about it? That's a big deal."

"No, because we never talk about anything," I said.

In the first of the *Final Destination* horror films, a teenage boy has a premonition that the plane he has just boarded will explode in midair, and manages to get himself and a handful of friends off the flight. The plane does indeed take off and then blow up, and in the days that follow the survivors die, one by one, in horrific freak accidents—until it becomes clear that Death is chasing each of them to take care of what the explosion did not.

What I did not realize at the time of the crash was that the summer of 1982 would not be marked by the fact that my family and I had cheated death. I would look back on it instead as a sort of high point for my family, a time when, as my mother said, we were lucky. Dad was on the upswing. And when he was happy, Mom was happy. For Dad, the conference in Orlando seemed important—it must have marked a peak in his engineering career. Kelley and I were finally old enough, me at eight and him at five, to travel without strollers, the threat of tantrums, or bathroom accidents. Mom had just started taking classes at the local community college while we were at school; a year later, she started working part-time. After arriving in a completely new country as an immigrant bride and, soon after, becoming a mother, she was finally coming into her own. She and Dad were clearly at ease with each other, shuttling us around Disney World, watching us make sand castles on the beach, packing lunches from supermarkets for our roadtrips. Mom popped orange sections into Dad's mouth as he drove the rental car.

On those warm Florida evenings, when the fierce sun retreated, we all hopped into the hotel pool, Mom and Kelley in the shallow area and Dad and me on a mission: He was teaching me to swim. We all spent hours in the pool, as the moon rose up over us, reflecting in the blue water—which was nothing like the blue of the warm salt water that lapped on the beaches in Miami, but no matter. Our fingers and toes looked like raisins and my hair bore the metallic smell of chlorine no matter how well I shampooed it with the little beige, cylindrical bottles from the hotel. Though his uncorrected vision was terrible, Dad was not wearing his thick, horn-rimmed glasses in the pool, and for once, he looked suddenly approachable instead of severe. At the start of the trip, I was barely dog paddling. By the end, just over a week later, I could make it all the way across the short side of the pool in a serviceable crawl, side breathing a few times to boot. Dad, who was a good swimmer (he had learned in the Taiwanese army), was ebullient, proud, and full of praise. His good mood, bolstered by having taught his daughter to swim, swayed him to yield to our Sea World entreaties. Usually, Dad was rigid, insistent on things being done his way and on his schedule.

This need for control, marked by explosions of anger, his "temper," was blissfully absent on this trip. If we convinced Dad to extend our stay in Florida and go to Sea World, this idyllic time for him and our family might last a bit longer. In the years that followed, Dad's "temper" got worse, he and Mom fought more—things had settled down after the fight at the restaurant, but it turned out to be a harbinger of things to come.

We didn't yet know we were glimpsing the beginnings of my father's bipolar disorder. When he had his first depressive episode after he left his engineering job amid frustration about his stalled career, he lay in bed, mostly, for almost half a year. We mostly ignored it and pretended Dad was just "resting" after many years of long hours and sleep deprivation. When he finally roused himself, it was for his new real-estate business and the "home improvement" projects that he worked on all hours, hardly sleeping, but never finished. Soon, our whole house was a construction zone, with walls torn down to the studs and piles of sheetrock and tools. I got used to falling asleep to hammering or drilling in the wee hours of the morning. The feeling that our home had been subjected to a series of explosions, that we were constantly tiptoeing around things for fear of stepping on a nail or dislodging some work in progress, mirrored our psychological states. We ignored things that were broken, stepping over them, pretending they weren't there – or that they were supposed to be that way. We latched on to what illusions of normalcy we could glean (don't all dads go on these home-improvement kicks?) and never acknowledged to each other anything was wrong.

The first time anyone in our family used the word "bipolar" (or "manic" or "depressed") in front of each other was after I went to college, took a psychology class, met people who said they were diagnosed with manic depression (as it was commonly called then), and I returned on a break. With the perspective gained by distance and a little bit of knowledge, I couldn't not say it. "Dad, you are NOT NORMAL!" I yelled at him on the final day of winter break my sophomore year. He was up on the roof, pulling shingles, as I craned my neck and shouted at him. "You have manic depression. You are manic right now. Do you know what bipolar disorder is?" He never stopped yanking at the singles with his inverted hammer, the fury building behind his thick glasses. "No daughter of mine calls her father crazy!" he yelled, kicking a pile of shingles until they came cascading off the roof onto the deck with a clatter. I jumped. The misshapen nails on the weatherbeaten brown shingles were rusted and bent into odd angles, like broken limbs.

But before that, years had passed during which we said nothing about Dad's behavior, about his illness, to each other. Because Chinese culture favored Confucian stoicism, because it was too painful to confront, because I had looked away in that restaurant when I was eight and felt I couldn't rewrite that decision, because my mother didn't say anything so we thought we shouldn't either. It was in this environment that I also never brought up the plane crash, or even our trip to Florida, which would just underscore the distance between Dad then and now. I thought no one else in my family mentioned it for the same reasons.

But sometimes I had wondered, in a *Final Destination*-like way, if maybe we weren't supposed to have all died. If we couldn't have just frozen it all like a portrait, when as a family we were maybe happiest, most loving and united: All of us splashing around in a Miami hotel pool, or posing with smiles on our faces at the southernmost point of the United States. A sweet Florida orange section, held by my mother's delicate fingertips and poised in mid-air, as my father opened his mouth while keeping both hands steady on the wheel. If my father wouldn't have been happier if he never had to experience the decline of his career, his psyche, and, finally, his marriage.

And that maybe, like the movie, we were now slowly dying as a family in another kind of way. We *were* lucky, then. But what were we now?

☙

The Shirzais's lost brother was named Mohammed, but in addition to rarely saying he was dead, they did not often mention him by name. He was always "our brother, who was lost," or "Mohib, Sarasa, and Mina's father."

What I learned about Mohammed, over time: He was clever, idealistic, but prone to fits of bad temper. Like my father, he wore thick horn-rimmed glasses and a thick black sweep of pomaded hair. Mohammed had a stern exterior, often harshly reprimanding or spanking his young children. Yet he was at heart a pushover, especially for his little daughters, and for no one more than his wife, a village girl who maintained her rural ways as much as he insisted on his urban Kabul ones. He found her naïveté charming, bought her bolts of fabric in the brightly printed styles fashionable in the late 1970s, to gently nudge her into updating her wardrobe.

His other passion, the radio. The relatively new technology to Shinzmaray had arrived when he was growing up, a tantalizing window into the outside world. When village women there had first heard a male voice emanating from the battery-operated radio, they had covered their faces with their scarves, thinking there was a small man on the other side of the speaker. Mohammed wanted to be in that outside world. Most of all, he wanted to be the man on the other side of the speaker. He, like his brothers before and after him, went to Kabul for boarding school, and studied to be a radio journalist. In 1979, when young intellectuals started organizing against the communists, he was working for a Kabul-based radio station. When the coup started, they had planned, he would take over the radio station and be in charge of communications.

He told no one in his family about the plans or his role, not even his wife. He had to protect them. When the planned coup was exposed by the communists, KGB-conscripted Soviet and Afghan soldiers came for Mohammed. He was taken from his home, in front of his wife, and never seen again. Maiwand once told me he thought Mohammed was so brave, maybe even reckless, because he knew his brothers would take care of his children if he died. "We never spoke of this," Maiwand said. "But we knew. It was a silent agreement."

The family only showed me one picture of Mohammed. It was the same one that had appeared in the newspaper, the one I had shown to Grandma upon arriving in Kabul. It was the last one he had taken with his children before he was captured, said Yusuf, who had reluctantly lent it to me (not because he didn't want it to be published, but because he didn't want to let it out of his hands). Over time, I saw copies of that black-and-white snapshot in his children's homes, and amid a stack of old pictures that Daoud kept in his office, secured with a thick rubber band. It was the way they wanted to remember their father and brother.

The image endures: Mohammed reclining on the bed. He's propping himself with an elbow and wearing that argyle sweater. Those horn-rimmed glasses, that side-parted sweep of black hair, set off by his long, straight nose. Though his lens are thick, his eyes—a moody intellectual's eyes, storm clouds on the horizon—shine through the glass. The three children gather on the bed around his blanketed legs, a pyramid of offspring: Mohib, six, with dark curls, lips in a petulant pout. Sarasa, four, in a pageboy haircut, a hint of mischief in her black eyes. Mina, a chubby infant in footie pajamas. Mohammed is not smiling, because that was Afghan convention for photos, but he is happy. His easy posture and luminescent eyes say so. And his beloved radio, with the antennae jutting out at an angle, sits on the floor at his side, close enough for him to reach over and adjust a dial without jostling the children.

I knew Mohib, Sarasa, and Mina as the children of Mohammed in that photo before I had met them in person as fatherless adults.

The three siblings shared an apartment, eventually having moved in together after Sarasa's break from the uncles. For years, they had been trying to sponsor their widowed mother to come live with them in the United States. In early 2004, the paperwork finally was approved. They knew their mother, used to living in a multi-family compound in an Afghan-refugee neighborhood of Pakistan, would never feel comfortable in a three-bedroom apartment with them. The three siblings pooled their savings and bought a two-story house far out in the suburbs west of Portland. Soon, their mother was on her way to live with her children for the first time in nearly fifteen years.

In Afghan culture, men are nicknamed by their professions—Daoud was called Ustad for professor, others *Doktor* or *Inginir*—and women are known by their roles within the family—*Majana* and *Dada* for "auntie" or *Randara* for "sister-in-law." All the Shirzais called Mohib, Sarasa, and Mina's mother "Mamoy," which meant "wife of my uncle," an acknowledgment of her late husband. The uncles, her own children, Stephanie and me—

everyone called her that, until the title became synonymous with her.

In May, one week before Stephanie and I were to leave to meet Daoud and Laila in Afghanistan, Mamoy, still newly arrived, invited the two of us over for a send-off dinner. Mina called me to deliver the invitation from her mother, who spoke only a few words in English, something that changed little even after she had been in the United States for years. Mamoy felt no compulsion to assimilate. I admired her for this. She was unrelentingly Afghan, barking at everyone in tirades of Pashto whether or not they understood her, feigning anger at people for not visiting her enough, not knowing enough Pashto, not drinking enough of her tea, or eating enough of her food. "Learn English? Why should I learn English?" she would say in Pashto, slicing the air with an upturned right hand. "Everyone else should learn Pashto!" Stephanie confessed to Sarasa and Mina that she was scared of their mother.

We arrived at the new house, remarkable in its sparkling whiteness, from the carpet to the walls to the tile countertop in the kitchen. Did Mamoy miss the deep crimson hues of the carpets and cushions in an Afghan household, the constant swirl of brightly hued scarves, dresses, and *shalwar kameez*? Mamoy flung the door open, and greeted us with outstretched arms. *"Salaam! Tsenga ye? Jora ye? Stere me se!"*—she embraced me and Stephanie as we crossed the threshold. Mamoy had unwavering black eyes in a pale face that had grown fuller but not softer with age, and an infectious smile. Her cheekbones swept under the wells of her eyes like knife edges. She hugged me tightly, kissed me three times on opposite cheeks, right-left-right, engulfing me into the soft cotton fabric of her white chador. She was short and round, hardly delicate, though her eyes and cheekbones bore a vestigial prettiness grief and time had not erased.

At her side was Sarasa, who wore a black *shalwar kameez* she had made herself. Her voluptuousness was not hidden by the untraditionally close fit of her traditional outfit. This was a constant source of tension between her and her mother. Mina flanked her big sister, wearing jeans. Despite a honeymoon period, during which everyone had been on their best behavior, the long-awaited reunion with her now-adult children had been jolting for Mamoy. She had been left behind in Pakistan when all three of her children were sent, in their early to late teenage years, to be raised by their uncles in Portland. Her daughters told me that Mamoy had always understood why this had to be, knew it was for the best, and didn't fret that the immigration processes to bring her to join them eventually took much longer than the Shirzais had hoped. Even so, in their years living away from her, Mohib, Sarasa, and Mina had transformed into alien, American creatures. They wore clothes, said and did things that puzzled, shocked, and chagrined their devoutly religious mother. Once, taking it upon herself to do everyone's laundry, she had found Mina's thong underwear and not been able to comprehend how a woman would wear such an article of clothing, and why she would ever want to. And on this night, Mohib was absent, which after the initial month or two following Mamoy's arrival, was more often the case. His frequent escapes to places and activities unknown had also become one of a growing number of conflicts in the newly united household.

Mamoy embraced and greeted Stephanie, then grabbed her hand in two of hers, and uttered an insistent question in Pashto. Mina stood at her side and chuckled as she translated, "My mom wants to know why you are scared of her."

Stephanie stammered, "Wha . . . *Why did you tell her that?*" Mina shrugged her shoulders guiltily.

Though her children favored eating around the coffee table as they had during Sunday dinners at Maiwand's, Mamoy had spread out an embroidered disterkhan cloth on the cream-colored carpet. She invited us to sit down on the floor around it. "You will have to get used to this," she said, as Mina translated. We ate from the platters of stewed meats and vegetables, homemade flatbread, as well as a big plate of a flat, stuffed pastry-like concoction called *parakee*. The handmade dough had to be rolled out and stuffed with a seasoned mashed potato and onion mixture. Then there was the danger factor of dropping and removing them from a pan of sizzling oil, which Afghan women did with their bare, toughened index fingers and thumbs. As I surveyed the crispy brown bubbles on the surface of the dough, I knew Mamoy felt our impending trip was very important.

We ate heartily, Mamoy joking that it was good we liked the food so much, because that's all we'd be having for a while. After dinner, Mamoy returned with two folded cotton squares. They were *chador*, just like hers, one white and the other pale yellow. They felt worn and soft, and had scalloped, embroidered edges. "You will need these," she said, handing one to each of us.

Stephanie and I each looked down at the folded scarves. Sarasa and Mina had promised us a couple of them before we left, and I had thought we'd just figure them out somewhere between Portland and Kabul, on the plane or during our layover. After all, Mamoy wore them with such ease, what skill or special knowledge could be necessary? But as I tentatively unfurled the unwieldy piece of fabric on my lap, I had no idea how to put it on my head or wrap it. It was so large—I could barely extend my arms to meet its full length. Mamoy shook her head, and unleashed a stream of Pashto that Mina translated to, "Oh, goodness, you're going to need a lot of help with that. Here, let me show you or you will never get by in Afghanistan."

She came to me first, the one who was not scared of her, and sat down on the floor cross-legged in front of me. Mamoy talked at me in Pashto the whole time, but no translation was necessary because she deftly took the chador in two hands, lofted it over my head as it billowed and came to rest with the front edge right at my hairline. She then adjusted it so that more of the fabric was on my right side. In a swift motion, she flung the longer end over my left shoulder. Her hands were soft and cool on my face and upper arms. She then fussed with the edges so that it was secure under my chin and over my chest, saying something emphatically. Sarasa translated, "It's really important to cover *all* your chest," with a sarcastic edge.

Mamoy raised her hands before me—voilà— and I sat there, frozen. A wrong move would certainly send the entire scarf architecture askew. Could I really do this for weeks? Mamoy moved on to Stephanie, unfurling and wrapping her scarf for her. After pulling down Stephanie's bottom edges safely over her bosom, Mamoy turned to check on me. I had instinctively folded my arms up below the scarf. "Don't tuck your hands in there!" she scolded. "It looks like you've stolen something." She laughed and pulled my forearms out.

I caught my reflection in the glass coffee table, startled by how different I looked without my unruly black hair framing my face. With my face naked against the light fabric, I felt strangely neutral, both in color and in appearance.

Mamoy reached over and unwrapped my scarf, handed it to me in a pile of fabric, and said, "OK, now you try." Her eyes fixed on me. She was more religious than any of the other Shirzai women in Portland, but even now she never spoke of Islam, or the scarf's significance. Whenever Mamoy could commandeer one of her daughters as an interpreter, she talked to me about one subject alone: family. She told me about all of the nieces, sisters-in-law, and children who shared her household in Pakistan. She had taught the younger women to sew, cook, and make jewelry, including the elaborate beaded dress ornaments a Pashtun bride had to prepare for her wedding. The heavy pieces could take up to a year to make by hand. She asked me about my own family, and I tried my best to explain the things that would ring familiar to her: my parents' immigration, my large extended family in Taiwan, how large meals and boisterous conversation always materialized when they were together, which was rare nowadays. Then I'd gently try to explain things that were unfathomable to her, such as living on my own, visiting my parents a few times a year. I skipped my father's illness, and my mother's struggle with the idea of divorce.

I wanted to learn to wear the scarf well—and I wanted her to think of me as family.

Nervous, I hurried through the motions, clumsy as I measured each side and threw it over my shoulder. Mamoy gasped. "No, no, no, not over the right shoulder!" she cried, caught the errant tail of my *chador*, and unwrapped me.

"The left, the left," she said, shifting the fabric, measuring out a length on my right-hand side, and inviting me to throw it over the correct shoulder.

Sarasa giggled. "Did I just make some kind of major faux pas?" I said.

"No one does it over the right," she said, offering me a pitying smile.

I fiddled with the fabric over my hairline, testing its purchase on my forehead, and then took the extra cloth on my right side and flung it onto my left shoulder. For this, I earned an exclamation of approval from Mamoy. "Keep it on for a while," she said. "Get used to it. You should wear it at home to practice." I began to move more freely, realizing that it was harder than I had imagined to dislodge the scarf from my head. If I did, she demonstrated, it would be simple to slip it back on in a single motion before any men caught a good look at my exposed hair. First, she did it with my scarf, and then with her own. Seeing her glossy black hair, streaked with filaments of silver, for the first time—how long it was. She wore it in two long braids on each side, the tapered ends coming to points like sable paintbrushes. Her pale face, framed by that long, straight hair, parted neatly in the middle. The blackness of her hair playing off her round, jewel-like eyes.

Now I knew why the young village girl, before the hardness brought on by the loss of her husband and the years without her children, had to cover her hair. She smiled sheepishly, and yanked her white chador back on, taking care to tuck the ends of her braids back into it.

As the evening came to a close, Mamoy placed our scarves into a shopping bag. It was time for Stephanie and I to say our goodbyes until we returned from Afghanistan. As we stood in the vestibule, Mamoy gave a little speech in parting, wishing us good luck and godspeed in lofty language that suggested we were embarking on a great journey. Her blessing. I hadn't mastered her scarf-wearing lessons just yet, but she was proud of me. As she and I embraced and cheek-kissed in parting, I held onto her right hand. She wore a gold ring with a large, square saffron-colored stone that had a small gold medallion embedded in it. "I like your ring," I said and Mina translated. "*Xaysta*," I said, using one of the only words from our Pashto language tapes that had stuck with me. Beautiful.

"*Tashakur*," Mamoy said. Thank you. "My husband gave it to me."

As Mina repeated these words about the father she never really knew, Mamoy's eyes grew moist and she smiled. I cradled Mamoy's hand in mine and stroked her cool, soft skin with the other, my fingers lingering over the glimmering stone. Her gaze was soft, not focused on me anymore. Was she seeing her husband's face, perhaps on the day he gave her the ring? I glanced over Mamoy's shoulder at Mina's straight, regal nose and that closed-lipped half-smile, and I saw her father's face too, from that black-and white photo. The three little children nestled in a mound on his reclining, blanketed legs, like their father was their life raft. Where had Mamoy been when that photo was taken? Maybe she had been in the room, her heart warmed by seeing her husband and children together. Maybe she had been preparing dinner, tending to her perfectly crisp bread or richly spiced stews in the kitchen, where she kept her long braids uncovered in the presence of women. Perhaps she stepped out to check on the children and laughed her loud, infectious laugh when she saw them quietly nestled with their father. Maybe Mohammed, in that happy moment, feeling the weight of his children on his legs, saw his bride, the mother of his children, with her shining eyes, glossy hair, and broad smile, and forgot momentarily about the communists, the coup, the danger. He might have thought, *We are complete, Masha'Allah.* Thanks to God.

This was the first time Mamoy had mentioned her late husband. She talked about him even less than her brothers-in-law did. Had I not seen that ring, the gift from Mohammed, on her finger before? Was it a coincidence? Had she been waiting for me to ask? She was smiling softly and studying the luminous amber-colored stone.

Her husband. That photograph. How, though Mohammed was trying not to smile, the corners of his mouth turned up like Mina's were now, as she studied her mother's ring. Mamoy wrapped her arms around me again, hard.

"Don't forget to practice," she said. "Wear the scarf at home before you go."

I knew then that my trip was not just journalistic, and not even simply an answer to Daoud's "And how will you help?" I was a pilgrim, an outsider, who had been granted the privilege of traveling a migrant stream of nostalgia, of love, and loss—of husbands, fathers, brothers, and a country.

7.
Thresholds

Four-thirty in the morning in Kabul: The first call to prayer. *Alarm-clock sales must be terrible in this city.*

Soaring voice of the muezzin, drifting through the pre-dawn haze from echoey, resonant speakers. The singing sweet and ethereal, vowels drawn out into aching, sustained notes: *Allaaahu Akbar.* God is greater than can be described. Then, after three repetitions, *Ash hadu an la ilaha illal lah.* I bear witness that there is no god but God. Again, a repetition. The voice filtering into my Lariam-distorted dreams like tea steeping in water: gentle, swirling, and warm. One consciousness slowly filling another. My favorite line, said near the end of the morning prayer only, was *As-salatu khayru min an-nawm.* Prayer is better than sleep. I often registered my disagreement by attempting to close my eyes and return to slumber, however uneasy it had been. But inevitably, the rooster in the courtyard would join the muezzin. Then the donkey from the neighboring nomad camp, its asthmatic bray like fiddling gone awry. Still, no matter how tired I was, dawn often came as relief. Distracted by the activities of the day, I noticed the side effects of the Lariam less.

As the family in Portland had done for Aisha, the call to prayer is said into the right ear of a newborn before the umbilical cord is cut; it is the first words a baby hears. From the start, those words are meant as a gentle awakening, a transition to a new day.

Each new day in Kabul brought new discoveries, new family members to meet. I got used to interacting with Daoud in this new context, catching him in white *shalwar kameez* as he stirred his instant Nescafé® (Afghans are not coffee drinkers, so he had to procure his own) in the morning before his driver arrived, or in the evenings as he stood in the cool courtyard with his battery-operated radio tuned to the BBC. We visited him at his work, an echoey Soviet-era building with formerly grandiose spaces, metal detectors at the entrances, and broken toilets. We toured campuses like Kabul Education University, for which Daoud was trying to overhaul curriculum. We met Nazo, Amina's youngest daughter, impish and green-eyed; she and her new sister-in-law Rochina shared a room with us. At twenty-two, Nazo had missed nearly a decade of education because of the civil war and Taliban. Now, she was attending the tenth grade at an all-girls' high school set up by a French NGO in a ramshackle building. Laila, Stephanie, and I were absorbed into Rochina and Nazo's daily rhythms at the house.

In the space of this home he had purchased for a life that never happened, Daoud let his guard down, speaking frankly of the personal toll extracted by his return to his country for the first time in thirty-five years. When he had left Afghanistan for college, Kabul had a modern streetcar system and stately trees lining the asphalt roads. Now, the roads had been reduced to an unpaved, dusty mess, with virtually no trees—they had all been destroyed by rockets or cut down for firewood. Daoud had developed the "Kabul cough," a chronic hacking, black-phlegmed affliction from the thick pollution of diesel, dust, and wood fires. New lines and furrows appeared on his face.

I had hesitated to ask him if we were going to make the journey outside of NATO-controlled territory to Shinzmaray. He could not go, because his role in the Karzai government, as well as his profile in the United States, had rendered him suspect in the insular village, even though it was his birthplace. But the decision was his, and I desperately wanted him to put the wheels in motion. I wanted to cross the next threshold of my Afghanistan journey, and enter those mud-brick buildings in the framed photograph on Maiwand's wall.

The first indication that we would make the trip was our introduction to Asad, the family's the next-youngest sibling before Nazo. He had been away for his job for a U.S. construction contractor. Daoud had told us that, if we were indeed going to Shinzmaray, Asad would serve as our escort and bodyguard. We were in the women's sitting room before dinner one night when there was a rustling in the entryway. A figure appeared behind the gauzy curtain in the vestibule. Amina and the male voice exchanged words in Pashto. Laila poked my leg discreetly. Barely turning her head toward me, she said through clenched teeth, "Do not . . . make eye contact . . . with my cousin . . . in front of his mother." She looked over at Stephanie to make sure she had heard also. The curtain parted and a young man stepped gingerly inside and eased himself next to Amina, across from us. I felt suddenly nervous, anxious to show Amina how well I could follow the household's rules, show respect for cultural protocol. I looked lightly down and off to the side, as I had seen women here do, allowing my *chador* to drape over the more-exposed side of my face. He was sitting cross-legged, with his arms wrapped around his knees, and had a dark, western-style button-up shirt and khakis on. Amina said a few words and gave Laila a cue.

"Angie, Stephanie," Laila said. "This is my cousin Asad."

"Hi, how are you?" he said, in accented English, with a hint of a British lilt. I was expecting a Salaam aleikum.

"*Waleikum.* Hi," I said. "I'm fine. How are you?"

Stephanie greeted him as well. Amina's dark eyes were on me. I concentrated on the repeating patterns in the carpet.

He had learned English in Pakistan, where schools taught it as part of the post-colonial curriculum. He said he provided local security for a large U.S. construction firm. He said he would accompany us to the village in three days—on Friday.

As we talked, I continued looking off to the side at Laila, then at his sock-clad feet, then at the ground. I didn't know where to look. I wanted to smile or say, "Great!" but I didn't. Then Asad excused himself to the living room, where the men ate. Amina had a slight smile on her face. Laila gave me a barely perceptible nod. Exhale. I had passed the test. And we were going to Shinzmaray.

On Friday, we were to meet Asad in the courtyard an hour before the first adhan to leave for the village. The night before, Laila took charge: She set Stephanie's cell phone alarm for three in the morning and warned us to drink as few fluids as possible because the car ride could take half a day and we would not be able to make bathroom stops. Leaving the vehicle outside of NATO control was dangerous and, even without the threats posed by insurgents and warlords, the roadside would be dotted with landmines. I slept fitfully, my Lariam dreams more ominous and vivid than usual. Right before I bolted awake at two forty-five, Maiwand and Yusuf had been chasing me through an airport in one of those wide electric carts that airline staff drive; no matter how fast I ran, the cart's incessant beeping, its flashing orange lights, Maiwand and Yusuf's mute and murderous-looking stares, were always right behind me. They wanted to run me over. The moment the cold metal edge of the cart brushed against my heel, bare in my sandals, I woke up. Heart racing, I met Laila's eyes, also open and groggy. She motioned for me to go back to sleep for a bit. I closed my eyes and tried to conjure up a more pleasant image of Maiwand, showing me the framed photograph of Shinzmaray: the starkness of the sunbleached mud-brick buildings against the blue sky. I imagined stepping through the door of the home in which Daoud, Maiwand, and the others were born.

Asad hailed a cab and took the three of us to a large taxi and bus depot on the outskirts of Kabul. The first rays of the rising sun stabbed at the indigo sky, illuminating dusty Russian sedans and minibuses painted in clown-colored patterns. "Cover your faces," Asad muttered to us before we got out of our taxi. Unlike the other night in the women's sitting room, he was tense, his movements stiff. I learned later he was wearing a bulletproof vest. "Don't speak English, not even when we get into our hired car. The drivers don't want to take Americans because it's dangerous."

Laila took the part of her scarf that was draped over her left shoulder, pulled it up over her nose and mouth, and held it there with her left hand resting on her face. Stephanie and I followed her lead. I stared down at Asad's hiking boot-clad feet as we followed him. He approached a driver, a thin, middle-aged man, and talked to him in Dari. I heard him say "Ghazni." They haggled a bit, and then the driver opened his car doors and motioned for us to step inside.

The first half-hour of our drive was quiet as the sun rose in pomegranate hues against the dusky sky. Asad and the driver made stilted small talk, and he occasionally exchanged a few words with Laila in Pashto. Stephanie and I kept our mouths shut. Laila dropped her scarf, pulling it up to her face again if we passed another car or someone on the side of the road. Stephanie and I did the same.

Then the ring road, a newly paved circular highway that linked Afghanistan's major cities, stretched out before us. The last buildings on Kabul's outskirts, many of them under construction with rickety bamboo scaffolding, faded into flat, dusty blankness. Asad's posture relaxed and he exhaled deeply. He had gotten us this far, and our fate was largely out of his hands now. Nothing left to do but wait until we got to Ghazni, where we would meet Uncle Hamid, who would set out from the village to intercept us at the appointed gas station.

Unlike the other cars we had ridden in, this car was rigged British-style, with the driver on the right side, even though people drove on the right side of the road in Afghanistan. Asad sat in the passenger seat, on the left. I sat on the leftmost side of the backseat. This allowed me to look in the sideview mirror and get a good look at Asad's face—something which I had not dared to do under other circumstances, after Laila's warning.

The mirror was encrusted with dust. But I could see that he had very dark, deep-set eyes and lashes so long they cast shadows as the dawn light washed over his brown cheeks. He had the slightest hint of a beard and an assertive, straight nose that gave him a regal profile. My face flushed warm under my scarf.

Suddenly, he turned around to face the three of us women.

"So, how are you doing back there?" he said in English, smiling for the first time all day.

"Asad!" Laila scolded. He had warned us not to speak English.

But he ignored her and kept chatting, telling us about the ring road construction project, sections of which his employer was in charge. We would see, he said, that the new asphalt was already falling apart in places, because foreign contractors had not been prepared for Afghanistan's harsh climate, nor for tanks and military vehicles constantly rolling over it.

We slowly, reluctantly, responded to him. Soon, we were all talking in English. Our driver started driving twice as fast.

"He realizes he's stuck with Americans and now he's going to drive as fast as he can so he doesn't have to be with us for long," Asad said wryly, and told the man in Dari to slow down.

I worried. Would the driver refuse to take us and leave us at the side of the highway? But Asad seemed unconcerned.

The rolling toffee-colored land stretched out as far as we could see, interrupted only by a smattering of scrubby trees here and there. Brown mountains, voluptuous yet austere, in the distance. Every now and then, a squat, rectangular building with "MDC" in red-and-white block letters.

"Mine Detection Center," Laila explained. The rocks all around them were painted white, and a few were red. "The white rocks are safe and the red ones mean there are mines."

Often we'd hit a detour where the road had started coming apart, just as Asad had explained. The detours took us on the bone-jarring rocky dirt alongside the road, often for miles. Sometimes, we rolled only a few feet away from red rocks. I sucked in my breath. I turned to Laila, her eyes wide too.

After about an hour and a half, in the middle of seemingly nowhere: a cluster of figures, a few ramshackle structures on the side of the road. The driver muttered something to Asad. Asad muttered back. He turned back to us, not smiling anymore. "Checkpoint. Cover your faces. Don't say a word."

We approached and slowed to a stop. *Keep looking down*, I told myself. All I could see through the window with my downcast gaze: The distinctly curved metal magazine of the AK-47. A wiry brown hand wrapped around it. Afghan army, Taliban insurgent, warlord, some random robber looking for money-laden foreigners? Don't look. My breath, captive in my throat. My mouth, sandpaper.

The driver's side window rolled down. The man with the gun approached.

"Please," the driver said apologetically in Dari, nodding toward the back seat at us, swathed in *chador*. "There are women in the car."

A shadow of a hand, waving us on. We were off again. Exhales all around.

We were silent for a long time after that.

We passed through one more checkpoint, and countless more MDCs and detours, Asad urging our driver to slow down about half a dozen more times.

Finally, a city of squat, concrete buildings appeared on the horizon. It had been three hours since we set off from the house that morning, though we had only traveled about eighty miles. The detours had slowed us. We had arrived in Ghazni. Laila warned me that it would take another couple hours still to negotiate the dirt roads between Ghazni and Shinzmaray.

Hamid was waiting inside his twenty-year-old white Toyota Surf 4x4 when we pulled up to the gas station. It was a relief to see his familiar bearded face, to no one more than Asad. Laila lit up at being reunited with her father, and they exchanged a quick greeting before he motioned for us to get into his car. Today, Hamid wore a turban of twisted gray patterned fabric over his white skullcap. He and Asad were businesslike as we hopped out of the cab, covering our faces, and into Hamid's car. Asad paid our driver a thick wad of Afghanis and the driver sped away. The baton, passed. Hamid greeted me and Stephanie with *salaam aleikums*. As we navigated a series of winding, treacherous dirt roads leading toward the village, we spoke freely in English. Hamid drove the roads with casual ease, as he had hundreds of times. Asad was more relaxed, giddy even. He chattered away about everything from the many roadside memorials for victims of various wars—simple structures made from wooden poles and flag-like strips of cloth—to the large, lavish compounds that belonged to local warlords. Then he began telling jokes.

"A donkey, a goat and a dog get on a taxi," Asad said, with a stand-up comic's flair.

"The donkey pays five dollars, the goat pays nothing, and the dog pays one hundred dollars and doesn't get any change."

He paused. "That's why today," he said, "a donkey stays still when a car passes by, a goat runs away, and the dog chases the car."

He burst into a fit of surprisingly high-pitched, cackling laughter. I laughed, as much at his joke as at his laugh. Hamid rolled his eyes, smiling to himself.

Every once in a while, a village would emerge from the undulating, bare land, as if the adobe structures had sprung up from the earth itself. Endless monochrome, then shocks of color: Jewel tones of women and children's green, blue, and purple clothes. The yellow and red plastic water jugs they brought to communal wells. Herds of goats and cattle, guided by black-clad nomad boys, floating by.

We then turned off the main road, past empty homes with no roofs, their jagged mud walls reaching upward like misshapen fingers. "Soviets," Hamid said. "They bombed many houses here."

Past those ruins, another cluster of adobe houses lay in the distance.

It didn't look different from the other villages. Asad wordlessly pulled a swathe of gray fabric and a skullcap out of a pocket and began wrapping a turban around his head until it looked just like Hamid's.

"The men wear their turbans in the village," Laila explained. "And look, there's Shinzmaray coming up."

There it is. So similar to all the villages we had passed. But the difference, exhilarating—Maiwand's silver-framed photo, that image I first laid eyes on nearly three years ago, here, all real.

We pulled into the double doors of the largest compound in the village, the Shirzais's new house that was built after Daoud and the brothers had settled in America. We were swept up by our hosts: Jumagul, the Shirzai brother born after Hamid but before Maiwand; his wife Fahima; and their four children. We were sat down, served tea, which my parched throat could not get enough of, and Afghan bread with jam and cream (a throwback to British occupation?), and warmly welcomed. Jumagul, who had been visually impaired since birth—Daoud had told me he was somewhere between legally and totally blind—had thick glasses and broad smile, and Fahima had embraced and kissed us warmly when we first arrived. The children, between two and nine, stared at us curiously. The oldest boy, long limbed and gangly, dutifully filled our teacups.

"We drink a lot of tea here," Jumagul said to us. I tried not to drain my cup too quickly to quench my cotton-mouthed dehydration. "I hope you can keep up."

Hamid told our hosts that he would take us to the family's old house and the village mosque before the midday prayer. He wanted us to stay low-profile, not attract too much attention. Even though we weren't obviously American in our *shalwar kameez* and with our Asian features, xenophobia was at an all-time high in the village. A couple weeks before, Laila had come here with a female cousin. Two girls, no older than thirteen, threw rocks and shouted obscenities at them as they walked through the village, Laila told me.

"Go back to Kabul!" the girls yelled.

"Little did they know I came from America."

༚

My father's father, Hsing-Te Chuang, was a high school principal in rural Fujian, China, in a village that was as rocky and arid as Shinzmaray. Frustrated by the poverty and lack of opportunities, my grandfather took his eldest son, Tien-Mu, with him to Taiwan after World War II, in hopes of buying some land to farm. Hampered by malaria in rural Taiwan's tropical climate, father and son finally settled in a small city of Hsinchu, choosing it over Taipei because my grandfather thought the rampant gambling by Chinese émigrés in the capital would be a bad influence on his children. In 1947, my father Tien-Yuh, barely five years old, crossed the Taiwan Strait with his mother and seven other siblings on a large sailboat, tossed violently by the sea. My father always said he had no recollection of China at all; all of his memories begin with the harrowing boat journey, throwing up the entire time and not being able to keep down a bite of food.

In the Hsinchu school system, my father was a top student from the start, the material coming too easily to him. He started cutting class, playing marbles at the local temple with his delinquent friends. Due to their skillful forgery of parent signatures on their report cards, it took some time for my grandfather to discover this, but when he did, an epic spanking was delivered and my father was back in school. He was put on a track for junior-high bound students (many stopped at grade school in those days, including elder brother Tien-Mu), and passed the entrance exam to the best school. My grandfather hesitated to pay the junior high tuition for my father, but did so at Tien-Mu's urging, even if that meant also losing the income that another working son would bring the family. My grandfather relented, and my father's life path was set: Education would be his ticket. My father thought he would aim for a government-sponsored high school so as not to burden the family more, and from there he might be able to become a primary school teacher after graduating. But one of his junior-high teachers, impressed by his intellect, urged him to consider a university track. "Don't settle for the government-sponsored school," he said. "Get a part-time job now and start saving up for it." My father delivered newspapers after school. Later, he always pointed out the irony that Kelley's first part-time job was as a paperboy in our suburban Bay Area neighborhood, and that I made a living in newspapers.

My father's after-school job, his teacher's encouragement, his high test scores, all pushed him on to a top high school. That in turn led him to

National Taiwan University, for which he made a strategic calculation to take the entrance exam in civil engineering, hearing that the Taiwanese government's burgeoning dam projects meant there were abundant, high-paying job opportunities. He always had said his true passion had been electrical engineering; his spare time in high school had been spent taking apart and putting together radios at a local repair shop. Because of the family's need for money, he had cheated himself from his calling.

What Dad didn't realize at the time was that, by choosing civil engineering, he had opened the door to another path. He took the National Taiwan University entrance exam in 1960, less than three years after the Soviets had launched Sputnik. The satellite, all of one hundred and eighty-four pounds, was unable to do much other than transmit radio bleeps. Yet those orbital signals, eerie in their meaninglessness, were heard by countless Americans, and set off a crisis of confidence about the nation's dominance in science and technology. Thus began the space race that launched NASA to the moon, and also drove earthly innovations: vast infrastructure modernizations like the rapidly expanding Interstate Highway system forced the United States to redouble its investments into science and engineering. The only problem? There were not enough American engineering school students and graduates to fuel this new push.

Waves of 1960s and 70s immigration from what was formerly known as the developing world were spurred by the offers of scholarships and visas to talented engineering students. Entire American diaspora from Taiwan, India, Japan, and Eastern Europe were built on this push, aided by Civil Rights-era shifts in immigration policy aimed at undoing historic favoritism toward those of Northern European origin.

My Asian American generation was made up of the children of those recruits; we grew up absorbing the idea that our fathers were a class of chosen people. They were the top scholars of their home countries who crossed the threshold from poverty to opportunity, with the power of their intellects and hard work. We were expected to build on that, to prove the genetic prowess and parenting abilities of our fathers by being even more accomplished, even more chosen. We were raised to believe that education was the key to everything, that the brain was more important than the heart, because success gained with the former would provide for the latter. We were told, either directly or in every implicit way, that failure was not an option. Our fathers had risked too much, worked too hard, and still had something to prove to those who had remained back home, relying on money sent to them. Was it any wonder that we second-generation immigrants got boxed in with the Model Minority label? It did not appear terrible as far as stereotypes go, often used against other people of color in the United States in a "they did it, why can't you?" kind of accusation. But like all stereotypes, it precluded the idea that we were not a monolith, that we were not inherently or culturally imbued with qualities other young people didn't have. We simply were under more pressure, with parents who made sure school was our first, and often only, priority. How I resented missing out on the team sports, swim lessons, church youth groups, afternoons spent loitering at the mall and developing budding social skills by flirting with boys—activiites around which many of my non-Asian classmates seemed to build their lives. Outside of a few close friends, I was socially anxious, viewed as a somewhat harmless nerd, neither worth bullying nor attention-worthy in other regards, like as a date to school dances.

Ironically, it was the onset of my father's depression at the beginning of high school that opened up those extracurricular worlds to me. With Dad in bed most of the day, and my mother too preoccupied to keep tabs on me, I was given the freedom to take non-academic classes like art and music, play in the band, spend long hours with the student newspaper, join a Chinese American organization for second-generation youth and, within that bubble, have my first deep female friendships and make out with my first boyfriends.

On the occasion of my junior prom, my group of non-Asian female friends at school, from band, knew they would not get asked by boys from our junior class whom they would actually want as dates. They took matters into their own hands and asked the cute, but non-threatening, freshmen from band, who were only too eager to go. My own social standing, even among them, was so precarious at the time, that none of them let me in on this plan. Before I knew it, all the available freshmen in band had been snatched up and I was dateless. But I resorted to my secret weapon: Mike, my best friend from my Chinese American youth organization, was a senior at a prestigious all-boys school in Oakland, and was unusually rebellious for our community. He liked to skateboard, DJ, tag (as in graffiti, but artful graffiti), and sneak out of the house after curfew to see his girlfriend.

At that moment, Mike had been grounded for months because of some combination of the aforementioned activities that had horrified his strict parents. But they trusted me, the goody-goody Chinese friend, so when I asked him to prom, it was like offering him a Get Out of Jail Free card. I felt like I had the most mysterious date at prom, and my freshman-escorted friends eyed me a bit resentfully for pulling a wild card. That evening was a microcosm of my high school experience: Not totally excluded, not totally included, but always on the edge, living between two alternate universes— Chinese American and white. This was a kind of freedom.

But my greatest freedom came as an unintended benefit of my father's depression. Because he was disengaged for most of my high school years, I was free to develop my heart as well as my brain and become an artist —a writer—while most of my Chinese American friends chose the more traditional tracks of medicine, engineering, law, science (or eventually married men who had done so). They were shocked that my father "let" me become a journalist, to major in English, to write for a living. Back then, I didn't tell them my father was simply too ill, too far off the track of his own American Dream, to care about mine.

At least that's what I told myself then, angry at my father for his depression, his checking out. Looking back, I underestimated how much his assumption that he could not pursue his passion for electrical engineering, his feeling that he was always in the wrong field, must have in part prompted the sudden quitting of his job and career change—and ultimately, been at the core of his depression. And that, even as his moods swung toward mania toward the end of my high school years and my entry into college, he never criticized my unconventional career choices. He remained unfazed in the face of pointed questions from his Chinese immigrant friends like, "Tien-Yuh, why would you pay Stanford tuition for your daughter to go into journalism? At least make her study law so you get your money's worth." (Never mind that I paid a large share of my own college education through jobs, scholarships, and loans; it was a point of pride among the immigrant community to pay for your child's expensive education.)

In the confusion of those early manifestations of his bipolar disorder, my father was never able to tell me, "Pursue your passions, because I wasn't able to." But I now know that was why he "let" me take the path I did.

Education was my father's threshold to a world his father never imagined for him, to one he never dared aspire to for himself. Yet the failure of his dreams, in many ways, was my threshold.

આ

Making our way through Shinzmaray, Laila, her father Hamid, cousin Asad, Stephanie, and I approached the original Shirzai home, across the small village from the new compound where Jumagul and family had welcomed us. It looked exactly like Maiwand's photograph: a simple, nearly windowless mud-brick structure in sunbleached dun. The door was wooden, heavy but sunbaked to a brittle dryness. It was raised so that we had to step over a six-inch threshold shaped from the adobe.

Following Hamid, I stepped over it, planting my foot carefully on the earthen floor of the darkened interior. The crossing over, the fulfillment of the promise made on that October 2001 night at Maiwand's house: *You should go with us.* Laila followed me, then Stephanie, Asad lingering back in protective mode, checking over his shoulder for unfriendly onlookers.

All that had transpired on this worn earth, burnished to a sheen by the Shirzais's maintenance, their living, for generations, on it. The new compound had concrete floors, but dirt floors of village homes like this one were carefully prepped and watered to keep down dust and provide a smooth surface on which to lay carpets.

"This is our family's old house," Hamid said. "*Zor kor,*" he added in Pashto. I recognized the word kor from my language tapes. One of the four words for home.

It looked larger than it had appeared in Maiwand's photo, but was still only a fraction of the size of the new compound. Laila, Stephanie and I walked from room to room as Hamid and Asad followed, offering up details about the home's design and history. Some rooms had built-in storage niches and latticework designs in the thick walls. A series of holes in the walls were vents for an intrawall channel system that distributed the heat from the wood-burning hearth during the winters. The hearth had been a pit oven in the kitchen, now just a charred, cylindrical hole with a wide ring of black soot around it. As we entered a small, unembellished room adjacent to the kitchen, Laila said, "My grandmother's old room."

"Most of us—Daoud, me, our brothers and sisters—were born right here," Hamid said to me, careful with his English.

I knelt down. The smooth, beige earth on which brothers Daoud, Hamid, Mohammed, Maiwand, and their sister Amina, took their first breaths, beneath my fingertips. Could I take its pulse, feel the traces of life that remained here?

Though it was nearly midday, the house was quite dark and the sun filtering in from the skylights lent the smooth dirt floors and walls a soft golden cast. Though Daoud had stopped coming back to Shinzmaray, it was his story, his youth, that circulated through the empty house as the warmth from the fire once did. His younger siblings, Hamid included, had spent most of their childhoods in a house in Kabul. But for Daoud, this was truly home. This was where it had all started—where he, the precocious firstborn of the village mullah, prepared to cross his threshold.

Daoud's father taught him to read the Qur'an in Arabic when he was five years old. When he saw how quickly the boy learned, he moved on to the great Pashto and Persian poets, from Rahman Baba to Hafez. Daoud absorbed it all, and by the time he was seven, the teachers at the village school were having him take over classes when they were sick. The village women, all illiterate, bribed him with sweets to read out loud as they sewed.

But Daoud grew restless. He organized fights between boys in the village, collecting wagers. Sometimes, he fought boys himself. When their parents put an end to the street-fighting ring by administering some beatings of their own, Daoud switched over to training the stray dogs in the village to fight.

But then the village got its first battery-operated radio when he was in fifth grade. It arrived at the home of a former governor's family, and everyone went over to listen. For the villagers, especially those who could not read, the radio was a lifeline. Daoud took it as a sign that he was meant to leave the village and find out what those disembodied voices were talking about.

A year later, he got his wish. At eleven, he had never set foot outside Shinzmaray. The village school his grandfather had founded stopped at sixth grade. The country was poor but peaceful. Afghanistan's leadership, under King Mohammed Zahir Shah, was instituting a program of democratic reforms. A new initiative aimed at mitigating inequities between rural and urban education offered free room, tuition, and board for middle and high school to the top three students in villages around the country. Daoud, the top sixth-grade graduate in Shinzmaray, was selected to attend boarding school in Kabul.

On the first day of spring in 1955, the beginning of the Afghan new year and school year, Daoud and two classmates started the two-day walk to the nearest city, Ghazni. There was still snow on the ground. As they were leaving, his father was proud, Daoud remembered. His mother simply said, "I know you'll be back quickly—because I know you'll get into trouble," as she held back tears.

Reaching Ghazni, the three boys hitched a ride on a truck, climbing on top of a load of wheat. The dust and flying wheat hulls choked them, and the cold made their faces sting. But the open road and unending sky stretched before them. The universe beyond Shinzmaray, the one that until then had only existed on the radio and in his books, was in Daoud's reach.

This was the threshold—to the life for which he had always sensed he was destined. And Daoud was not just stepping over it; he was flying over it faster than he ever imagined.

8.
The Limits of Vision

When I was in college, Big Uncle Tien-Mu hanged himself, inside his home in Taiwan. Big Uncle was what we called Dad's oldest brother, the one who had first immigrated to Taiwan from China with my grandfather. He was the one who had insisted that my grandfather pay my father's middle-school tuition, so that Dad did not have to quit grade school and go to work as he had.

I had always been closer to my mother's extended family, and I barely knew *Da Buo*, Big Uncle, as we called him. After finishing grade school, he had apprenticed with a butcher and eventually opened his own small beef jerky factory in Jungli, Taiwan. The upstairs had been converted into apartments for him, his wife, and his six daughters and one son. When I was in middle school, he had once taken me, Kelley, and Dad on a tour. It ended with *Da Buo* pulling seasoned chunks of stringy dried beef out of large stainless-steel tumblers for us. I was charmed by the simplicity of his occupation—I had never understood what Dad did as an engineer, but *Da Buo*'s work was not only tangible, it was tasty. At that young age, I hadn't understood it was a product of Uncle Tien-Mu's sacrifice, that his dropping out of elementary school and working had made it possible for my father to go to middle school and beyond. That the life of a small-time beef-jerky maker in an industrial Taiwanese city was a world apart from that of a civil engineer with a Ph.D. in the suburbs of San Francisco. If *Da Buo* had any resentments or regrets, I never detected them as he proudly pulled samples of the various batches—regular, spicy, fruit-flavored—from the shiny tumblers and insisted that we try them all.

After that, he had visited us in California once, by himself, staying in our home for a few days. He mostly talked to my father and was polite and formal with us. As Dad sunk into depression, we didn't hear from or about him for years.

And then, he was gone forever. Mom had told me over the phone in a quiet voice, as I sat in my dorm room. She didn't want Dad to hear her tell me. Dad didn't talk about it, or appear to react.

"He didn't want to burden his children and wife with the Parkinson's," Mom said, barely above a whisper. *Da Buo* had just been diagnosed within the last couple of years. He had been doing fine so far, physically. "He was a proud, self-made man. The illness was too much for him."

But hasn't Dad been depressed? I wanted to say. Isn't depression, or bipolar disorder, why people kill themselves—not Parkinson's? What about his grown children and his grandchildren? Or his wife, whom I learned later was the one who found him? Or the fact that people were living self-sufficiently for decades with Parkinson's? Could this be something hereditary?

I didn't ask any of those questions. Dad had been manic at the time, so maybe, as had been the case through other cycles, Mom hoped the depressive phase was permanently a thing of the past.

Later, when Mom and I came to talk more openly about Dad's illness, we would often have a pointless debate about which was worse: Dad's mania, or his depression. At their most extreme, they were both intolerable. But we eventually both agreed depression was worse.

In fact, it was his first depressive episode five years before Big Uncle's suicide that really forced us to acknowledge something was wrong. During my freshman year in high school, my father suddenly quit the government-lab engineering job he had held for more than a decade and announced he was becoming a real estate agent. He wanted to change careers, and getting licensed in real estate took only a few months' worth of courses. Mom, Kelley, and I were baffled, but Dad's "temper" had been flaring for months prior, and we knew better than to get in his way.

But, after coming home with a couple of boxes full of pilfered office supplies and two "Thank you for your service" plaques from the lab that— unlike his diplomas and other awards proudly displayed in his home office—went straight into a desk drawer, Dad slept. He changed out of his engineer's uniform of a polo shirt, with pens in the pocket, tucked into wrinkle-resistant slacks, and put on a gray sweatsuit with red trim. And he went to bed, nonstop. For days, he just got up to go to the bathroom and bolt down meals silently with us. When Mom urged him to take a shower and change into real clothes, he begrudgingly lifted himself out of bed with great effort, turned on the water for a couple minutes, and changed into a gray sweatsuit with blue trim. And went back to bed.

"He's resting," Mom said, jaw tight. "He didn't sleep well when he was working."

I took her word for it, and waited for his piles of binders from the realtor's association to be opened. The only thing I really knew about being a real estate agent was from a television news segment I had watched, about the boom and bust cycles of the market and how realtors suffered greatly during downturns.

"Dad," I said once during dinner, as he stared wordlessly into his plate. "Why did you quit your job? I heard on TV that being a real estate agent is hard, because the market goes up and down."

My words came out scolding, a tone I would not have dared use with him even weeks earlier. I really wanted to ask why he hadn't spent more than a couple hours a day out of bed in the past couple weeks, but Mom's discomfort about what was happening kept me from bringing up the obvious.

Dad made a guffawing noise, harsh and bitter in his throat. A few grains of rice escaped his mouth. Mom's jaw got even more tight.

"You don't support me," he grumbled, barely audible. "I'm trying to start a new career and you don't support me."

Then he got up, pushed himself away from his barely eaten dinner, and went to bed.

When Dad finally arose and started spending time in his office, the real-estate binders remained untouched. He sat in front of our late-1980s-model IBM PC, with the white-on-black-screen type and floppy disc drives. Dad then spent most of his days playing games, the same ones Kelley and I played, at which he used to scoff. He fixated on J-Bird, a knock-off of a popular arcade game in which a hopping bird-like character must be guided down a pyramid, over and over again. The game's repetitive whirrs and bleeps became the soundtrack of my father's decline. When J-Bird misstepped and fell off the pyramid into the black void, he did so headfirst, with his little bird feet straight up in the air. The fall was accompanied by a precipitous dropping noise as J-Bird was swallowed by the blackness, never to be seen again. Until the next turn.

Dad alternated his activities: J-Bird for a few hours, then back to bed to watch television. *The Price is Right*, reruns of *Bonanza* and *The Andy Griffith Show*—as if he were trying to relive a better time in his American life. He hardly talked then, and if I tried to say something to him during that time, the reply came from an expressionless face in the glow of the television screen, head propped on a pillow. If I tried to get his attention during J-Bird, he just ignored me.

Mom stuck with the "resting" narrative for a while, but after a couple months, I noticed her standing over him in bed, her thin body (getting thinner these days) in front of the television screen, trying to talk quietly so Kelley and I wouldn't hear: "What's wrong with you? Just do something, anything. Do you want your son to see you this way?"

Embarrassed at overhearing, but stung by being left out of my mother's entreaty, I slunk away from the master bedroom. In truth, Mom was right to worry about Kelley, who like most eleven-year-old boys was trying to find his reflection in his father. What he saw was confusing and humiliating, as much for him as for Dad. An introvert, Kelley internalized it, becoming more shy, making few friends in middle school for fear that they might want to come over for a visit. Lacking any explanations from Mom, Dad, or me, he started calling Dad a "couch potato," a term that he learned from watching Al Bundy on *Married . . . with Children* on the family-room set that Dad hadn't commandeered. "Dad's being a couch potato again," was the closest he got to being accusatory. And then he'd withdraw again.

As Dad became more unkempt, his two sweatsuits more threadbare, Mom's insistence that he shower and get haircuts regularly more futile, it became difficult—embarrassing—to be around him. His hair stuck out in salt-and-pepper tufts and was flattened in the back where it came in contract with his pillow. He smelled of dandruff and old sweat. His skin became sallow, and his eyes listless behind his thick glasses, always reflecting the TV or the computer screen.

I stayed out of sight, out of earshot of it all, not wanting to hear my mother yell at him to get out of bed or hear my brother bemoan his couch-potato father. As a new high schooler, my busy schedule of classes and extracurriculars provided a convenient excuse. Band practices went late in to the night, especially during the fall when we marched in competition and at football games, incurring the disdain of the popular kids in our bottle-brush hats and polyester uniforms with epaulets. The relief of being away from home on nights, weekends, and even for occasional overnight trips, outweighed any potential social liabilities.

Later, I discovered that the school newspaper was an even better year-round time suck, with constant deadlines and even later nights in the dank production room, laying out galleys on light tables with X-Acto blades, running pages through the hot waxer. As an editor, I wielded my red pen for hours, and volunteered to do more than my share. Fueled by warehouse-store-size tubs of M&Ms and cinnamon-flavored jawbreakers called Atomic Fireballs, we toiled past midnight on some days, to a late-Eighties soundtrack of Led Zeppelin and Violent Femmes on the boom box. In those late-night hours, I felt totally immersed in something productive, something apart from my family, among people who knew nothing of what I faced at home. All we talked about was the next issue, the top stories, the layout, and our aspirations to be real reporters or editors someday. In those late-night hours, friendships formed, romances blossomed, and rivalries flared. I was more witness than participant, happy to let other people enact the dramas while I found my rare slice of peace. After a while, our little staff felt like a family, and this made me happiest of all. My love of journalism started, in part, because of my need to escape.

I'd get home so late, Mom and Kelley would be in bed already when I stumbled in, a teenager past curfew for legitimate reasons. Such peace to slink into my room, slide into bed, without interacting with a single member of my family. Without fail, twenty minutes later, my door would softly crack open and Mom, her movements dull and sleepy, would peer in, confirming my return in one piece, and let the door close. Sometimes, she'd linger with the door cracked open, breathing, the weight of her loneliness in the air. She wanted me to wake up, to say a few words to her, to break the stagnant silence she endured day after day in the master bedroom. I'd open my eyes and prop my head up.

"I'm home," I'd mumble.

"I know," Mom would say. "So late—again."

"We had a lot of work to do. Deadline's this Friday. They asked me to edit the cover story this time."

"They must think you're good," Mom's mouth turned up at the corners but her eyes were dull and lined. "Of course you are."

"Yeah, even though I started on the newspaper later in high school than everyone else, our advisor thinks I can be a professional journalist if I want to be."

"Do you like it?" Mom smiled more genuinely now. "You must, you spend all your time there."

"Yeah, I do. I really do," I said, smiling back. "How's everything here? What's Kelley up to?"

Mom looked away. She blinked. I knew her eyes were teary. "The same," she said. "Everything is the same. Kelley had a soccer game today. You should ask him about it."

I had withdrawn from Kelley along with the rest of my family, for much the same reason I couldn't make eye contact with him in that restaurant years earlier—if we didn't acknowledge what was happening, it was easier to ignore it. Mom never spoke of what was wrong with Dad either. She simply stopped talking about him, period, soldiering on by going to work, making our meals, coming up with excuses to their friends about his absence at Chinese School and social events. No one questioned her, or openly wondered why a man who almost never got sick suddenly kept catching colds or getting food poisoning.

It's often said that mental illness is a taboo in Chinese culture. Surely that was what motivated my family to blame Big Uncle's suicide on his Parkinson's and not his mental state. But to say that there is a taboo around such things is not entirely accurate. For Chinese people, the denial is so complete that it's not even a possibility. We can do that with any and all uncomfortable truths—anything that falls out of the narrow bandwidth of Chinese norms. Better to shut them out completely than to get into the messy business of acknowledging them. Around that time, my childhood friend Johnny Wang had attempted to come out to his mother. "Don't you know there is no such thing as a gay Chinese person? Oh, sure, *wai guo ren* do that kind of stuff," she said, referring to white Americans as "foreigners" in Mandarin, a habit that followed our parents from Taiwan, "but not Chinese people." Likewise, there was no such thing as a depressed or bipolar Chinese person. My mother just said Dad was lazy, resting, stubborn, or had a temper.

After months of lying in bed and doing very little but playing J-Bird, Dad got a call from a friend of a friend, inviting him to join his small real-estate brokerage, as soon as he passed the licensing course and exam. Without fanfare, as if the last half year hadn't even occurred, Dad got out of bed, changed the sweatsuits for his polo shirts and slacks, and began to work, non-stop. We were too relieved to question it. He put in fifteen-hour workdays, completing the course and passing the licensing exam in record time. Soon, he had a handful of Chinese-speaking clients and spent Sundays running open houses.

Business continued growing, and Dad rarely took a day off. If he did, he worked on new remodeling projects he had started in the midst of this rebirth. First it was the old master bath, then the other upstairs bathroom. He didn't finish any of them. We stopped using certain rooms. Inviting people over was out of the question. In my later years of high school, I often finished homework, or came back from newspaper production, at midnight or one in the morning, and then was lulled to sleep by the sound of sheet rock against my dad's table saw or hammering in some distant room. He boasted that he only needed three hours of sleep a night. Once, he had to be rushed to the hospital after slicing off the tips of three fingers on the table saw.

And my dad's temper grew more unpredictable, erupting in ranting conflagrations that now often occurred in public, or were directed at friends or my mom's family members. They started avoiding us, isolating my mother when she needed support the most. By then, I was starting to understand my father was manic, and that his swings between barely being able to get out of bed and non-stop working were the manifestations of bipolar disorder. But I didn't say anything to my mother or even my brother for years, even when a white neighbor whom I babysat for told me she was bipolar, and on medication. I couldn't help but notice her house looked a lot like ours: Piles upon piles of unfinished projects—in her case, craft kits and women's magazines dating back five years—in every available space of the house. But, like Johnny Wang's mother said, some things were trappings of the *wai guo ren*—foreigners'—world, not ours.

Eventually, in college, I mustered up the courage and vocabulary to confront Dad about his illness, to instruct Mom to say "bipolar," "depressed," or "manic," instead of "temper," "resting," or "workaholic." But the one thing that we did not talk about for years even after that was the most obvious thing of all: Uncle Tien-Mu's suicide, and the possibility that bipolarity or depression ran in the family.

I couldn't say it to Mom or Kelley, not then. Because to say it meant one thing: Dad could kill himself. It was too much. So I did what had become familiar since that restaurant meal twelve years earlier, when five-year-old Kelley had looked at me with those pleading eyes. We looked away: from Dad, from the truth, from how this was hurting us all. We looked away from each other, our willful blindness shielding and wounding at the same time.

ত

After our visit to the Shirzais's original family home in Shinzmaray, Hamid and Asad ushered us back into the Toyota Surf and showed us the village school and mosque, both erected and maintained by generations of Shirzais. Because it was Friday, the day of rest, it, the school and the rest of the village were nearly empty. Some children gathered near the well and when they looked at us curiously, Hamid motioned for us to get into the car. The catch-22 of our visit: We were here to see the village, but it was potentially dangerous for the village to see us. We were disappointingly cut off from the people around us.

As we returned to the compound, the morning's tea was catching up to us, and Laila led me and Stephanie up a set of stairs to the roof, where the outhouse was. From there, the rest of the village stretched out before us, more mud-brick homes which offered glimpses of courtyards, vegetable gardens, animals, behind their high compound walls. What unseen lives and faces existed behind the other compounds and beyond, into the unending dun landscape?

Laila's small grip around my arm. She motioned toward another house, another rooftop like the one we were on. Two heads, male and young, were peering over the wall, staring straight at us.

"We've been spotted," she said, voice tight. "I don't have a good feeling about this. Let's go back downstairs."

For all that Fahima and Jumagul had made us feel warm and welcome in the red carpet-lined interior of their home, the village's insular paranoia rendered me and Stephanie—and even Laila—prisoners in our moment of greatest freedom. Here we were, defiantly venturing beyond where State Department Advisories, *The Crosslines Field Guide*, NATO control, paved roads, and better judgment would have us remain. Yet we were confined to remain out of sight, because of fear. I heard it in Laila's voice as the two figures looked at us over the wall, and saw it in in Hamid's posture when children at the well had stared at us. It wasn't until later that I really grasped that this danger—an intense distrust of any and all outsiders borne of a quarter-century of war, and counting—was as tangible as those red-painted rocks or the AK-47s at the checkpoints.

Fahima had cooked all of us a hearty lunch of beef stew, *rice pilau*, more bread, yogurt, and we all ate together on the *disterkhan*, men on one side, women on the other. This was a nice change of pace from Kabul, the men and women in the same room. Village customs were generally more conservative, but not always predictably so.

After lunch, I followed Fahima to the kitchen, where she did the dishes squatting next to large, cylindrical water containers with spigots. Every day, she and Jumagul filled those containers with water from the well in the courtyard. Poorer families went to the communal wells we had seen dotting the landscape. I offered to help, but she laughed me off. In a brief lull before afternoon chores needed to be done, Fahima sat down with the three of us women in the now-empty eating area. Laila translated.

"My aunt was told you wanted to learn about women in the village," Laila said as Fahima talked. "What do you want to know?"

Where to begin? I wanted her to tell me her story, her dreams, and whether she could ever fathom the world in which Laila—they were born the same year, a couple hundred miles from each other—now existed. "What time do you wake up in the morning?" was all I could muster.

"Three-thirty in the morning," she said. Just before the first milking of the cow, with enough time to pray before the start of her day.

She described her days of nonstop physical labor: milking the cow, pumping water, heating water, cooking, cleaning, washing clothes, patching walls, looking after the children, churning butter, baking bread. "As soon as

I go to bed, I fall asleep. I am exhausted, always," she said. "But it is not the work that I mind. It is that my life is the same one day after another.

"I would have liked to go to school," she said. "I did, for a little while."

But, she explained, her father was killed by nomads and as the oldest child, she had to leave school to help her mother. Her deep-set brown eyes began to well up. She stopped and inhaled sharply, choking back a sob. Laila grew quieter as she continued interpreting. Fahima had been so deadpan. From where had this sudden emotion surfaced? She lowered her head to compose herself, her face hidden in the looseness of her headscarf. Should I reach out and comfort her? I didn't know how. Laila was tentative as well.

Just as the old house had made me think about Daoud's breakthrough moment, the world and its opportunities opening up before him, Fahima's grief was the opposite. The death of her father, and her fate to be born as a woman of modest means in rural Afghanistan, had meant that the threshold always eluded her. In its place was monotony, the inability to see beyond the endlessness of her routine. In fact, in this large, relatively modern compound, provided for by family overseas, she and Jumagul had it pretty good. Fahima had had few run-ins with the Taliban (once, she said, a couple of Talibs came to the house and demanded that she provide a meal for them; she did, and then they were on their way), and no interactions with U.S. or NATO forces. Still her life, physically demanding but relatively comfortable, had not changed in a decade, even as other Shirzais had migrated around the globe, gone to college and graduate school, and, in the case of Daoud, taken a position in the new Afghan government.

She had composed herself when Jumagul came into the room. He shyly approached Laila to ask if we wanted to ask him any questions. Fahima slumped back against a cushion. Jumagul was eager to tell me about his time living in Pakistan, before he got married and was asked to keep up the family compound here in Shinzmaray. He had liked city living, and had hopes that his brothers could fly him to the United States for a surgery that would give him better eyesight. But post-September 11, obtaining a visa for an adult Afghan male under fifty was virtually impossible.

Here in the village, his days were filled with caring for the animals and crops outside, from the chickens and cattle to the vegetables and animal feed they grew themselves. He also maintained the mosque and school on behalf of the family. His eyesight didn't hinder him from these duties; he knew the village and the family's land so well he didn't even need what little vision he had to navigate it. But his vision, or lack thereof, had stopped his education earlier than his brothers'. He spoke matter-of-factly about his arranged marriage with Fahima after he returned to the village from Pakistan. I read between the lines and understood that a wife from a poorer family, the daughter of a widow, was chosen for him because her family's status somehow compensated for his disability. *Do you love each other?* I wanted to ask. But it felt like a hopelessly naïve question.

For Jumagul, village life also was a mind-numbing routine, laced with a taste of what might have been.

"Unfortunately, I got stuck here. Why is everyone gone and I'm here?" he said, still smiling. I tried to look past his glasses to see his eyes. Was he being wry? Or bitter?

A long, uncomfortable silence followed. I thought about my father's family: Was Jumagal like Big Uncle Tien-Mu, the brother left behind in the equivalent of the beef-jerky factory while the family's favored son traveled the world, got a doctorate, and lived the American Dream? Had that disparity, the sense of being left behind, contributed to Da Buo's despair and depression?

As with Fahima, I wanted to say something encouraging, but was at a loss for words. I wasn't sure what I had expected to hear from Jumagul and Fahima, but I had romanticized the idea of village life. Daoud, Maiwand, and Yusuf liked to speak of Shinzmaray as their true home—they were country people, real Pashtuns needing nothing but the land, a few animals, family, and tribe. Many other Afghan American immigrants, mostly Tajiks, were "Kabulis," a word they uttered with a hint of disdain for uppity city folk. But for them, and for Laila and her cousins, Shinzmaray was a place they visited for a while, and then a car and a plane could whisk them back into lives of opportunities and experiences of which Jumagul and Fahima could barely dream. Was I unsettled by Jumagul and Fahima's honesty? Uncomfortable with how it made me reexamine my own extended family? I had to admit, I had wanted to find them happy, espousing the virtues of a simpler life and their connection to their roots. Now, I was not sure how their dissatisfaction, Jumagul's sense of injustice, fit into the larger Shirzai family narrative. Or my own family's.

Why is everyone gone and I'm still here?

While Jumagul talked, Fahima heard the lowing of the cow, and quietly excused herself to go milk her. The animals seemed to need more attention from her than the children, who were remarkably self-sufficient. Once in a while, one of the children clamored briefly for their parents' attention, but for the most part, the two older sons took care of their younger siblings.

Jumagul sighed and said, "Let me tell you about Afghanistan before the wars and the drought."

He waxed eloquently about when the village was full of trees and streams, and people's farms were so big and prolific they could not see all their crops from any one spot on their land. His voice swelled, and his words tumbled out so fast Laila had trouble keeping up. Watermelons, grapes, cucumbers, wheat, nut trees – people had so much, and they always shared with each other. There was a time when people were welcoming to, not afraid of, outsiders, he said.

"I apologize for the state of my country," he said, his dark-eyed gaze so piercing that I could make it out through thick lens.

"I fear you've found it a letdown," he said softly. "Please know that Afghanistan wasn't always like this."

"I know," I said.

"Have you ever seen a country in worse condition?"

"No, I haven't," I replied in honesty.

∾

The family busied themselves with afternoon chores, and Laila, Stephanie, and I explored the expansive compound on our own. I marveled at how large it was, how well the design compensated for the lack of plumbing and electricity. Basins with drains had been built for giant metal water containers with spigots, creating working sinks. The latrine was on the roof, built into the house for easy access, but not directly over the living spaces. The walls were a couple feet thick, providing natural insulation.

The compound had been meant for far more people than just Jumagul, Fahima, their children, and Grandma. Daoud had told me once that when they first started planning for the bigger house about fifteen years ago, he and his brothers envisioned multiple family members returning and living there for part or all of the year. He, his brothers Maiwand and Yusuf, all had projects they wanted to start in the village, whether it was to re-launch the girls' school or to catalog all of their father's letters, many of them containing original poetry. They envisioned the younger generation returning, fulfilling their answers to Daoud's query, "And how do you plan to help the country?" *Watan.* So this huge, many-roomed compound, as expansive as the old house was modest, was erected. It had been a boon for local labor, an empty vessel for the Shirzais's hopes and intentions, that they would return to their source. That they would reconnect with the land that was birthplace, homeland, and home.

But the new house remained mostly empty. Grandma settled in here, and Jumagul and Fahima watched over the house and land. War and life—that is, war in Afghanistan and life in America—prevented the other family members from returning for more than brief visits. And now Daoud didn't come back at all.

The old house had teemed with stories, full of the history and spirit of the Shirzais. As Laila, Stephanie, and I walked through the new compound, I wanted to find that, to find what new chapters of the family's story might be inscribed within these walls. But there was little but nearly empty rooms. Surely this house must have a heart. Jumagul, Fahima, their children, and, especially, Grandma could not live in this space, large though it was, and not leave their mark. Laila had just finished showing us a small room filled with carpets and cushions, not unlike the women's sitting room in Kabul, that was Grandma's.

"Come this way," she said, waving us into a side room adjoining Grandma's. "You'll like this."

The small room had a mantel-like shelf and a skylight that let in a swathe of sunlight against that wall. The only things in the room were five framed black-and-white photographs on the shelf. In the middle, the largest, was Daoud's college graduation portrait, in a dark cap and gown.

"Wow," I said, stifling a gasp.

"I know," Laila said quickly, embarrassed, trying to prevent me from saying the obvious out loud.

But it was Stephanie who did: "He was so . . . *handsome.*"

All of the features were familiar: his dark, intense eyes, the furrowed brow, the thick black hair. Yet something else on this younger, smooth-faced incarnation: A soft glow. A quiet confidence. The barely perceptible head-tilt of an old-Hollywood headshot. It was impossible not to stare.

To his left was a photo of Hamid, clean-shaven. He was wearing a wide-lapeled jacket, large sideburns, and a pompadour. His topaz-like eyes held a glint of mischief, like he was about to tell a joke. Laila chuckled at the dated image of her father. "Total seventies," she said.

To the right was Mohammed.

His horn-rimmed glasses. The sweeping side-parted hair. Mina's long, elegant nose anchoring the angular contours of his face and the kindness behind his brooding brown eyes. Behind his stern expression, the hint of a slight smile.

I inhaled sharply. Stephanie tucked her camera by her side and Laila grew silent.

The lost one. Here he felt real. For all that he wasn't talked about by the Shirzais, this photo spoke the proverbial thousand words and more. I could smell the pomade he used to style his thick hair, not unlike my father's Brylcreem. I could see his pores, almost feel the smoothness of his just-shaved face the way it must have brushed up against Mohib, Sarasa, and Mina's cheeks, the way it felt under Mamoy's loving touch, those many years ago. This visceral Mohammed brought shape to the contours of his loss, why it still felt so close to the surface for Mamoy and Grandma. Why Grandma had set up this room, a shrine of sorts. And why, of all the Shirzais, Grandma was content to remain here. For her, life was not about the next threshold, the future, but rather, about the past and what no longer was.

To her, all of the sons in this room were departed, in one way or the other. When she had said goodbye to the eleven-year-old Daoud with, "I know you'll be back quickly," she had, despite the joke, thought he would return after high school. Then he went away to the United States, and thought he would come back after working for a few years. Then the Soviet War started, Mohammed was taken, Maiwand and Yusuf had to flee, Hamid moved his wife and children to Pakistan, and Daoud could not come back. The family wanted her to think of Mohammed as "lost"; in some ways, all of the sons in this room had become lost to her. Two smaller photos, of Maiwand and Yusuf as teenagers, flanked the three big portraits, as if to underscore this point.

Here, the heart of this big, empty house. And contrary to Daoud's hopes that this structure would contain the Shirzais's future contributions to Shinzmaray, its core was still rooted in the past, frozen in a time before unspeakable loss. And while Daoud's photo occupied the center space, Mohammed's presence in this room grew tenfold for every silence, every omission, every time the word "died," or even his name, was not uttered. Until there was nothing else left on this shelf, in this compound, in this family.

Jumagul's blindness, which allowed him to see things only when he held them right in front of his glasses, was a fitting metaphor for the limits of vision in the village. We left Shinzmaray as a swirling dust storm engulfed the area. It was as if the sky and wind had manifested Jumagul and Fahima's myopic world. We couldn't see more than a few feet in front of us. The dust swept over herds of camels and sheep, their nomadic keepers leaning into the barrage like sparse, skinny trees. We bounced along on the treacherous dirt roads, deep gullies on either side. Hamid was driving his Surf 4x4 by memory, not sight. When we had said goodbye to Fahima, she had nearly crushed me in an embrace with her strong arms. She didn't want what our visit had brought briefly into her world—a diversion, a chance to be listened to—to go out the door as we did.

We pushed forward into the wall of dust, dark like coffee grounds. Hamid was confident at the wheel, Laila and Asad relaxed, if a bit impatient about our slow pace, and irritated by the dust that crept in past the closed windows of the truck. Now, we women kept our scarves over our faces for protection, not modesty.

The storm subsided as we arrived in Ghazni. It was startling to have a clear view all of the sudden, like waking from a dream. Gone were the village's adobe and rolling earth. We were on the city's asphalt roads, amid cinderblock buildings. We stopped at the same gas station, and Hamid waited for a driver-for-hire to take us back to Kabul.

As if to make the scene even more jarring, a tan U.S. Army Humvee rolled by, full of soldiers holding M16s, which seemed long, unwieldy, and unused compared to the battered, compact AK-47s I had seen on the road. The soldiers' desert camouflage, blond buzz cuts and sunburnt faces were so out of place there. They looked so young and so lost. What did they see as they patrolled the city? The chaotic throngs of turbaned and bearded men walking, riding bicycles, and driving cars must have seemed impenetrable and threatening. Their eyes lingered for no more than a second on us three women in the backseat of the old Surf 4x4, with our scarves pulled over our faces. Hamid and Asad milled around outside of the car, in turbans and shalwar kameez like all the other men around them. In the midst of Ghazni's hubbub, we didn't warrant a second look. To them, only three sets of brown eyes peering out from behind our scarves were visible.

I had more in common with those soldiers than I did with Fahima, Jumagul, or any of the Afghans around us. Yet, seeing myself through the eyes of these men, probably no older than nineteen or twenty, and no doubt wanting desperately to go home, I felt less American than I ever had in my life. To them, I was no different than any of the residents of Shinzmaray from whom the Shirzais kept us hidden. But to the villagers, we were as alien as the soldiers. The boundaries of us and them, of local and foreign, of safe and dangerous, had become impossibly blurred. It was a lot like trying to see the world through the blinding dust storm.

After we had returned to the United States, we would receive a stark reminder of these boundaries, and how we had crossed them. I would learn from Daoud that Jumagul had gone to sweep the mosque the day after we left, and had found an anonymous note intended for him and Fahima. It roughly translated to, "Those who harbor foreigners should watch their backs." I felt ill. I imagined the smooth-walled mosque, the angry script of the note peeking out from under one of the prayer mats. Should we have gone to the village at all?

"I'm sorry," I said to Daoud, not knowing what else to do. He shrugged. It happens, he said. If the author of that note had really wanted to hurt them, he would not have given them a warning.

But on that day, careening toward Kabul on the ring road as the sun set, amber behind imposing steel-gray clouds—this particular driver was racing to arrive before dark, when being on the highway was far more dangerous—I was relieved that our trip and stay in Shinzmaray was concluding safely. Exhausted, all four of us were quiet on the ride home. I wondered how Daoud felt, not being able to visit his birthplace anymore, for fear of his and his family's safety. By crossing too many thresholds,

Daoud had rendered himself unable to return.

Finally, the driver, being guided by Asad, began winding through local streets in Kabul and we pulled right up alongside the familiar white compound wall with the blue door. I sighed.

I could already feel the warmth and the pull of what lay on the other side of the blue door. Asad held it open for us. I stepped over the threshold, my sandaled feet longing for the cool softness of the courtyard's green grass.

I'm home.

Part Three:

Watan / **Country**

Many of us are at home both in the East and the West, and yet in neither place. We travel by intercontinental jet, and arrive disoriented and culture shocked on both ends. Interestingly, it is going home, in whatever direction, that is the most disorienting.

—Debra Denker,
Sisters on the Bridge of Fire: Journeys in the Crucible of High Asia

9.
The View from the Sitting Room

In Afghanistan, the only person I ever saw with any kind of planner or datebook was Daoud. He tucked a full-sized American wall calendar, the kind you get free from a bank or hardware store, into his beige canvas briefcase. Every space was filled with his neat printed script in blue ballpoint pen, appointments and To Do lists threatening to burst out of the square boundaries of each day. The people whose names he had hand-printed in the squares next to appointment times had not taken the same care, since often Daoud found himself waiting on people who were late —sometimes by an hour or more—or who never showed up. Daoud had unsuccessfully tried to hide his irritation when I was a few minutes late to our very first meeting in Portland, two and a half years ago. Afghan time was maddening to him. "This," he grumbled, "is the problem with Afghanistan. How do they expect to rebuild the country this way?"

To Afghans, the spontaneous rhythms of human interactions mattered more than the clock or calendar. Afghan time was ticked off, not by minutes and seconds, but by prayers, cups of tea, and conversations that spilled over into long, sumptuous dinners. Since the wars had started, life was, by nature, unpredictable. People learned not to plan. Who knew if there'd be a bombing, a funeral, a government overthrow tomorrow? Who knew if you'd even be around? Instead of planning, they learned to be patient. A Taliban commander once warned former U.S. Ambassador Zalmay Khalilzad, "You Americans may have all the watches. But we have all the time."

I, too, had to shed my own conditioning about planning, getting used to not knowing what I would do each day when I woke up. Since the Shinzmaray trip, every morning brought some discovery, even if it meant we spent most of the day at home with Rochina and Nazo, Laila's cousins, helping them with chores, or chatting. Other days brought surprises, like the time Daoud sent his driver back to the house to take the three of us to the National Archives for the afternoon. Nazo volunteered to escort us, but directed the driver on a long detour—through one of Kabul's shopping districts, where we looked at dress shop after dress shop with her. Each one was more dazzling than the one before, with beaded, glittery Indian-inspired garments that had come into vogue when Bollywood movies arrived on the heels of the Taliban's departure. Finally, we arrived at the Archives, where a special display of posters for the upcoming Afghan presidential election was on exhibit. Word of our circuitous trip got back to Daoud, and Nazo was soundly reprimanded. We were never sent the car again. Though other opportunities came to us, and we took them: An offer from Daoud to introduce us to the Minister of Higher Education, a request from Nazo for us to visit her school, an invitation to a graduation party at Kabul Education University from one of our newfound professor friends there.

I came to regard our plans and schedule like the weather: They seemed random, but everything we expected to happen eventually did. Flow was more important than precision. But the Lariam side effects distorted time, particularly when sleeping, and sometimes upon waking I'd feel like I had been in Afghanistan for months. Other times, as our activity-filled days flew by, I couldn't believe our month here was almost over. Only one week left. I had learned so much about the Shirzais, and had certainly collected enough for my article on Daoud's work at the Ministry. But there was still an unspoken gap in the Shirzais's story: Mohammed.

The black-and-white photographs in Grandma's shrine-like room in Shinzmaray had told me something about the family that I had not known before—about the silent space that Mohammed's absence occupied, the unacknowledged power of this loss. It was tucked away, not shown to guests along with the hospitality of bottomless tea cups and trays of bread. But it was there, in the heart of the house, well-maintained and not a speck of dust on the frames or a single smudge on the glass.

And every Shirzai knew where this room was.

Now, back in Kabul, I wanted to ask people about those photos, to know more about the day Mohammed was taken. But I knew there were some things, even as a journalist, and especially as a friend of the family, I should not ask directly. Daoud and Maiwand already had told me that they were not in the house when it happened; Daoud was in Oregon already and Maiwand had been jailed for writing anti-communist graffiti in the bathroom at his university. They had told me Hamid was not there either. Yusuf, who was a teenager at the time, had already told me his account. That left Mamoy—and Amina, the Shirzai brothers' only sister in Kabul.

But ever since that first day of our introductions, Amina had been somewhat elusive. She greeted us when she saw us, asked about our days. But she was more a watchful presence (as when she kept an eye on us during the meeting with Asad) than a friendly one. After our return from Shinzmaray, Amina was warmer, more at ease with our presence in the house. One evening, after dinner, as Rochina and Nazo were cleaning up with Laila and Stephanie helping, I brought my laptop to the women's sitting room. Stephanie had downloaded photos from our trip to the village on it. I offered to show them to Amina, who patted the cushion next to hers for me to sit. Without an interpreter, we were reduced to a handful of Pashto words and phrases that I knew: "*Kha da*" (It's good). "*Der kha da*" (It's very good). "*Wo*" (Yes). "*Xaysta*" (Beautiful). "*Zor kor*" (Old house—or home). "*Nawe kor*" (New house). "*Ghat kor*" (Big house). These served us well for the photos of Jumagul, Fahima, and the children, as well as of the old house, and the new compound.

I deliberately saved one photo for last: the one Stephanie had taken of Grandma's photo room, in which all three large pictures—Daoud, Hamid, and Mohammed—were visible. I silently clicked on it and tilted the screen at her. Amina made a small sound of recognition and stared for a long time. She made regular visits to Shinzmaray and must have known the room. But seeing this photo told her that I had also seen this room. She touched the screen image of Mohammed and looked at me quizzically, asking a question softly in Pashto. I wanted to summon Laila. But, wait: I knew what Amina was asking me, if not the words, then the spirit of the question. "*Wo*," I said, catching her dark-eyed gaze for a moment, and then turning my eyes downward respectfully. She had asked if I knew what happened to him. "But I want to know more," I said, just above a whisper, in English. Then, heart pounding, barely audible: "What did it mean to you?" I mustered the courage to ask only because I was sure she would never understand me. Amina nodded gently and said "*Xa*," the Pashto equivalent of "Oh," or "Uh-huh." Startled, I clicked the photo closed. Had she understood me? Or was she just making a polite acknowledgement of my English jibberish?

"*Khlas so?*" she asked, motioning toward the screen. Finished? "*Wo*," I said. "*Tashakur*," she said, and placed a firm hand on my shoulder. Then she got up, smiled, and took leave of me.

I heard Laila and Stephanie's laughter from the kitchen as the sounds of running water and clanging pots and pans resonated through the wooden door. Laila would understand better what had just transpired with her aunt. A delighted shriek from Nazo, and footsteps, rustling. A long silence. "Angie!" Laila yelled. "Where are you? Come in here!"

I pushed my way past the swinging kitchen door and saw what they were looking at: The cat, the wily calico that always tried to get into the bread when no one was watching, had made a little nest of pilfered towels and fabric scraps in the corner behind the refrigerator and given birth to a litter of tiny kittens. Their eyes were still closed. Nazo reached for one of them and Rochina batted her hand away as the mother cat bared her teeth. Laila, Stephanie, and I looked on in awe. As we were going to and from the village, as Rochina and Nazo were busying themselves with cooking, as I was preoccupied with Mohammed's death, new life was happening right under our noses. I wondered how many of those kittens would survive. Life for animals in Kabul, even for this semi-domesticated cat that was fed table scraps, was brutal.

"Hmph," Rochina said, unimpressed. "I was wondering where that naughty cat had gone. She hadn't tried to steal the bread in a few days."

She went back to her washing as Nazo cooed at the kittens. And, as the evening wore on, I forgot to bring up my conversation with Amina.

The next morning, the women in the house awoke with a particular sense of purpose. After morning prayer, when Nazo would usually roll drowsily back into bed and sleep in as long as she could, Rochina nudged her sister-in-law and marched her toward the kitchen. I heard Amina's voice in the kitchen, which was unusual. Eventually my curiosity got the better of me.

I came into the kitchen, blinking away sleep. White clouds of flour swirled in the dawn light streaming in through the windows. Rochina and Nazo squatted on the kitchen floor with their sleeves rolled up, their strong, limber legs supporting them, each kneading a glossy, pale mass of dough on cloth laid on the linoleum. The air was thick and yeasty. They began forming balls the size of large grapefruits. This continued without their usual chatter. Nazo, who looked decidedly groggy, did not like being up this early in the morning, and Amina paced between them, checking on their progress. She noticed me looking on, and asked me something in Pashto. I shook my head, wishing Laila were up with me. Amina said something else to me that began with "Laila," and I said, "*Wo*," enthusiastically, hoping I had just agreed that she would ask Laila. Did this have something to do with our conversation yesterday?

"My aunt wants to know if we want to come with her to the bread bakery," Laila said a bit later. She explained that this "bakery" was a public wood-burning oven where families brought their own dough to be made into the puffy flatbread that we ate every day. "And then she's going to the old house on the other side of town that our family rents out. Our tenants moved out, so now my aunt cleans it and takes care of it."

I masked my disappointment. I didn't mind running errands with Amina, since I had wanted to get to know her better. But—why would I have even thought she had understood me the evening before?

"Of course," I said. I knew better than to ask Laila when we were leaving. Now, we were on the bread dough's time clock. We lingered in the women's sitting room as Rochina and Nazo periodically checked on the rising dough, lifting up the cloth covering the blobs and giving them a poke or two.

As if on cue, Amina came into the vestibule, found her blue *chadori* on its hook, threw it over her head in a practiced motion, and walked, now strangely faceless, to the kitchen. It was time to go. Rochina and Nazo had arranged balls of dough around a large, flat, round basket with an indentation on the underside for the carrier's head. A white cotton cloth was draped over the dough. Amina bent down and Rochina and Nazo carefully set the basket in place on top of her head, then stood up, looking around for us as much as her load would allow her. I smiled at her, and could see her dark eyes smiling back through the mesh opening of the *chadori*. The three of us were in our headscarves. About half of the women in Kabul at that time wore *chadori* like Amina, nobody had ever suggested that we should do so. I asked Laila why Amina wore the veil outside, instead of the headscarf she wore at home. "Does her husband want her to?"

After Laila translated the question for her aunt, I heard a loud "Ha!" followed by deep laughter from behind the *chadori*. Amina's reply sounded sarcastic.

Laila smirked and said to me, "She says she doesn't know or care what her husband thinks. But it's too troublesome to deal with a headscarf when you have to carry the bread or do any kind of work. The *chadori* just sits on your head without falling off and you don't have to keep fixing it."

I blushed, wishing I hadn't asked the part about her husband. She was right—not only did I constantly readjust with my scarf, but I also noticed that Rochina and Nazo did too. It was second nature to them, as habitual a gesture as tucking my hair behind my ear.

As her blue-draped form stepped through the blue door into the unpaved street, effortlessly balancing the bread basket atop her head, Amina said something else to Laila.

"Besides," Laila relayed, "if she doesn't wear it, other women will talk."

I wished I could have seen Amina's face as she said that. It was hard to get used to conversing with a disembodied voice coming from behind a wall of fabric.

"Wow," I said. "So it's the women, huh?"

Seeming to understand the gist of my comment, Amina said something else and Laila translated, "Men may make the rules, but women are the police."

I had tried on Amina's *chadori* once and walked around the house in it, just to see what it was like. I expected it to feel heavy and oppressive. I thought I'd be bumping into walls. But the fabric was lighter than it looked, and the mesh face screen actually allowed me to see surprisingly well, peripheral vision and all. Looking in a mirror, I saw that transformation I had begun the first time Mamoy taught me to put on a *chador*, and continued when I put on a *shalwar kameez*, was complete. I was not myself, but a faceless and armless figure. For that reason, and not for the perceived physical impediments, I couldn't imagine going out of the house like this, though Amina and countless other women here did every day.

Yet to most Afghan women I had met, the *chadori* was not a high-priority issue. "I'll wear whatever they want me to," one female student at Kabul Education University had said to me, "Just give me electricity twenty-four hours a day, and a promise that my children will grow up with functioning schools and no war."

Amina was striding far ahead of us, not slowed down in the least by her *chadori* or the basket, and we jogged a few steps to keep up. We wound our way through a maze of unpaved, unmarked streets, taking so many turns—left, right, then right again, left—that had we become separated from her, we'd never find our way back. As we reached a larger intersection, a low, swaying blue shape sat near the middle of the street, barely out of the way of car traffic. I looked closer. A woman, wearing a dirty *chadori*, smeared with black stains like a mechanic's coveralls, sat cross-legged on the road. She extended one upturned, gnarled hand from behind the veil, fingers misshapen and knuckles swollen. As we approached, the tempo of her rhythmic high-pitched warble, in time to the constant swaying of her body, increased and her hand reached toward us. Her smell, sour sweat and ammonia. I wanted to step away, but my feet slowed against my will and I stared. Kabul had countless beggars, many of them amputee landmine victims hobbling on makeshift crutches, waving stumps of arms, or dragging themselves around with their hands, calloused beyond recognition (the double amputees), and children, boys and girls. But I had not yet seen a grown woman. But I had not yet seen a woman. This beggar's claw-like hand, her stained veil, and her bird's voice grasped at my throat and pushed tears into my eyes, which I blinked back. Stephanie murmured a soft sound of pity.

Amina strode past the beggar without a second look, mumbling to Laila. Laila whispered, "A widow. She's here all the time."

Falling behind again, I rushed to catch up with Amina, grateful for a reason not to keep looking. Then guilty for feeling grateful. That was the thing about Kabul: Just when you thought you had steeled yourself against all its human misery, it found a way to pierce your armor. I would need Amina's decades here to have her fortitude.

As we stepped in front of the bakery, enclosed on three sides with a roof but open in the front, a tide of warmth swept over us. The oven's heat rippled forth, wave after wave. At the back of the building, right next to the wood-fired pit oven, two women in headscarves and simple dresses worked on either side. Though perspiration was beading on my nose and forehead, they didn't seem affected by the rippling heat. In the front, two more women sat on the ground shaping dough, slapping round blobs, like the ones in Amina's baskets.

Even before she knelt down to remove her basket and then flipped up the front of her *chadori*, the women recognized and greeted Amina. Embraces and cheek-kisses were exchanged with the front two women, and the two at oven waved. Just as their eyes landed on us, Amina quickly motioned to us and said a few words. The women nodded. We nodded back. Later, I'd learn from Laila that she had said, "This is my niece, and these are two sisters from the North who are visiting us." Sometimes Stephanie and I were cousins, and sometimes we were from Pakistan. The story always changed slightly. But the implication remained that we were Afghans from one of the northern ethnic groups, who looked Asian—or from Pakistan, which could explain our lack of understanding of Afghan languages—and that we were definitely not Americans. I was secretly pleased that I could "pass."

The women's hypnotic bread-making rhythm echoed the cadences of their speech as they chatted with Amina. The women in the front, once they finished slapping the dough balls flat, laid them on a floured surface, coaxing each piece into a long oblong and pressing water-dampened fingers along the dough to make vertical grooves. Then those pieces were passed back to the two women by the oven, who slapped the flattened raw dough onto the sides of the cylindrical pit. The result looked like a misshapen featherbed, perfectly browned, filling the hot air with yeasty aroma.

Amina left the basket there; Rochina or Nazo would come pick it up along with the finished bread later. She flipped her *chadori* back down over her head and motioned for us to follow. Once we reached a main road, Amina hailed a taxi. The driver rolled down his window and she leaned in, her eight-square-inch mesh face-window a couple feet from him. The two talked, more and more animated, until it was clear that Amina was raising her voice, and she was gesturing forcefully with her right hand from under her veil. "Bargaining," Laila explained. "My aunt's a tough one."

Once again, I thought of the wars and regimes she had lived through in Afghanistan—and, most of all, her presence in the room the day Mohammed was taken. And my unanswered, perhaps not-understood, question: "What did it mean to *you*?"

The cab driver hung his head in resignation, and then motioned for all of us to get into the cab.

We got out in a neighborhood northwest of the city's center. The houses were smaller, more vertical—most were two stories—and closer together. We approached a double-doored wooden gate on the outer wall of a saffron-colored house. Amina opened a padlock and let us in. As I walked past her, she caught my gaze through her mesh face screen and said something.

"She wants you to know that our family lived in this house all together through the Soviet War, after people moved from the village," Laila said. "Maiwand and Yusuf grew up here."

I nodded. I had thought this was just a rental property. *Through the Soviet War*. That meant that the family had been here when Mohammed was taken in 1979, just before the war started. The last time they saw him was in this house.

Was that why she had taken me here? Or maybe this trip was just a coincidence. After all, she had to come and clean the house sooner or later. Judging by the ease with which she pulled off her chadori and hung it on a perfectly hook-shaped branch of a gnarled, dead apple tree in the concrete courtyard, this caretaking of the past was routine for her, like taking bread to the baker. The twisted, lifeless tree stood, defiant, providing a trellis for grapevines someone had trained around its branches. The vines were so well embedded that their flat, pale-green leaves appeared as if they were growing out of the tree.

Through Laila, Amina said she had lived in the early 1990s, during the civil war that followed the Soviet War, with her husband and six children. In those chaotic days, rockets screamed through the streets—once shattering a downstairs window—and stray bullets claimed random victims, including a neighbor's twelve-year-old son, the same age as her youngest at the time. The neighbor boy's bloodied body lay in the street for nearly half a day before someone carried him away for burial. Soon after that, she and her husband decided to move the whole family to Peshawar and enroll their children in the refugee schools run by other Afghans there.

But eventually, they returned to Kabul, eager to reinhabit and protect the family's properties, and live in their country.

The house extended far back from the street. The floors and walls were concrete and cool, coated in a thin film of dust. The main sitting room was beside the front entryway, looking out onto the courtyard. Amina ducked into another room. The door opened and slammed, followed by a muffled jingling sound. When Amina emerged, she gave Laila a handful of keys, some attached to a ring and some loose, wrapped inside a red-and-black checked handkerchief. Then she found a broom and started sweeping. Laila's cupped hands were full of keys, the old-fashioned kind, with flat, round heads, cylindrical shafts and little square ends with finger-like protrusions. There were many more keys than there were doors in the house.

Laila, Stephanie, and I clambered up the stairs and began sticking keys into locked doors. Laila was determined to find her Uncle Maiwand's old room. We jiggled keys and peered inside keyholes. The echoey house reverberated with our every move. I imagined Maiwand and Yusuf, a couple years apart, playing in the courtyard, like in a black-and-white picture Yusuf had shown me of the two boys standing there. They were wide-eyed, gangly, and entranced by a single bicycle wheel, rolling it together. As teenagers, they had watched from within these walls as a revolution took hold, as the nation reeled from the 1978 assassination of President Mohammed Daoud Khan and most of his family by the communist People's Democratic Party of Afghanistan. Known as the Saur Revolution, for the Dari name of the month during which it took place, the overthrow threw the country into months of instability under warring communist factions. Concerned about the precarious communist rule, the Soviets gradually increased their presence in Afghanistan, starting clandestinely with the KGB, escalating to the full Red Army occupation in December 1979.

Laila, Stephanie, and I, after trying all of the keys upstairs, found that none of them opened any of the doors. We gave up and went downstairs. We walked all the way out the back door and into a narrow roofless corridor that separated another section of the house. In that part, there were two outhouse-style bathrooms. The rest of the back section was a large, low-ceilinged room. I craned my neck inside, but it was too dark to see. "This is where Mamoy and her family lived," Laila said, "where Mohib, Sarasa and

Mina grew up. I think some of them were born here." This was where that black-and-white photo of Mohammed and the children had been taken. It smelled dusty; I couldn't make out its size or shape.

As Stephanie took pictures open-air corridor, aiming her lens at a slant of midday sun against the golden walls, Laila and I went back into the main house, where we tried the keys in a couple rooms tucked under the stairwell. Finally, one gained purchase on a lock, and Laila turned it with a satisfying click. We swung the door open to the corner room. There was an oval "AFG" sticker in the window, the kind you would put on a car. "This is it," Laila said, excited. "Uncle Maiwand's room. I know he had that sticker. I've seen pictures." I walked its small perimeter, peering out the window. Laila filmed the room with her camcorder, zooming in on the sticker. I stepped out of the room so she could have an unobstructed recording, and time to contemplate this space that had belonged to the man who was like a father to her.

Amina was now upstairs, attacking cobwebs with a smaller broom. I walked past the stairwell, into the front sitting room. It was larger than any other space in the house, and had a big window looking out at the courtyard, the apple tree, and the double-doored gate that we had entered. I paused in the middle of the room, staring at that gate, its brown vertical wooden slats contrasting with the ripples in the yellow plaster courtyard wall. That gate. Why did it feel as if I had seen the view from this room before? It was quiet. I only heard the rhythmic bristle of Amina's broom against the upstairs ceiling, Laila's soft footsteps in Maiwand's room, and the whirr of Stephanie's camera shutter in the corridor.

Then I knew: This was the window through which Yusuf last saw his brother on the day Mohammed was taken. It was just as he had described, when he had told me the story two and a half years before. I had just met the family then, in early October 2001.

Daoud and Maiwand had been terse about Mohammed's capture, each telling me they hadn't been there and didn't know the details. The first time I met Yusuf, he also cut a wide berth around the topic. The second time, he showed me the photo of Mohammed and the children. As I studied it, he began telling me the story.

He talked about the time after the Saur Revolution, before Soviet invasion, how in 1979 the KGB was everywhere, and intellectuals and anti-communists began disappearing. It happened slowly at first, he said, so they weren't that worried. Mohammed hadn't told his family that he was helping organize the anti-communist coup; he didn't want to implicate them. A radio journalist and producer, Mohammed had aligned himself with a Muslim nationalist group. His role, to take over the national radio station if the coup took hold, was no small responsibility in a nation where large numbers of illiterate people without access to electricity depended on radio as their only means of contact with the outside world. What the family did know at the time was that Mohammed had been involved in various causes since he was in college, and that his fellow activists often came to the house and whisked him away to important meetings.

"Then the coup was foiled," Yusuf had said. "The communist government started sweeping."

He fell silent for a while.

"Friday was our day of rest," he began again. "We had guests at the house. I was sixteen. At eleven-thirty in the morning, there was a doorbell."

Everyone was in the front sitting room. They had cushions for sitting set up in a semi-circle, facing the front window, with a view of the courtyard, with the apple tree, the peach tree, and the other greenery there. There used to be flowerpots in the room, lined up along the windowsill. The flowers filled the room with their sweet fragrance, which mixed with the scent of tea steaming in glass cups on the table. The women were in one of the back rooms, busy preparing lunch for the guests. Someone opened one side of the double-doored wooden gate and greeted three men, two Soviets and an Afghan. The Afghan had a big mustache, Yusuf remembered. They asked for Mr. Shirzai, whom everyone immediately understood to be Mohammed, because people came for him all the time. Mohammed calmly got up and walked to the gate to talk to them. Nothing seemed to be awry with this conversation in plain view of the family and guests. Surely Mohammed would tell them he was about to have lunch with his family and he could meet them later. Then he walked with them, through the gate and out onto the street.

It was when they turned around that Yusuf saw them—the Kalashnikovs slung over each of the three men's backs. Only Mohammed was unarmed. They were headed toward a Jeep, parked around the corner a block away, barely in sight. Everyone else saw this too. None of the men were grabbing him by force and they weren't walking particularly quickly. But Mohammed wouldn't want to make a fuss in view of his whole family. The men hadn't parked in front of the house because they had anticipated a struggle to get him into the car.

A terrible realization seeped through the room, through the teenaged Yusuf, like a growing stain.

"There was nothing I could do. They were armed. We started breaking out—in screams, in tears," Yusuf said, his eyes faraway. "Our guests disappeared. Our sister was hysterical. His wife was hysterical."

More than twenty years later, when he told me about that day, his brother, the Kalashnikovs, Yusuf was somewhere else. My presence had suddenly felt irrelevant.

"That was the last time I saw him. I knew he was gone."

A long silence.

"What was the first thought that went through your head, when you saw the guns, the Jeep parked around the corner?" I asked softly.

He met my eyes, almost startled to see me there.

"Thought? Thought?" he said, grasping. "I wasn't thinking."

"What were you feeling?" I corrected myself.

He put his bearded face in his hands and closed his eyes for a long time. Was he thinking or crying?

Then he looked up, straight at me, dry-eyed.

"It was like lightning strikes you over the head," he said, "and goes through your whole spinal column, paralyzing you."

I stood in the sitting room, staring at the wooden gate, smelling the empty room's dust and abandonment, thinking of Yusuf's words. I saw the cushions in a semi-circle, the half-finished green tea on the table, dishes with pistachios, golden raisins, and the cubes of rock sugar people would wedge against their front teeth as they sipped tea. Where had Yusuf been sitting? He, the lanky teenager, trying to look grown-up among all the men, admiring the gravity of his big brother's activism: *Oh, here comes someone else for Mohammed again.* Mamoy must have been helping prepare lunch, with Mohib, Sarasa, and Mina in the room, playing. Her expressive, round eyes and pale, smooth skin in the flush of youth and motherhood without the weight of grief—how lovely and vivacious she must have been. The braids she liked to wear, black and glossy, threatening to slip out from under her scarf, and Mamoy feigning exasperation as she tucked them back in. Did she see her husband walk out the door and not catch his eye for modesty's sake, since there were guests there? Or perhaps there was a brief, barely perceptible exchange that only a married couple could detect?

And Amina, "our sister"—who must have run out with Mamoy when the men's shouting and wailing in the sitting room started. Yusuf had said they were both "hysterical." I could hardly imagine the Amina of today shedding a tear, much less wailing. But this was her younger brother. She had lost other siblings in the village, but they had died young, a fact of life there. Mohammed was different. He was a college graduate, a professional, a husband and father. He had made it past the threshold, out of the village. Kabul then was a modern, peaceful place. The Saur Revolution, the assassination, the Soviet presence—they all felt like a passing storm contained within the world of political people. And, until that day, they had not realized they were political people.

I looked out on the empty courtyard, with the dead apple tree—twisted like the beggar woman's hand—and the double-doored gate, shut. This is how Amina must have seen it that day: without life, a door forever closed. And now she was the caretaker of this vacant house, sweeping out the dust, the way Grandma's photo room was kept clean. Both places shrines, in their own ways. Her sweeping continued. She was on the steps, making her way down with the broom. Amina – who had brought me here. Maybe she had understood my question, "What did it mean to you?" Whatever the case, she had answered it.

This private revelation felt like too much to hold to myself, just standing there. But what could I do? It would be unfair to burden Laila and Stephanie with this, on an outing that appeared to have nothing to do with these memories. I pulled my digital camera out of my purse and took a picture, out the window, focusing on the double doors of the gate, catching the vine-covered dead apple tree in the frame. Holding onto this view.

I turned around, startled, to find Amina just a few feet behind me, staring. My face burned. She had an indecipherable look on her face, a hint of a smile. I wanted to say so many things to her in that moment. Laila was not there, so it would have been impossible for Amina and me to understand each other anyway. I did the only thing I could think of to do. I showed her the photo I had just taken on my digital camera: the view from the sitting room.

"*Xa,*" she said, nodding.

And because the memory was theirs, not mine, it was fitting that I didn't know what she was thinking. After all, in clothes that were not my own, I had "passed" at the bakery—and at passport control, the checkpoint on the way to the village, and in the eyes of those U.S. Army soldiers in Ghazni—as someone *like* an Afghan. Just as the Shirzais in Portland had taken me in as someone *like* family. But, coming to Afghanistan, I had begun to know the boundaries between seeming and being. I had been grasping for the knowledge of exactly what it was like to lose Mohammed, as if it would finally seal my insider status with the Shirzais. That grapevine could stubbornly cling to the apple tree in the courtyard until the two were nearly indistinguishable, but they would always be two, not one. Today, whether Amina meant for me to or not, I had gotten as close as an outsider could. I had felt, if not known, completely. And the view from the sitting room, like this house, felt empty—truly lost.

I knew, from that first meeting with Maiwand, that the family had maintained hope that Mohammed was still alive for nearly a year. They sent clothes and food for him to Pul-e-Charkhi Prison, where countless anti-communist intellectuals were being held. There was no sign any of it was getting to him, but Mamoy insisted they keep dropping off the packages. Then one day one of the guards at Pul-e-Charkhi gave Mamoy his clothes and wedding ring. "Stop looking for your husband," they told her.

That was the day he became lost.

A mass grave unearthed in 2006 near Pul-e-Charkhi by NATO forces contained about 2,000 bodies, which had been shot in the head and then buried. Many had broken bones. In total, tens of thousands of Afghans were tortured and executed in similar ways during the Soviet era. As many as 50,000 other Afghan families lived on with similar silences, without a body to bury or a grave to visit. Their placeless grief lay in quiet rooms like this one, in countless other empty houses being swept, framed photographs in hidden rooms, and in the soundless echo of the word "lost," uttered by those tens of thousands of families.

For so many here—women especially, the ones who stayed behind, after the death and after the exile of men—post-Taliban Afghanistan was not post-anything; wars and murderous regimes blurred together into present tense. How would the Americans be remembered? Amina's reluctance to let the bakery women know we were from the United States offered a hint.

Soon, Laila, and then Stephanie, came. Laila was holding a sheaf of browned, parchment-thin paper. She showed me how there was English writing on it—the careful, round script of someone who was learning to write foreign words. The sentences were complex, with dependent clauses and adverbs. They appeared to be some kind of English exercise. She wondered out loud if it was her father's handwriting, since Hamid had been an English teacher.

"I bet it is. You should show it to him tonight and ask," I said to her, as her face brightened at the possibility that she could return a piece of his youth to him.

"This house has so many stories," Laila said, looking out the window.

Amina signaled to us that she was ready to go. Laila and Stephanie followed her out. I lingered, the last one in the house. I looked out the window one last time, pictured the partially open gate that Friday morning in 1979—the glimpse of the three Kalashnikovs, the unarmed Mohammed between them, and the Jeep, a block away. Shortly after 11:30 (Yusuf had remembered the exact time) all those clues crystallized into a single, irrevocable conclusion.

It was like lightning strikes you over the head.

I turned toward the front door, feeling the strong afternoon sun at my back, and stepped out, jogging to catch up with Amina. Laila and Stephanie were outside with her, scrutinizing the faded handwriting on the browned papers. Amina had already thrown her *chadori* back on and was faceless again, holding one of the gate's double doors, ready to lock them behind me.

10.
Ice Cream in a War Zone

From the time we had arrived in Afghanistan, Laila had talked about ice cream. All around us were cesspools, amputee landmine victims begging for *bakhshesh*, and crumbling walls scarred by trails of bullet holes. Yet there was ice cream, she had assured us. Kabul was not a place for trucks with tinkling music to attract kids; here children worked, begged, or starved, and a kid carrying an ice cream cone down the street would soon find the frozen treat coated in the mix of dust and diesel residue that painted everything in the city—if he didn't first get beat up and have it stolen.

It was during that first car ride from Kabul Airport when Laila had brought up ice cream. We were talking about *chadori*, a topic which segued to that of ice cream more easily than one might think. As our driver steered his Volga sedan down the unpaved roads, women in *chadori* moved alongside us like dusky-blue shuttlecocks, faces hidden behind small mesh ovals.

"What was it like wearing *chadori* here during the Taliban time?" I had asked. She last visited Kabul in 2000.

"It wasn't that big of a deal," she said, shrugging. "Just hot. It was the other restrictions that made me mad."

"Like what?"

"For instance, we went to this ice cream shop in our chadori, with male escorts, like we were supposed to—but the man wouldn't serve us because we were women."

The Taliban's infamous Department for the Prevention of Vice and the Promotion of Virtue, the same government agency that had been responsible for beating women who showed their ankles or polished their fingernails, had also outlawed selling ice cream or French fries to women. The religious police scoured the city in their Toyota pickup trucks, shutting down stores or beating shopkeepers if they suspected them of serving female customers. The man who refused to serve Laila probably was alarmed to encounter a woman openly ordering ice cream. He wasn't taking any chances.

Ice cream and French fries. I found it puzzling that Vice and Virtue, as they were known, would have chosen to outlaw these particular foods, which happen to be two of my favorite foods, as well as Laila's. Was it the phallic nature of a French fry? The suggestive quality of ice-cream licking? Did Taliban leadership hold a *jirga*, a traditional tribal council, to discuss the vices and virtues of particular foods before deeming ice cream and French fries worse than, say, peaches (with apologies to T.S. Eliot and LL Cool J) and cucumbers?

Eve Ensler, the playwright and activist, wrote about a group of women in Taliban-ruled Jalabad sneaking behind a wall of hanging sheets in the back of an abandoned restaurant, lifting their burqas and taking a few furtive bites before the roar of pickup trucks sent them fleeing— abandoned bowls tipped over, spoons akimbo, melting rivulets of cream providing evidence of their crime. A woman caught with ice cream could be punished by flogging or even execution, Ensler's guide told her. In her 2002 memoir, *Zoya's Story: An Afghan Woman's Battle for Freedom*, Zoya (a pseudonym) writes of life under the Taliban, "something as mundane as eating ice cream became a ridiculous undertaking," as much because of the physical limitations of the chadori as because of Vice and Virtue regulations.

Similar stories are never told of French fries.

"It's like no ice cream you'll try anywhere else," Laila said.

"What's so special about it?" I was sweating in the un-air-conditioned Volga sedan and felt cooler just hearing about it.

"Well, first of all, it really tastes like cream. Like it came right out of the cow," she said, her voice quickening against the lethargic, stale air. "Every shop makes its own right there in the back. And it doesn't have flavors;

it's just pure sweetened cream. Then there are little extras—rosewater, pistachios, cardamom—just to make it interesting but not to cover the rich taste.

"It just glides on your tongue like butter." Her large, round eyes took on a dreamy softness.

"Plus, there's just something about that ice cream that takes me back," Laila said. "It's part of my childhood."

She had been born in 1979, the year Mohammed was taken—she had been too young to remember any of it. But she did remember trips with her father, brothers, and her cousins Mohib, Sarasa, and Mina to the ice cream shop. She'd closely guard her portion from her greedy brothers, neatly devouring it as the boys made a mess.

"This time," Laila said, "I'm going to find some ice cream."

Outside the car window, I saw cratered concrete and buildings flattened like cardboard boxes. Two wiry men pushed a cart full of vegetables being pulled by an emaciated donkey too feeble to contribute noticeably to the men's efforts.

There was something necessary about discussing ice cream while driving through a war zone. As our time in Afghanistan progressed, and moments and images began to weigh on me—Fahima's tears, Grandma's photo of Mohammed, the beggar woman, the view from the sitting room—I came to understand that better than ever. Laila's quest became my quest: I would not leave Kabul until I tasted that ice cream.

It was hard to leave the house. Sure, we went out for our meetings at Daoud's office or the universities he was helping rebuild. And accompanying family members to school or on errands, as we had with Amina, wasn't a problem. These were things only we Americans were interested in. But a purely social outing was another matter, one that would become mired in the politics of the household. We had to figure out how we would get there, and who would go with us. The dress-shopping detour en route to the National Archives had pretty much ruled out using Daoud's government-issued car and driver. We'd have to take a cab, which required a male escort. Amina, an older married woman could venture out on her own.

But we were younger, unmarried, and unfamiliar with Kabul. Safety, if not propriety, would require the escort.

Asad could take us; but the problem was that if we brought him, it would become an outing with family members, in which case it seemed unfair to leave Nazo and Rochina behind. When Laila and I had first broached the idea of finding ice cream, her cousin Nazo's green eyes had lit up and a smile had crossed Rochina's elegant, serious face. Then they hesitated and looked at each other cautiously—Amina would expect one of the women to stay home and help prepare dinner.

"No, no, you go," Rochina said to her sister-in-law.

"No, no, you go," Nazo said.

"That's OK, we'll figure it out later and go another day," Laila said quickly. When we hung out with them in the kitchen that afternoon, there was an odd quiet between the two women as they chopped onions and okra.

"That was a bad idea," Laila whispered to me.

Even if both Nazo and Rochina managed to get away, with a male escort there would be six of us, and we wouldn't fit into a cab. We'd have to take two, which would require two male escorts, not to mention skillful coordination through Kabul's unmarked, congested roads to ensure we ended up at the same place. Nobody had cell phones, and the networks were nascent and spotty anyway. Finally, there was eleven-year-old Ihsan, Asad and Nazo's nephew from Kandahar who was living at his grandparents' house for the summer. He'd be crushed if we all went out for ice cream without him.

"I'm beginning to think I'm going to spend another trip in Afghanistan without ice cream," Laila said, sighing. Her narrow shoulders slumped under her bunched-up scarf, which she had allowed to slide off her head inside the house. As guests, Stephanie and I were too intimidated by Amina to test the limits of propriety. After I saw how she looked at her westernized niece's exposed, ponytailed hair, I dutifully kept my scarf on my head.

Now, the ice cream-deprived Laila just sighed. I reached over and lifted her fallen scarf onto her head just as her aunt walked by. Laila rolled her eyes at me.

"It's okay," I said. "There are more important things than ice cream."

"Oh, you have not tasted this ice cream."

From that day on, Laila would reminisce about ice cream—the fresh cream, the cardamom and rosewater—once or twice each day. I sometimes wondered if I heard the call to prayer from the local mosque's loudspeakers as often I heard Laila talk about ice cream.

One scorching hot day, on our way back from a visit to Kabul Education University, she and I, against her family's warnings, bought some cold cherry juice from a street vendor. Stephanie, still recovering from some suspect chicken she had eaten at the graduation party, declined. Parched, Laila and I gulped down its icy, sour-sweet goodness, sharing some with Daoud's driver. By that evening, we were violently ill, and the next day the driver called in sick with food poisoning. Laila and I could barely stomach meals, and alternated between lying down and using the toilet. Yet Laila still talked about ice cream. She made it sound appetizing even then.

Soon, I had imagined it so many times, I could feel the cool, just-milked butteriness in my mouth. Some days, I forgot I actually hadn't eaten this ice cream, until I heard the note of longing in Laila's voice.

It seems silly, looking back now, that the family politics, and not the Vice and Virtue Department, would have prevented us from fulfilling this goal. But within the high, white plaster walls of the family compound, those obstacles felt as real as Taliban rules.

Night was not one time in Afghanistan, but three. I dreaded sleep on Lariam in Kabul, but I loved evenings in the courtyard.

Fig trees and large rose bushes crowded the small space. Their shadows deepened the Kabul night, marred by neither skyscrapers nor streetlights. The cool damp grass brushed against my sandaled feet.

In Pashto, there are three words for night: *maxam, makhustan,* and *shpa. Maxam* is evening, *shpa* is late night, and *makhustan* is the middle time between those two. As the sun set each day, the night's three stages unfolded.

Maxam was dinnertime, a time that brought everyone together, the culmination of all the other rituals of the day—prayers, women cooking, young people returning from school, men returning from work. As we ate in the women's sitting room, with the pomegranate-colored cushions and carpets, I studied the contrast between the warm overhead lights in the house and the first steely shades of night outside the window.

Maxam was spent eating dinner in the sitting rooms, and *shpa* was for sleeping in the bedrooms. *Makhustan* was the time to stand in the courtyard. Everything changed at *makhustan*.

After dinner, everyone went their separate ways—to wash dishes, pray, study, or chat over tea. The rigid lockstep of the household—to each activity its time, and to each person his or her place—relaxed, and family members floated throughout the L-shaped house, their soft steps criss-crossing the courtyard grass. When the nightly power outages dimmed the house's interior and generator power kicked in, people congregated in the courtyard.

Inside the house, one sitting room was for men, and one for women, but the courtyard was a gender-neutral zone, where I could approach any member of the family without feeling as if I were trespassing. For me, this freedom carried an edge of danger: With a dozen people in the house of seven rooms, nearly all of which had windows facing the courtyard, I was under constant scrutiny. No eye contact with men, and don't stand too close, I would remind myself.

I remember one particular night when Daoud, as he often did, stood in the courtyard with his battery-operated short-wave radio to his ear, listening to the news on BBC. It cheered me to see him there. Like him, I missed twenty-four-hour news stations and the internet. Asad, his nephew, hovered near him. Both men's *shalwar kameez* were stark white against the shadows. I approached them, as if I were just wandering by and happened upon them. Asad nodded a silent, shy greeting to me. I stood as close as I dared, straining to hear the crisp British voices over the hum of the generator's diesel motor.

Daoud relayed the news to us: Israeli tanks killed ten Palestinian protesters in Rafah refugee camp. The standoff in Najaf, Iraq, between Moqtada al-Sadr and U.S. forces continued. Accusations of the U.S. military abusing Afghan prisoners followed in the wake of the Abu Ghraib scandal. Daoud added his own commentary to each news item, such as "This is very bad," and "But of course we can't trust the official account of the casualties." Normally, back in Oregon, Daoud and I would discuss events like these in his Mt. Tabor office. I missed those conversations, the freedom I had to talk with him there.

Stifling a yawn, Daoud announced he was going to sleep, collapsed
the antennae of his radio with the flat of his palm, and walked back into
the house. Others still lingered in the courtyard, but the diesel generator's
constant hum stole the words of all but the closest person. Asad and I were,
in effect, in a rare private conversation.

An awkward silence hung in the night air. "You know," Asad said, his
brows furrowed. Another pause. "I have really good aim with an AK-47."

"Wow," I said, stifling a nervous laugh. Was he trying to impress me?
"Really?" My usual barrage of reporter's questions—How did you learn to
shoot one? What did you shoot? Are they hard to aim? Does it even matter
how you aim a semi-automatic rifle?—eluded me.

More silence. Our eyes followed Daoud through a window of the
house.

"He seems tired," I said. "It must have been a long day for him."

Asad and I had stepped closer, in order to hear each other.

He looked in the direction of the small room he was sharing with
Daoud. "*Ustad* wakes me up in the middle of the night sometimes," he
said, in his precise, careful English. He referred to Daoud by his family
nickname, Pashto for "professor." "He wakes me up with his shouting in
his sleep."

"Really?" I said.

"We share a room. It's very loud when he yells. It wakes me up."

Asad looked away. Why was he telling me this?

I couldn't imagine him talking to Daoud about it, even if they were
roommates; everyone treated Uncle Daoud—*Ustad*—with such reverence.

"What does he yell?" I asked.

"I usually hear him shouting things like, "Help!' or 'Don't kill them!
Leave them alone!'" Asad said. "I think he's talking about his family, our
family."

As I looked out over the trees and into the darkening night, I
tried to scratch the surface of this revelation. In his dream, was Daoud
encountering the KGB-conscripted soldiers who had taken his younger
brother? The warlords whose compounds flanked the village? A Taliban
insurgent? Some monstrous hybrid of the three? I wondered if they carried
knives or guns, if he were running after them or they after him, and if
anyone was caught, shot, maimed, or killed. I had always associated Daoud

with a world of books, international dignitaries, and navy-blue blazers. He was the one who had gotten out before the wars started, who didn't directly experience what he called "the butchery and slaughter." Daoud constantly reminded me that it was not him, but those like Amina, Hamid, Jumagul, and Grandma, who suffered through it. He was the lucky one. Yet, seeing how the bullet- and rocket-scarred city depressed and haunted him, I had begun to doubt that. In Kabul, he had bags under his eyes and a heaviness in his voice that he didn't in Oregon.

Were Daoud's dreams like my Lariam nightmares—or worse? Did he wake in a cold sweat, with the images of his family lying in pools of blood, the sounds of their pleas for help? Asad had waited until no one else was there to tell me about his uncle's nightmares. I wanted to ask questions, but he excused himself to go inside, sensing that we shouldn't linger in conversation too long. Someone was always watching.

That night, I lay awake in the room I shared with the young women, across the courtyard from the one Daoud and Asad shared, wondering if I would hear something if he yelled in his sleep. I didn't. If makhustan was a shadowy time, in which boundaries could be crossed, or at least stretched, then late night, *shpa*, was pitch black, impenetrable. Asad had shared a glimpse of something with me, had given me a window. But was it meant as an invitation to see deeper into the Shirzais—or into him? But even he had felt the watchful eyes from the house on us, known when it was time to retire into the night.

The family had opened their home to me; taken me into their lives; made a place for me at maxam dodai, the evening meal; they had allowed me to wander freely in their courtyard at makhustan. Yet, as the generator and lights went out, and the home plunged into true darkness, *shpa* remained theirs and theirs alone.

❧

On one of our last nights, Asad ducked into the women's room during dinner and announced to us that he had been told—by whom, we didn't know—that Stephanie and I would want to buy some souvenirs and gifts before we left. He could take us, with Laila, shopping on Chicken Street if we'd like. Souvenir shopping hadn't even crossed my mind. Landmines, militants, and the precarious state of my digestive system had overshadowed the prospect of buying knick-knacks. But now that it was nearly time to go home, seeing the famed Chicken Street appealed to me.

"That would . . . be nice," I said, looking at Amina; her nod was barely perceptible.

Laila nodded vigorously between mouthfuls of rice. We both had just recovered from the cherry-juice incident, and were eager to get out.

We left the house the next day with little drama; no one else was very interested in souvenir shopping, though Ihsan joined us. Nazo and Rochina waved at the five of us as we stepped out the door. "Chicken Street is for tourists," Rochina had scoffed. "But you guys have fun."

Asad flagged down a taxi. Ihsan didn't want to be jammed in the backseat with the three women, so Asad propped his nephew between half the passenger seat and the car's parking brake, the boy's knobby knees high in the air as he slouched down. Then, as soon as we zipped away from the house, we were stuck in Kabul's unrelenting traffic.

By now, the routine was so familiar it hardly fazed me: First, the dust and diesel fumes washed in through the car's open windows. Then we couldn't stand it anymore so we rolled up the windows. Then we began to roast as the sun beat down on the taxi and the exhaust from the gridlock swirled around us. So we'd roll the windows down again. The driver was merciless on his clutch, jerking forward every time the traffic moved an inch. Without traffic signals or road striping, various streams of autos were not so much merging as consuming every available space on the road, a slow-moving stampede of steel cattle.

Ihsan bellowed something in loud Pashto. The driver slammed on his brakes, which made Ihsan yell the same thing again. Asad quickly rolled down the passenger-side window and patted Ihsan on the back. The driver eyed the boy.

"What did he say?" I asked.

"He said, 'I'm going to throw up! I'm going to throw up!'" Laila said.

We reached a busy intersection and Asad asked the driver to stop. We climbed out, stepping over open sewers to the sidewalk, and rounded the corner onto a bustling street full of shops. Each storefront on Chicken Street was full to bursting, wares dangling from overhangs and doorways —a richly loomed rug here, a patina-coated goblet there. Every centimeter of the window displays was filled with lapis, turquoise, and silver jewelry, tea sets, miniature maps of Afghanistan carved from semi-precious stones, little decorative boxes of every imaginable shape and style. Some were coated with a thick layer of dust that must have dated to the Taliban days.

Still, the most distinctive part of each store was the shopkeeper himself. Often wearing a certain cap or turban to indicate his ethnic and tribal affiliations, he beckoned in sweetly intoned Dari for passersby to come in and behold his wares. Crowds of men, women and children walked quickly in all directions, jostling into each other but never losing pace. We moved much more slowly than them, stopping to look at everything. People bumped into us from behind and sidled past, exasperated.

This place felt too public, the kind of place where car bombs went off, where militants looked for foreigners to kidnap. A gnarled old man in dirty *shalwar kameez* brushed close to me and shouted his beggar's cry, "*Bakhshesh, bakhshesh.*" Laila planted a hand on my elbow and we veered away from him.

Hours passed with shopping and bargaining. Once we were inside the stores, drinking green tea and haggling with the chatty shop owners, the outside world felt far away. We headed away from the shops with our packages: The triumphant weight of a small rug, a brown one with a simple Persian pattern, pulling down the plastic bag in my right hand, a bagful of jewelry and knick-knacks in my other. Stephanie carried in her bags an assortment of intricate boxes inlaid with semi-precious stones and a crisp new dove-gray *shalwar kameez* for her boyfriend. Asad had giggled nervously when she held a *kameez* up to him—keeping a safe distance, of course—to see how it might fit. But once he got over the initial discomfort, he was a good sport about suggesting the soft gray over the more-traditional white, explaining that it was a very stylish color in Kabul now. Ihsan, who had been an equally good sport about waiting for us to bargain and make our purchases, was now starting to drag a bit as we made our way back to a main road.

After all the ducking in and out of storefronts, rounding corners into alleys and descending into basements, all of us but Asad were disoriented. We blindly followed him; he seemed to be searching for something. He was leading us to a block with restaurants—was he hungry?

We stopped at a nondescript storefront. Asad walked in, motioning for us to follow. Ihsan became very animated, practically skipping inside. Asad exchanged brief words with the man in charge, and ducked past the crowded main room, poking his head into an empty back room painted electric-blue. He said a few more words to the man, who nodded and motioned for us to sit back there.

Asad had been searching for a table where the five of us, a mixed-gender group, could sit together comfortably without coming under scrutiny. In the main room, only men sat with men, or women with women.

We settled in—Laila, Stephanie, and I on one side, Asad and Ihsan on the other. The vinyl chairs had light aluminum frames and the table had a faded faux Formica top. Laila pulled out her camcorder for the first time that day, grinning so widely that the skin around her big brown eyes crinkled.

"What?" I said.

"Don't you see? Look where we are!"

This was an ice cream shop.

"I'm so happy," she said. "Just wait until you try this."

The man came in to take our orders. Asad turned to us. "What kind of ice cream do you want?"

I looked at Laila, waiting for her to recite her mantra: cardamom, rosewater, pistachios . . .

Giddy, she fumbled with the laminated menu in front of her, at a loss for words. Turning to her cousin, Laila said, "Just order for us."

He did, and Ihsan chimed in with his own choice.

We all sighed at the same time. Ihsan fidgeted in his chair. It squeaked on the linoleum. Asad shushed him.

Suddenly Laila's smile faded.

"Umm, do you think the freezing process kills bacteria?" she said quietly to me. "Because I don't think this milk is, you know . . . "

"It's not pasteurized is it?" I said. My stomach knotted at the thought of the cherry juice.

"Nope, it's like right out of the cow. That's what makes it so good," she said grimly.

"I think only heating kills bacteria," Stephanie said. "Maybe the freezing just stuns it for a while."

We laughed nervously. We had waited too long, wanted this experience too much, to become rational now.

Asad and Ihsan were immersed in their own conversation. They had no interest in our bacteria paranoia. It was a bit mysterious to everyone in the household, who pitied us our weak stomachs and immune systems, our dependence on Lariam and complaints about its side effects. They dutifully boiled our drinking water every day, and asked after our health as if we were elderly.

"I don't care," Laila said. "I have to eat this."

As if on cue, the waiter brought in three glass dishes and set them down in the middle of the table, and another followed with two more. The ice cream, a vanilla color, was molded into shapes. Three of them looked like a doughnut stood up on end with crushed pistachios and cardamom sprinkled over it, and the other two were cylinders covered with moist strands of fresh coconut. Ihsan grabbed one of the dishes holding a cylinder and dove in.

We distributed the rest among ourselves. Laila sat with her doughnut-shaped one in front of her, spoon poised.

She feigned a stony expression. "I fear for my life," she said, giving the potential bacteria one last nod with the same joke-phrase she always uttered before taking plastic slippers to the giant cockroaches in our bathroom. We laughed. She had never used that phrase when we rode near minefields or passed through roadside checkpoints outside of NATO-controlled territory.

With that, she stuck her spoon in, careful not to topple the doughnut. Then she wedged a bite out of the frozen concoction and tasted her first ice cream in Afghanistan in more than twenty years. She closed her eyes and smiled.

"Mmm," she said. "That's even better than I remember."

Awaking from her reverie, she suddenly fired up her camcorder, and pointed it at me. "Eat, eat," she commanded. "We have to document this. Your first Afghan ice cream."

I too had the pistachio and cardamom. I carved out a small amount, and wiped thoughts of bacteria from my mind. The cold steel of the spoon hit my mouth before I tasted the surprising flavor of pure, sweet cream. I had been expecting vanilla because of the color. The texture was impossibly dense yet smooth, rich and delicate, buttery and fatty, and quick to melt on contact. It had the heft of Devonshire clotted cream with the fragility of panna cotta.

The crunchy pistachio and cardamom bits were just afterthoughts to this odyssey in dairy. After savoring a few more bites, I wrested the camcorder from Laila's hands so I could film her eating her ice cream. She obliged, bringing the spoon to her mouth theatrically. I turned to Stephanie, who waved her spoon at the camera. As a photographer, she hated being on the other side of the lens, so I mercifully turned to the boys' side of the table, filming Ihsan as coconut shreds and melted ice cream dribbled from his mouth. Unlike the rest of us, Ihsan gobbled his treat, eating it the way any eleven-year-old boy would—quickly, and with equal amounts of gusto and mess.

As I raised the camera to Asad, I realized that, through the small-screen viewfinder, I was looking at him face-on for the first time. The absence of an audience—whether other restaurant-goers or his mother—and the shield of the camera afforded me this brazenness. Much as I had in the sideview mirror of our Ghazni-bound hired car, I studied his face again. Today, his toasted-wheat complexion was clean-shaven. His dark eyes were fringed with long, straight lashes and framed with thick, arcing eyebrows.

He looked back directly into the lens, unflinching. Feeling the weight of his gaze, I realized that this was not the sideview mirror. We were, in fact, looking at each other, just through a lens. Heat rose to my face, despite the cold buzz of the ice cream I had just eaten.

"So," I said, trying to sound like a television reporter. "How would you rate this ice cream?"

What a dumb thing to say, I thought.

"Very good," he said, with a broad smile and a spoonful of ice cream. For all that I was flustered, and for all that his mother would not have approved of this, Asad seemed perfectly at ease. Should I bring up his AK-47 aim? Probably not.

He and I made some more small talk as I stared into the viewfinder screen: A hair-thin scar bisected his left eyebrow. His teeth were white and straight, and he was doing a lot of smiling and laughing as I continued my patter for the video.

Suddenly, a small, cool hand slipped under the camcorder: Laila. She was stifling a giggle.

"Your ice cream is melting," she said, raising her eyebrows.

She had cleaned her dish right down to the pistachio and cardamom bits, bacteria be damned. I got to work on my ice cream doughnut, which had now collapsed into a mound, albeit a very delicious one.

I turned to Laila, who was in her own quiet meditation, taking in the odd shade of paint on the walls, the hubbub outside our little room, and the tiny milky puddle at the bottom of her glass dish. We exchanged smiles.

"We don't even need that," she said, motioning to her camcorder on the table. "We are never going to forget this ice cream."

She was right. Not just the ice cream, but also the blue walls, the squeaky chairs, and the goofy grins on everyone's faces. And watching Asad's long-lashed dark eyes through that camera viewfinder—Asad, who had figured out how important tasting ice cream was to us, and orchestrated this trip to make it possible.

We would remember this as our reprieve from the rest of Kabul, a small haven away from misery, pollution, and strict gender protocols.

What was necessary about ice cream in a war zone: The luxury and the impracticality of this food, transient by nature, demanded our attention. Ice cream was the taste of being fully in the present.

But for Laila, it represented the past as well. Ice cream was the Afghanistan she wanted to remember. And on that afternoon in Kabul, she had found it again.

It was about tasting survival, about savoring the durability of childlike wonder.

11.
Learning to Pray

The yellow door was made of wood that felt too light. Every time we, the Americans—Laila, Stephanie and I—swung it open, we pulled or pushed too hard and it flailed wildly on its hinges. Back and forth, back and forth. It had a large, crooked black English letter painted on it. "What does the K stand for?" Stephanie asked, puzzling at it like it held a secret code. Rochina smiled: "It stands for kitchen." Our laughter echoed through the room.

This was our space within the Kabul house, the place where the five of us young women had spent most of our waking time together. The sisters-in-law Rochina and Nazo enjoyed the company as they did their chores. It was not a kitchen for the faint of heart. Kabul's endless dust blew in, necessitating diligent sweeping. Hot air made it stuffy; the cold air chilled it. That wily calico watched the pile of flatbread tucked under a cloth, diving into it the moment it went unmonitored. The "stove" was two waist-high butane tanks in the corner with burners on top of them. The women wrenched the tanks' handles, waited for them to hiss for a while, then lit a match from a large box, and threw it at the burner as eyebrow-high flames burst to life with a deep *foomp!* sound. Rochina and Nazo calmly stepped back, and then sidled up to the fire, and twisted the knob until the flame was low enough to cook on.

The men had their own spaces, such as the *saloon,* or sitting room, where the family would discuss and make important decisions. But the kitchen was the women's space—specifically the younger women's. Amina rarely went in. Nazo, Amina's youngest child and only daughter, now had the company of Rochina, who had just married Nazo's brother, so there were enough hands in the kitchen for Amina to enjoy the fruits of being the matriarch and leave the cooking and cleaning to the younger generation. The men, though not forbidden there, usually steered clear. The kitchen was a place where secrets could be shared, with little worry that someone would walk in and overhear. In the kitchen, Rochina and Nazo could be themselves.

As sisters-in-law, Rochina and Nazo's relationship bore far greater importance and closeness in Afghanistan than it typically would have in the United States. Rochina had moved a year ago from Pakistan to wed Nazo's brother Ayub, in a union arranged by their families. The two young women did all of the cooking and most of the housework together. They spent more time with each other than with anyone else. They moved in the kitchen with practiced synergy. Rochina, with her liquid brown eyes and straight black hair, was serene and serious. Nazo's startling green eyes had an impish glow, and her curly dark hair was always trying to escape from her *chador*. They chatted, bickered, and laughed with such ease, I sometimes wondered if Rochina's marriage had been arranged for her compatibility with Nazo as well as with Nazo's brother.

Ayub had been on a business trip to Kandahar when we first arrived, which was why Rochina, Nazo, Laila, Stephanie, and I shared the room usually occupied by the newlyweds—the only one in the house with access to a western-style flush toilet. The room barely accommodated the newlyweds' double bed (western-style beds were in vogue now, often given by the bride's family as part of her trousseau) and the three sleeping mats. I became accustomed to sleeping by Rochina and Nazo's sides, and falling into the foreign yet comforting rhythm of their lives.

Our days varied, but nights we were always together, the five of us. Some evenings we sat on the edge of the concrete-covered well in the house's courtyard, learning into each other under the fig trees as we chatted. Back in our room, we chased cockroaches the size of small mice out of our bathroom and bedroom curtains with plastic slippers. We listened to Bollywood tunes and Persian pop songs on Radio Arman, one of the first post-Taliban pop music stations, and danced in our tiny room, bumping into each other and giggling. Then we laid out our sleeping mats and stayed up late talking. We drifted off to sleep, shoulders almost touching—until the next day's call to prayer.

One morning, I had gotten up earlier than usual and lingered with a cup of tea in the kitchen as the household prepared for its day. Nazo came in, wearing her school uniform of a black *shalwar kameez* and a white headscarf. Her English was not as fluent as Rochina's nor her brothers Asad and Ayub—the latter three had been educated in Pakistan, where English was part of the post-colonial curriculum. Nazo often asked me for help with unfamiliar words. Once, when the city was abuzz about the Karzai administration's practice of giving ministry positions to family and friends of high-ranking officials, Nazo asked me what "nepotism" meant.

That morning, she had said, "I have forgotten the word that means you are sleeping but you are seeing things like you are waking."

"Dream," I said.

"Ah, yes," she said, with a sly giggle. "Drreeam."

She paused, a glint in her green eyes.

"Did you have a dream last night?" I asked.

Her pale cheeks turned pink. "Yesterday I dream about Yellow Pants." She covered her face with her hands.

"Yellow Pants" was her nickname for a black-haired young man whom she had spotted in Rochina's wedding video, wearing goldenrod trousers and a black shirt. The men and women had celebrated and danced in separate rooms. A week ago, Nazo had shown us the video, which depicted the men dancing in their room, and told us that she was having her friends at her girls' school inquire about the man in the yellow pants. There was no dating in Afghanistan, and chances were, Nazo would have an arranged marriage like Rochina and her brother. But if she happened to spot someone, she knew how to put the wheels in motion in her circles of girls and their older sisters, mothers, aunts. Once she inquired, a vast and seemingly invisible network of women might consider the question of whether he happened to be from a family of which her family would approve, and vice versa. If so, the women of her community might contact Nazo's mother, and the two of them might be able to meet in a formal setting, in the presence of the two families. Rochina had barely met Nazo's brother before they consented to marry each other. Their families were distantly related and had been talking about the match for quite some time.

The match had been negotiated by family members, as well as exchanged photos and word of mouth. Rochina and her family had considered other potential suitors—she was a classic Afghan beauty and well educated, the latter a rarity in Afghanistan because of the lack of girls' education during the civil war and Taliban years. None had felt right, she had told me, until Nazo's brother.

Nazo, by scoping out possibilities on her own, was clearly trying to take a different, yet acceptable, route to marriage.

"What was Yellow Pants doing in your dream?" I said, and playfully nudged Nazo.

She shrieked from behind her hands and pretended to run out of the kitchen. Then she returned, looked me in the eye, and deadpanned, "He was dancing. Just like in the video."

I wondered if she really meant that, or if "dancing" was a euphemism. It was hard to know sometimes how innocent she and Rochina were, what they understood of relationships, love, sex. Rochina and Nazo had asked me, Stephanie, and Laila about our love lives, but American-style dating was unfathomable to them. When Stephanie explained that she lived with her boyfriend, Rochina and Nazo immediately started calling him her husband. They could not imagine it being otherwise, if a couple shared a home. As for Laila, she always changed the subject quickly, not wanting to tell them about Tim. I told them about relationships I had in the past—one with a man whom I wanted to marry, others with men I had no intention of marrying. The truth was, I hadn't been in a serious relationship for years. My career had provided a welcome distraction and barrier; I dated, reveled in the ambiguity of friends-with-benefits relationships, and then allowed my reporting trips, or immersion into work, to provide a natural ending to them. In fact, watching Stephanie's boyfriend fret about and try to talk her out of this trip to Afghanistan, I was relieved to be unencumbered. I had also unknowingly set up another barrier as well: I would get close to men for a while, and then imagine trying to explain my father to them, or worse, introducing them to him. That always put a hasty end to my desire to move forward.

But trying to explain this—even some of it—to Rochina and Nazo, who furrowed their brows with compassion as I described various breakups, I started wishing that I had a simpler answer for them. Would Rochina and

Nazo would judge me as morally loose? No—as with Stephanie, they just didn't understand. "Why not ask your family to find someone for you to marry?" Rochina said. "It is best that way."

They watched Hollywood movies, but even those were viewed through the lens of their experiences. After the Taliban were overthrown and movie theaters returned to Kabul, *Titanic* was a runaway hit, because the tale of early-20th century American romance felt almost like an early-21st century Afghan one. A young, upper-class woman, Rose, is forced by her family to marry a man from her social class, but falls in love with Jack, a poor man of whom her family disapproves. Even the unhappy outcome—the two lovers are parted eternally by the shipwreck—rang truer to Afghans than the typical Hollywood fare. Love-conquers-all endings seemed unrealistic to them. Disaster, they understood. Of course, the version that was shown in Kabul theaters was censored. Scenes that American audiences came to think of as *Titanic*'s signature moments—Jack sketching Rose in the nude, or the two lovers fogging up the windows of her fiancé's Renault—were unceremoniously deleted.

Rochina showed me pictures of her and her husband, Nazo's brother, at their wedding. He was tall, square-jawed, and handsome, with a trimmed beard and deep-set eyes. She wore the heavily beaded, multi-colored dress of a Pashtun bride, piles of gold jewelry, and a mournful expression. "A bride must not smile, even if she is happy," she said. "She must act like she is sad to leave her family." Her husband had landed a lucrative wartime job with the United Nations. He was sometimes was on road for weeks at a time, as he was when we had arrived in Kabul.

Their wedding had been less than a year ago, and Rochina was now entering her second trimester of pregnancy, her lithe body just beginning to show under her *shalwar kameez*. Did she miss her husband?

"Yes," she said, sighing. "But when he comes back it is very nice."

A coy smile played on her face. "Very nice?" I asked.

"Very nice," she repeated, looking down and blushing. She straightened herself up. "Now I must go do the laundry," and breezily took leave of me. As she swung open the kitchen door, she glanced over her shoulder with her big brown eyes and winked. Then the door swung back, and I couldn't see her anymore.

A couple days later, Rochina skipped her usual afternoon nap, and dragged Nazo into the kitchen to prepare an extra-elaborate dinner. They had gotten fresh beef from the butcher earlier that day. Then Rochina took a shower, picked out a new outfit, a soft pink silk *shalwar kameez*, then put on perfume, makeup, and tried on five different *chador* before settling on one. As we all sat in the kitchen, watching her put the finishing touches on dinner, I caught her eye. "You're nervous today," I said. "And pretty."

"*Inginir,*" she said, using the family's nickname for her husband—the Pashto word for "engineer" was used to describe an educated man—"is coming home today."

Then, turning to me so only I could see it, she took her delicate hand, balled into a fist, and bit down on her pinky knuckle. She gasped softly, feigning breathlessness, grinned at me, then returned to stirring the stew.

This was sexier than all of the deleted scenes from *Titanic* combined.

We saw less of Rochina after that evening, though the five of us still slept in the couple's room. She joined us at night, just later than usual. Nazo, on the other hand, announced to me that she was having friends inquire about another young man she saw at the birthday party she took us to. "White Suit," she said, eyes dreamy. I remembered him—he was, indeed, wearing an all-white suit with a bright red shirt. He had a smooth face and was a flamboyant dancer.

"What about Yellow Pants?"

She laughed. Yesterday, we had contemplated some questionable meat in the freezer after one of the city's frequent power outages. Even families well off enough to have refrigerators couldn't rely on them. I taught her the word "expired," explaining the labels in American grocery stores that indicated when something should be discarded.

"Yellow Pants," she said, flipping the end of her *chador* dramatically over her shoulder, "has expired."

ཚ

Nazo wasn't the only recipient of English vocabulary lessons in the kitchen. Asad began making occasional visits to the women's space to ask me about English words he picked up at work. This did not go unnoticed by his sister and sister-in-law.

In fact, they already had been watching him closely. A day before we had left for Shinzmaray, Rochina had said to me, "So many hours with Asad in the car tomorrow." Her pointy elbow had found my side as we stood next to each other in the kitchen.

Was she really teasing me about her brother-in-law, the one Laila told me not to look at? I wasn't sure how to respond. "So many hours in the car with Laila and Stephanie too," I rebutted. She just shook her head gently with that secret smile of hers, busying herself with slicing onions.

A week and a half after our trip, Asad starting stopping into the kitchen with a thick, leather-bound notebook in which he wrote down words important to his security work, such as "Forward Operating Base" and "MREs, a.k.a. Meals Ready to Eat," in neat ballpoint-pen script. The phrases intrigued me. They were a disjointed snapshot of the United States' War in Afghanistan. I looked forward to the visits, though they were brief, and didn't even mind the women's good-natured ribbing out of Asad's earshot. It made me feel like I was in junior high and the girls were making fun of me because they thought that he *liked* me. I wanted him to—sort of. But then there was the delicate balance of my role as a journalist, guest, and most importantly, a woman, in this household held together by rules unfamiliar to me.

Whenever Asad was around, I felt Rochina watching us. She stopped her cooking and turned an ear toward us, growing particularly quiet if we were laughing at a joke. Did she understand what we said, or was she carefully reading the body language and facial expressions? I always sensed that Rochina knew a lot more than she let on—about the English language, about what happened under this roof, about sex, and about me. It made me feel closer to her and, lately, nervous around her.

Our days continued as they had, and each passing day the routines became more a part of me. I started doing more work in our room as our days wound down, plugging my laptop in when there was power and trying to capture what seemed impossible to confine to words: I was supposed to be writing about Daoud's work with the Ministry and higher-education reform in Afghanistan. But I found myself dwelling instead on Rochina and Nazo's symbiosis, a sisterhood born of marriage, and how it was so powerful, the three of us Americans were almost instantly absorbed into its rhythms, complete with inside jokes. With Asad in the picture, Rochina and Nazo had found a perfect way to treat me like one of their own. "If we're polite to you, that means you're an honored guest," Laila had once told me. "If we tease you, that means you're like family."

Over time, I learned to take it in stride, and it seemed the two women found other diversions. Nazo's birthday was coming up, and though Afghans didn't traditionally celebrate birthdays (since so few of them were born in hospitals and actually knew their birthdates), Rochina orchestrated a celebration among the five of us. She dispatched her husband to get a frosted cake and procured a large taper candle to stick in its middle. We sang "Happy Birthday" to Nazo in English. She forgot to make a wish the first time she blew out the flame, so we did it again.

"White Suit or Yellow Pants?" I asked her after she opened her eyes. She blushed deeply and giggled.

Soon, our last night in Kabul arrived. It was just the five of us in our little bedroom. Rochina's husband Ayub had left for another work trip, as had his younger brother Asad. Both had slipped out without saying goodbye to me, Laila, and Stephanie. I was disappointed about Asad, but also a bit relieved that we didn't have an awkward parting. What would I have done? I couldn't hug him, so would I have shook his hand? Would I have tried to exchange email addresses with him? What would Rochina and Nazo say about that?

As darkness fell upon us, I was relieved to be in that safe space, where we had spent so many hours talking late into the night. Tonight was no different. In the last few days, the Lariam's effects finally started tapering off and I was sleeping better, dreading nights less. We were sprawled across our sleeping mats and cushions. Nazo was in a silly mood, asking us to make a list of qualities she was looking for in a husband, in case we spotted someone in America for her.

"A little fat . . . " she said, as Laila, Stephanie, and I giggled. In Afghanistan, chubbiness meant wealth and thinness, poverty.

" . . . with lots of money in one pocket, and a radio in the other," she said, with confidence. We laughed some more.

"Radio?" I said.

"I like music. And dancing," Nazo said, and with just her arms and head, did an accurate rendition of White Suit's signature dancing style.

I laughed. Rochina looked impatient. She kept trying to catch Nazo's eye. Nazo was starting to describe the wardrobe of her future husband, a cacophony of brightly-colored suits, when Rochina interrupted her.

"I think it is Angie's turn," she said. "Stephanie has a husband. Laila is . . . what do you call it when someone does not want to talk about things having to do with husbands?"

"A prude," I said, chuckling. Laila glared at me.

" . . . a prude," Rochina repeated. "So we must ask Angie for her list so we can find a husband for her."

My cheeks grew warm. "I don't have a list."

Rochina crisply grabbed the notebook Laila was writing Nazo's list on, and slipped the pen out of Laila's hand. She made a great show of flipping to a new page, writing my name on the top (she spelled it "Angy," which was how it was spelled in Pashto), and holding her pen poised above the paper.

"OK, Nazo and I will help you write your list," Rochina said. "Number One: Name begins with 'A.' Ends with 'D.' Do we know anyone like this?"

Nazo giggled.

"Rochina!" I said, face growing hotter. "You're teasing me again."

"You like my brother?" Nazo said. Her cartoonish green eyes danced.

What could I possibly say? To say "no" would offend her—and would be a lie; to say "yes" would be too brazen.

"He is very nice," I said.

"She says he's very nice," Nazo said in English to Rochina, though Rochina had heard me perfectly well.

Something passed between the two sisters-in-law. A look. A plan. My heart was pounding. What was I so nervous about? Rochina, sitting on her sleeping mat, scooted closer to me and leaned on one knee, her face close to mine.

"You like him. You like us. You should marry him."

Rochina's face could look so serious, with those big eyes, that naturally downturned mouth. *But surely she's joking.* Nazo nodded, looking earnest herself. I turned to Laila, but she just kept a close-lipped smile on her face. Stephanie sat next to her, whispering, "I sure am glad I have a 'husband.'"

"What? Marry?" I said, voice strained. "You're kidding."

"No," Rochina said, her uncovered black ponytail flipping emphatically over her shoulder. "You marry him. You will be our sister. He wants to go to America. You are an American citizen. Perfect."

If I didn't know her, and Afghan culture, better, I would have taken this for a green-card scam. But here, marriage was still more about practical aims—making family alliances, settling debts, or helping people emigrate —than romantic love. It didn't make the marriages shams; in Afghan marriages, *kofa*, or parity, was more important. That meant, in part, that both parties would benefit equally from the union. If *kofa* existed, love would come with time. Rochina was looking out for her brother-in-law and his dreams of studying in America. After September 11, his hopes as a young Muslim male of ever getting a student visa in the United States had all but evaporated. And she was thinking of me, perceiving (rightly) that I liked him and could probably use a little help in the marriage department (also correct). That is, if she were serious. Was she?

"I can't marry him. I hardly know him!" I protested.

"You have known him for twelve days. You talk to him so much," Rochina said. *She had counted the days since our roadtrip to the village.* "That is more time than I knew my husband before I decided to marry him. And look, we are happy."

They were. After her husband left again, Rochina had moped the entire day. I rarely saw them interact; they were a properly discreet Afghan couple. But when I did, I could sense the electricity between them, the way her eyes danced, and his usually stern face grew soft. On the one hand, it was hard for me to imagine how this kind of attraction—and yes, love— had developed after they had married barely knowing each other. It felt ludicrous to discuss Asad and marriage with his sister and sister-in-law when I had only had a handful of conversations, never really alone and often avoiding eye contact, with him. I wanted to tell them I had slept with men after less time, but the thought of marrying them would have never crossed my mind. But why? To shock them? To drive home the contrasts between their world and mine? To tell them they were naïve?

I pictured Rochina in the kitchen, turning her head toward me to bite down on her pinky knuckle. Her soft, barely audible gasp. The slight swell of her pregnancy under her *shalwar kameez*. Who was the naïve one?

"Well?" Rochina said.

I had no answer for her.

"OK, OK," Nazo said. "You can marry my other brother?" Another unmarried brother, younger than Ayub and older than Asad, lived in Kandahar.

"But I've never met him!" I said.

Rochina and Nazo shrugged at each other. *So?*

Rochina straightened herself up. "I know you do not want him. Because you like Asad. But Nazo is saying that it doesn't matter which brother you marry.

"We just want you to be our sister."

Rochina had said "sister" once already, but now I began to understand. Rochina and Nazo, their rapport so easy, like a married couple, even when they occasionally bickered. How they moved in the kitchen, never bumping into each other. Nazo told me once that she and Rochina would have a say in whomever their remaining single brothers married, because they would be taking on a new sister as well.

"You already feel like sisters to me," I said. I had never become so close to women in such a short time. But with this talk of marriage, why had they not brought up the obvious? "I just can't marry your brother, because I'm not Afghan and I'm not Muslim. I wouldn't be acceptable."

"It is no problem," Rochina said. "You will not have to become Muslim right away. You can take your time. I will show you how to pray. Then you convert, and it will be OK."

I had not grown up religious nor been particularly drawn to religion, but Rochina made it sound so simple, so essential—a foregone conclusion. Learn to pray, and the rest would come. Sometimes, I had watched her pray, so consumed by the moment that nothing, not even the sonic boom of an F-16 screaming past, could disturb her. Other times, she would pray half-heartedly, sit up in the middle of her prayer, and ask me what I wanted for dinner.

Speechless, I rolled my head back on the pillow, meaning to make a playful gesture of surrender to my interrogators. But I realized just then that I was tired. We all were. Even Rochina and Nazo looked sleepy. All five of us had stayed up extra late on our last night, taking pictures and savoring our dwindling time together.

Rochina tilted her head toward me sympathetically.

"You think about this. Tomorrow, before you go to the airport, you tell us your decision. Yes or no."

❧

I cried big, fat tears, like a baby's, when I said goodbye to Nazo the next morning before she left for school. She hugged me so tight I couldn't breathe, which only made me cry more. The sensation of so much moisture in my eyes, on my face, dampening Nazo's black and white school uniform, my breath coming hard and ragged, shocked me, because I hardly ever cried back in the States. Not at movies. Not at weddings. Rarely over a man, and only when he was not watching. I was so preoccupied with my own tears that I was doubly surprised, as I pulled away from her, to see her own electric green eyes swimming and feel my own scarf damp with her tears. We both wiped at our runny noses and laughed.

And then she was gone, late for school, as usual.

Rochina accompanied Stephanie and me to the airport. Laila, who would to stay in Kabul with her family for a week longer before returning to Portland, joined us as well. The four of us were jammed in the backseat of a Volga sedan. A wiry, nervous driver and, inexplicably, a stocky second man in the passenger seat who kept barking orders to the driver, took us down Kabul's unpaved, dusty roads. My melancholy soon gave way to panic; we had driven into yet another traffic jam—this one a true Gordian knot that, compounded by the lack of traffic signals, marked lanes, and any apparent laws or courtesies, looked like it could take hours to untangle. Our driver cursed the traffic in Dari; we cursed it in English. Caught in the stagnation of dust, blaring horns, and foul air, there was nothing to do but wait.

It was then that Rochina turned to me—we were on opposite ends of the backseat, with Stephanie and Laila wedged between us.

"So," she said, breezy despite the heat and racket around us, "Did you make your decision? What is your answer: yes or no?"

"Decision? About what?" I played dumb. Maybe she would leave me alone to contemplate the implications of our plane leaving without us.

"About marrying Asad," Rochina didn't miss a beat. "You have had time to think about it. Yes or no?"

I blushed and looked imploringly at Laila.

"Don't look at me," Laila said, a sly smile on her angular face. She was getting me back for encouraging Rochina to call her a prude last night. "It's your decision."

Rochina grinned.

"Laila!" I snapped. "Tell her she's being crazy. The poor guy doesn't even know he's being talked about this way."

"That's how it always is. Plus, in our culture, it's easier for woman who's an outsider to marry into a family," Laila said. *Aha. Ulterior motives—Tim.* "I say, you get it started for our family, and it'll be easier for the rest of us."

"Should I ask him if he wants to marry you?" Rochina offered.

"NO!" I said, too loudly. "Please don't."

"OK, OK," Rochina said. She reached across Stephanie and Laila to grab my hand with her slim, cool fingers. "But I would like you come back and see us, and if you married him, you could."

I told her I'd come back and see her and Nazo even if I didn't marry him. I was getting choked up again. Then I caught a glimpse of my watch and realize our situation had become dire—we were down to forty-five minutes before the plane was going to take off.

The rest of my time in Kabul was a blur, as the traffic jam miraculously cleared up, our driver raced us to the airport, and we rushed in. Our luggage was inspected by hand, we were searched in a private room to protect the modesty of women, we paid a slew of obscure fees and taxes that felt more like bribes, and then had to argue with an airline representative who insisted that we had arrived too late to be let onto the plane. We barely had said goodbye to Laila, just calling out, "See you back in Portland!" My goodbye to Rochina had been hurried but tender; as we hugged goodbye I could feel the swell of the life growing within her beneath her loose-fitting clothes. I hesitated, wanting to say something meaningful in parting. Rochina shook her head and pushed me toward security.

Stephanie and I stood on the tarmac as our luggage was checked in—or rather, thrown directly into the Azerbaijan Air plane's cargo hold. The engines roared to life, and a male flight attendant poked his head out the door impatiently. We clambered up the stairs, plopped into seats in the mostly-empty plane, and both sighed loudly. Stephanie and I didn't speak to each other. Instead, we each scooted over to window seats on opposite ends of a row and watched Kabul and Afghanistan recede from below the aging Tupelov jet.

Kabul's sprawling brown grid, its rolling feminine hills, gave way to the indisputably male Hindu Kush mountains, jagged, foreboding, and ice-capped. They had taken my breath away once already, and they did so again. They had been a constant presence during my time in Kabul, ghostly sentries asserting their presence through the polluted air. Tomorrow, and the day after, and the day after that, I would not see them again.

Stop this plane, I wanted to yell, though none of the Russian-and-Azeri-speaking crew would have understood me. Turn it around. I didn't want this to end. What if I had said yes to Rochina? What if she had been serious? What if I did marry Asad? In the thin air of Neither Here Nor There, it all felt possible—or at least more desirable than returning to the complacency of American life and losing that closeness, that sisterhood, I shared with Rochina and Nazo.

Had that rickety jet been equipped with one of those credit-card phones on the seat back and had the house in Kabul had a phone, I might have called Rochina at that moment and declared, "YES! I want to marry your beautiful brother-in-law, learn to pray, and learn to *live.*"

Yes or no. Tell us your decision.

But was it about Asad, about Islam, or about a lifestyle and culture? To Rochina and Nazo, all of these were secondary. To them, life revolved around their sisterhood, around these tight bonds between women in cultures that observed purdah. Behind the curtain, women lived, laughed, cried, danced, and prayed together, as Rochina and Nazo did in their little room. Women praying together had a special place in Islam, so much so that they were encouraged to pray shoulder to shoulder to "bring them closer together and prevent shaytan (Satan) creating hostility in between the gaps." So wrote Ruqaiyah Abdullah in the modern religious text, *The Importance of Sisterhood in Islam.* Women praying together is "twenty-seven times superior to the prayer said alone."

When Rochina envisioned me praying with her, it was the most basic and profound gesture of acceptance and love she could have offered. If I had that credit card phone, my answer really should have been, simply, "Yes, I want to be your sister."

But there was no phone. By the time Stephanie and I had landed in Baku, Azerbaijan, spent a sleepless night there in another mosquito-infested hotel room, endured a seven-hour layover in Frankfurt, and crossed twelve and a half times zones to get back to Portland, Rochina, Nazo, and Asad felt so far away. A phone call to my mother awaited; I needed to ask if she had filed for divorce as she said she would, but I could only bring myself to lift the phone out of its handset, then set it back down. I wasn't ready.

I dreamed that Rochina was teaching me to pray. She appeared in my dream exactly as I remembered her in real life: heavy-lidded dark eyes, straight nose, and slightly downturned mouth. Calm elegance. Long black hair swept up into her *chador*. Usually she wore the headscarf loosely draped over her head, one end thrown over her left shoulder. But for her five daily prayers, she pulled the creased fabric forward and tight around her face, anchoring it around her chin so that her hair and long, graceful neck were properly covered. She knelt, and I knelt next to her. She lofted a large cotton scarf just like hers in my direction. It billowed white and soft through the air, and landed on my outstretched hand. I wrapped it around my head with ease.

Sitting on my heels at Rochina's side, on a crimson patterned rug she had rolled out for me, I rehearsed the flow in my head—stand up, bend down, stand up, prostrate, kneel, prostate, stand up. "Don't worry," she murmured in her accented English, words clipped just so. "You will know what to do. I told you I would teach you." Her voice comforted me.

Dawn bathed us in its soft light and we heard the call to prayer from a distant muezzin. I expected to hear the resonant male voice over the mosque loudspeaker that had stirred me from sleep every morning in Kabul. But the singer in my dream was female. In the real world, I know of no woman muezzins. Yet this aching soprano climbed toward God as it rose in pitch. As she finished the incantation, now familiar to me, the air vibrated, silent and expectant. I turned to Rochina, searching her face for her promise: *I told you I would teach you. You will know what to do.*

And then, as unexpectedly as it had come to me, the dream ended.

I woke up, groggy in the pre-dawn gray of Portland. I heard only the muted sounds of traffic on Northwest Irving Street. I was alone in my small apartment, with beige walls and tan hardwood floors—not nestled amid the plush red carpets of the Kabul house. It was so quiet. My own clock radio's red LCD numbers stared back at me: 4:30, precisely the time of the first call to prayer. I had three more hours before the alarm would go off.

Over the next few weeks, I got over jet lag, returned to the office, gratefully finished the last of the Lariam I was required to take, and learned that Mom had completed the divorce paperwork and Dad had been unresponsive to requests to sign it. I felt disembodied. The dream had felt more real than my waking life.

A traffic helicopter over my apartment would conjure the U.S. Army choppers that flew overhead as Nazo and I had leaned into each other while sitting on the courtyard's covered well. I'd recall the expectant way Asad ducked into the kitchen, past that swinging yellow door, with his notebook of English phrases already open. Nazo's tears, wet on my chador, and my own on hers. Rochina's cool fingers around my hand in the car.

Yes or no. Tell us your decision.

I replayed the dream about Rochina in my head before I went to sleep, in hopes of having it again. I never did. Over time, thoughts of Rochina and Nazo, and of Afghanistan, faded as I found my way back into the rhythms and comforts of American life.

I didn't realize until later that, in my dream, I must have already answered the question Rochina had posed to me before leaving Kabul. She was, after all, teaching me to pray. I must have said yes.

Part Four:
Tatobay / Homeland

  Often a sweetness comes
as if on loan, stays just long enough

to make sense of what it means to be alive,
   then returns to its dark
source. As for me, I don't care

where it's been, or what bitter road
   it's traveled
to come so far, to taste so good.

—Stephen Dunn, "Sweetness"

12.
Drive

I turned fifteen and got my learner's permit at about the time Dad was coming out of his first depression, just starting to get into the real estate business as he had promised. Mom, Kelley, and I were so relieved that he was up and about, so convinced that we would never witness the humiliation of his "couch-potato," J-Bird-playing phase again, that we instantly, instinctively forced ourselves into normalcy, or what felt like it. Like actors taking our marks, forgetting whatever had occurred during the break. Mom was ecstatic when I brought home the paperwork from my Driver's Education class.

"Time to teach Angie to drive," she said, practically pushing us both out the door, handing Dad the keys to the Volkswagen Rabbit in the same motion. Cars and driving were his element, and he prided himself on teaching newcomers to the United States: Friends from graduate school who had arrived later than he did, Mom, Mom's sister Wendy, his nephew. He had a simple doctrine of driving instruction: manual transmission only, from Day One. No easing into it with automatic; that was for wimps.

"If I teach you to drive an automatic," he said as he drove us to the local college parking lot, his preferred classroom, "you'll never want to learn to drive stick."

I hadn't even asked. I knew better than to think I might be like my friends, who spent twenty minutes learning to steer and brake in a parking lot, and within a couple hours were whipping around the town, maybe even on the freeway. I would spend multiple sessions in that parking lot, starting and stalling, and starting and stalling, until I got it right.

" . . . And then someday you'll be stuck somewhere and the only car you can drive will be a stick. And then what will you do?" Dad continued, still unprompted.

Our family's diesel Volkswagen Rabbit would become my hand-me-down vehicle; Dad had bought it for his long commute to the government-lab job because of its extreme fuel efficiency. It choked out foul clouds of exhaust and ran with the signature sputtering of diesel engines. When I stalled it, as I did often in those first parking-lot lessons, the four-cylinder engine jarred the tinny exterior with a force it had for no other task. Dad was unfazed.

"Don't worry about it. It's part of learning. When you learn enough times what doesn't work, you'll know what does," he'd say. I had rarely seen him so even-keeled. With all other things, he was quick to criticize, reluctant to give second chances or encourage trial and error. "Now, more gas this time. Easier on the clutch."

Driving a manual transmission was a balance, of forward momentum versus release, of go and stop. Dad always preferred complicated machinery to ease of operation, hard-earned skill over rote motions anyone could do. But his own machinery was the most complex of all, temporarily stable, but only as a way station between opposite extremes. This brief and precarious balance Dad achieved between depression and, unbeknownst to us, what would soon be mania, was like the elusive friction point between clutch and accelerator. Dad had found an unnamed fuel that lifted him from depression, and we were relieved. But he would accelerate without any checks as he ramped up his new business—right into an irrational, sleepless frenzy.

The first sign: He had just purchased a new BMW, a luxury our family had never had and could not really afford. He insisted he needed it to take clients around; a lesser car would send the wrong message. It was wide, with a leather-lined interior, a 500-series model that didn't offer a stick-shift option. A luxury sedan, not a sports car. It was metallic blue, shiny, and accelerated with a deep thrum that made the Rabbit sound like a lawnmower.

I longed to drive the BMW, and not just for its superior performance. At my school, the rich kids were getting their own BMWs for their sixteenth birthdays. As a studious Chinese American girl with a troubled, unemployed father, I found it easier to talk to teachers than to popular kids or most boys; I couldn't help wanting to fit in a bit more.

"No," Dad said firmly. "I told you, no automatics until you get your license."

He didn't know of my social-climbing aspirations or demonstrate awareness of anything at my high school except the grades I got. He wasn't even very protective of his car—once I did get my license, he was happy to let me drive it if he wasn't, claiming that anyone he taught how to drive should be trusted with any car. But he would not deviate from his driver-training dogma.

Dad insisted not only on my learning manual transmission, but also that I tackle the tough parts of stick-shift driving right away. As I finally got comfortable with driving around town, even rolling through stop signs in second gear, Dad always threw me another test to make sure I never grew overconfident or complacent. He'd watch me ride my brakes downhill with disdain before telling me I should have shifted to a lower gear to save them. I took each lesson in stride, trying not to forget all the tricks that would distinguish me in his mind as a competent driver from an unskilled one, like my peers with their automatic transmissions.

One day, Dad directed me to a semi-steep hill in a neighboring town, one with a stoplight at its crest. Without telling me why he was having me drive there, he had me pull over until the light turned red, then drive to the top of the hill.

"Foot on the brake and clutch," he said.

The light turned green. Dad peeked over his shoulder; no one was behind us.

"OK, green light," he said calmly. "Go."

I released the brake with my right foot. The car rolled backward about ten feet. I let out a yelp and slammed on the brake again. My heart was pounding in my throat as I turned to him, bewildered.

He pointed forward, telling me to keep my eyes ahead of me.

Then, slowly—so methodically that I had to wait for the next green light to try—he talked me through the use of the handbrake when starting on a hill. I had so much adrenalin coursing through my body when I did try it for the first time that I performed a perfect start, foot depressing the accelerator in synced opposition to right hand releasing the hand brake. The Rabbit's gears caught smoothly and we were off and over the hill.

Still, as we drove home after our lesson, I fumed.

"Why didn't you just tell me that the car would roll back?" I said, shoving the gearshift harder than usual.

"It's logical that it would. I was waiting to see if you would figure that out," Dad said.

"So I failed," I muttered.

"You failed to understand how the engine works," he said. "But the rolling back gave you enough of a scare that you'll never forget to use the handbrake on a hill again. I've saved you from a future accident."

He was smug. Maybe even a little cruel. But he was right.

Within the first month, I also had tackled getting on and off the freeway, parallel parking with no power steering, and checking the oil, coolant, and tire pressure. I performed dozens of other handbrake-assisted starts from a standstill, even from the exact same stoplight Dad at which subjected me to the demo, always with that memory of free-falling, back-rolling panic.

I passed my driver's test easily and, as promised, drove the BMW occasionally, even to school a few times. But I came to feel like the Rabbit was an extension of myself, its modest engine and finicky clutch a metaphor for my own humble social status at school and for the fine balance that my own wheels allowed me to achieve—between coming and going from my unhappy home and family.

As he was with teaching me to use tools, Dad had always envisioned me in his image, as capable and stubbornly independent. In time, being self-sufficient gave me the power to detach myself from him, so as not to be suffocated by his illness. It became about knowing how not to roll backward in my attempts to move forward, keeping my eyes ahead and on the road, without fear or remorse.

☙

A couple months after I returned from Afghanistan, I went to a national journalism conference, fresh off the publication of my story about Daoud Shirzai in Kabul. It was August 2004; an unspoken maxim among the hiring editors and conference-goers was that stints in Afghanistan or Iraq were the new calling cards for up-and-coming reporters. I had felt less engaged with journalism and the newspaper ever since I had returned. Though my editors ran my story on the front page, they were eager for me to move on to more pressing topics, like the Iraq War. I bristled at the idea that Afghanistan was now passé, though I knew from a news perspective, all the attention had shifted to Iraq. Embedded posts with the U.S. military were all the rage, one of my more-senior colleagues suggested helpfully; perhaps I could leverage my Afghanistan experience to get one.

But I felt different. I wasn't interested in journalistic trends or climbing the career ladder anymore. I couldn't stop thinking about the Shirzais in Afghanistan, what would become of Rochina, Nazo, Asad, Grandma? I couldn't help feeling that all newspaper journalism was superficial and cold. This included my own just-published stories, which brought me little of the pride or satisfaction I had felt when the earlier ones about the Shirzais in Portland had come to fruition. Either I had failed to tell the stories from Kabul and Shinzmaray vividly, deeply enough—or journalism had failed me. I think it was both. And why would I want to embed with U.S. troops in Iraq when I had embedded with real people in Afghanistan? Not just people—the Shirzais. I didn't want to move on from them.

Yet, at the conference, my newfound status among my industry peers, as the label of "reported in Afghanistan" followed me, opened the doors to meet-and-greets in presidential suites with free-flowing cocktails and fancy multi-course dinners that could have fed Jumagul and Fahima's entire family for a week. I longed to be back in Kabul, in shalwar kameez and barefoot in the red-carpeted women's sitting room, not in a skirt suit and heels in a beige, fluorescent-lit conference hotel.

All the things that I had always wanted as a journalist started materializing, just when it seemed they had ceased mattering to me. I met the biggest names in the newspaper industry and they actually wanted to talk to me. I was getting invitations to interview for jobs at their papers, major national dailies. And an offer to be considered for what I had wanted most of all: a foreign correspondent post, from editors at a major national paper who were eyeing me for Hong Kong, where my Mandarin skills would be useful. A couple years there, they said, and we could send you to Beijing.

As I made my way through cocktail party after power lunch after reception, I started buying into it again. Of course I wanted to report overseas, to cover the monumental changes happening in China. Maybe it was time for me to get closer to my family's true roots; though my parents were raised in Taiwan, both of their families were from my father's birthplace, Fujian. Such a move could propel me to the next level, of my career, of my life. Afghanistan had shown me how much more there was to the world than my life in Portland.

At the very least, an overseas move would put even more welcome distance between me and Mom and Dad. I noted this with irony—the idea of connecting with my family's Chinese heritage became even more alluring because doing so would allow me to get away from my actual family. I hadn't even been back to Taiwan in nearly a decade. Ever since Dad became ill, Mom went alone. Somehow, if we went without Dad it would seem like something was wrong; we found it easier not to go than to acknowledge why we could not arrive in Taiwan as a family of four, as we always had when I was younger. Dad was always too depressed to travel or too manic to subject to Mom's family over there. Ever since his father died in his late nineties and Uncle Tien-Mu's suicide, he lost interest in returning to see his own family. During his manic periods, he often called his siblings one by one and ranted at them, criticizing their children or their religious beliefs, or threatening to sue them for the money he had sent home to them. They stopped taking his calls.

As I was at the journalism conference, Mom was making the heartbreaking move to her new condo, wracked with guilt to leave Dad in his depressed state and tormenting herself over questions like which pieces of her life with him to leave behind and which ones to bring. Even the photo albums he had compiled since they had arrived in the United States took up an entire room's worth of bookshelves. She had to winnow down to a representative sample of the albums that would fit into her one-bedroom unit. Kelley offered to fly home from medical school to help; I half-heartedly said I could make the trip too. Mom insisted on doing everything on her own, being cagey about her move date so that we wouldn't come. I was secretly relieved I didn't have to. The idea of packing up boxes around Dad, in bed, so that Mom could leave him, made me queasy. I wanted her to leave him; I just didn't want to watch it happen.

I'd call from Portland, ask her if she felt settled in, if her condo management was taking care of repairs, if she liked her shorter commute to work. Things I didn't ask about: Her relentless insomnia after she moved out, which carved hollows out under her eyes and made her slim frame gaunt. Dad's silence after the divorce proceedings were final, even though he had initially refused to sign the papers and only did after she threatened to subpoena him in court. The weight of his continuing depression on us all.

I had always leaned on a certain kind of detachment afforded by my traveling, my all-consuming career. Now, as I waited for word about a job interview in Hong Kong that might propel me there by the end of the calendar year, I felt more removed than ever. I waited a very long time after Mom moved out to call Dad, to check on him, to have the same one-way conversation with his monosyllabic responses we always had when he was depressed. Neither of us acknowledged Mom's leaving. I asked if he was eating well, what he was eating, how he was getting food—a habit I gleaned from my maternal grandparents who, like most Chinese of their generation, asked after your well-being by asking, "Have you eaten?" He said yes, he was cooking a bit; he knew how, from his grad school years. And ordering takeout from restaurants in Oakland Chinatown, taking home a few days' worth of food at a time to refrigerate and reheat. Food stood in for the emotions that were difficult, or impossible, to talk about. Hearing myself talk to Dad the way my grandparents talked to everyone, especially their grandchildren, made me miss them. It was time to see them. I had been away too long, hiding behind the cloud of my father's illness.

Then I got the call: a job interview—in Hong Kong. It was September, and Mom had already planned a solo trip to Taiwan in October, the first since the divorce. Instinctively, I asked the recruitment director, "Could it wait until early October?" Then, without telling Mom yet, I started looking up Asian airlines that had flights to Taipei with layovers in Hong Kong.

"Really? You want to go?" Mom said, when I called her a few days later. I was sitting at my desk in my small Portland apartment, about a half a dozen windows open on my computer screen: Cathay Pacific, EVA Air, China Airlines . . .

"You won't get bored at *Wai Gong* and *Wai Po's*?" Mom said. *Wai Gong* and *Wai Po* was what we called her parents, old patriarchal Mandarin terms that literally meant "Outside Grandpa" and "Outside Grandma," to indicate my mother's status as having married *into* my father's family.

"Mom, I'm not a high school kid who finds Taiwan boring anymore," I said. Surely Mom was recalling a trip, not the most recent but close to it, during which I had been an *ennui*-ridden, hormonal, eye-rolling mess. "It's my home too, in a way. And *Wai Gong* and *Wai Po* are getting older. I should see them."

"OK. Come with me," she said, her voice brightening. "They'll want to see you. Maybe we can travel together, just the two of us, somewhere on the island . . ."

Her voice flattened again and trailed off. The weariness—how did I not hear it until now? She didn't have the energy to even think of a destination in her birthplace she'd like to take me to. But that brief glimmer I had detected was her desire to spend time with me, to reconnect.

Tears were clouding my view of the computer screen, open to Cathay Pacific's route maps page. The spider web of red arcs spanning out from the Hong Kong hub bled into a crimson pinwheel, a blooming poppy.

"Mom, let's go together," I said, speaking quickly, breathlessly, so she would not hear my tears. "Let's fly from San Francisco to Hong Kong and stay in the hotel the newspaper will provide. I'll do my interviews and you can play tourist. The next day, we'll have high tea at the Peninsula Hotel. We'll go get the best dim sum in the world. We'll go to the top of Victoria Peak. Then we'll fly to Taipei to see *Wai Gong* and *Wai Po*."

Was I overcompensating? The world traveler (I had been to all of these places in Hong Kong en route from a reporting trip to Vietnam a year prior), offering a deluxe tour when I could not give my mother simple emotional engagement.

Mom demurred, saying she'd be a distraction, she didn't know her way around Hong Kong and would get lost by herself, we could just meet up in Taipei.

"Mom," I said, insistent. "I could be moving to this city by the end of the year if things go well. Don't you want to see where your daughter might be living for the next few years?"

Mom barely left the hotel without me in Hong Kong. I gave her a map and marked the places within walking distance she could see, encouraged her to take the sparkling clean, super-efficient subway, and reminded her that she was fluent in two of three of the languages spoken here. Still, she spent the entire day of my interview walking in a park adjacent to our hotel, and visiting a Chinese pastry shop across the street that sold the most perfect egg custard tarts, flaky on the outside and almost liquid in the center. She ate an entire box in lieu of breakfast and lunch, and saved me two to sample when I returned. When my final interview with the bureau chief went half an hour longer than scheduled—a very good sign, everyone in the office told me—Mom called the office to check on me. They were charmed. I was slightly embarrassed and baffled. How had Mom hardly ever blinked when, in high school, I broke my late curfew over and over again, or when I went to Afghanistan for a month—but now was worried because I was half an hour late in calling her?

I was concerned about and annoyed by her sudden lack of self-sufficiency. She had become self-reliant, even to a fault, in the fifteen years of Dad's illness. Now divorced and living in her own place for the first time in her life, she was at her most independent. But she had also become fearful. In matters outside the divorce and her move, she desperately wanted to rely on me, or Kelley, or, as I would soon see, her parents, in ways she had never before. It was like she had used all of the gumption she had to leave Dad and start her new life. She had none left for Hong Kong, which for her was not about the Peninsula or Victoria Peak. It was about me. She wanted me to take over, to navigate, to make the decisions. She had made enough of her own already.

The next day, I took us on the subway and the Star Ferry to dim sum, the Peninsula, to Victoria Peak, through all of which Mom floated, disembodied almost. I wanted her to love the city, its contrasts: The sculptural mirrored and neon skyscrapers of the Island side, springing up off a steep, lush mountainside like science fiction. The old, gritty Chinese alleyways tucked behind grand colonial buildings in Kowloon, where live chickens were still slaughtered on the streets and vendors offered every ware imaginable—from the "most fresh" fried green onion pancakes to the "most sexy" prostitutes—in loud Cantonese or English tinged with Chinese, Indian, or British accents. I wanted her to envision me there with the same excitement with which I envisioned myself. But I knew she really didn't want me to go, not now.

She became animated the next morning, as we got ready to head to the airport for Taipei.

"Let's get a box of the egg custard tarts for *Wai Po*," she said. "If we get them on our way out they might still be warm when we get to Taoyuan."

Mom was doing something decisive; I relished watching her march into the tiny shop that couldn't fit both of us and our suitcases, walk out with a bakery box tied with red string, set it down on top of a newspaper vending box, and pull out two egg tarts.

"Here," she said, handing me one. "You haven't tried them hot yet."

I bit into the crust, which separated into delicate layers on contact, only to allow the warm filling to slowly ooze out. It was a perfect, authentically Chinese specimen: bursting with the most delicately sweetened egg flavor. Just egg, no hints of cream or vanilla or anything else.

"See?" she said, lips pressed together in a smile. "You carry the box. Don't let it tip."

The warm weight of the tarts pressed through the box as it rested on my forearm, braced against the crook of my elbow. I took my rollerbag handle with my other hand as Mom stepped out toward the curb and, with a single wave of a thin arm, confidently hailed a taxicab.

"To the airport. We have a flight to Taiwan to catch," she said to the driver in Mandarin. "My daughter and I are going home."

When I was three going on four, around the time Kelley was born, Mom and I used to walk to the park together. Kelley was still little enough to feel more like a tiny new appendage on my mother rather than a full-fledged younger brother; I still thought of myself as Mom's only child. As a stay-at-home mom in a country and language that were still unfamiliar to her, my Mom's days, after Dad went to work in San Francisco, were solitary. She was in her early twenties and had left home for the first time only a few years ago. Now she had two tiny human beings to care for, a new husband to cook and clean for, and a new country, culture, language to learn.

Every morning, she would cut a Red Delicious apple in half for me, carefully sectioning out the core with a paring knife, the middle part coming out in two domes, the rest of the core in angled, pyramidal pieces so as not to waste any of the edible flesh. After the tropical abundance of

Taiwan, the lack of variety and freshness of fruit in America must have come as a shock to her. Yet her childhood had taught her food was not to be wasted. Her parents used to raise pigs, much as the Chinese pictogram for "home" depicted, but the pigs were not theirs—they reared them for the Taiwanese army in order to supplement my grandfather's then paltry income.

The apple carefully sliced, Mom would hand me half, the pale yellow flesh gleaming against the deep red peel. As soon as it left her thin, elegant hand with the shining diamond and white-gold wedding ring, and into my little grubby ones, the apple would start to turn brown. The half apple felt like such a daunting task, so much fruit to chew through, a race against time before it browned so much it wouldn't be appetizing.

But I knew the deal. "Eat your apple half by the time we get to the playground, and you can play," Mom said. So I did, walking and chewing, walking and chewing, with determination. Often, she'd let me walk out ahead with my apple half while she finished putting Kelley into a stroller. Sometimes, I'd get all the way to the playground before her, and sit on the edge of the sandbox, finishing my apple and waiting for Mom and Kelley.

"I can't believe I used to let you walk out on the street alone. You knew the way, and we'd catch up with you," Mom recalled later. "But how different things were then, before kidnappings and such."

To me, Mom was embodied by those morning walks and the apple halves. She was beautiful, composed, elegant, always providing me encouragement to do things that I should do—like eat apples—but gently. My father's energy was gruffer, more volatile, but I always felt at ease with Mom.

From early on, she innately trusted me. Knew, as she did the day I stuck my head through the chair back, that I was the explorer, the one who would find my own way—in the world and out of my own messes. As Kelley grew up, he never was granted, nor even wanted, the freedoms I was given. He never walked anywhere alone—I became his guardian in Mom's absence, when she went to work while we were in grade school. In high school, he always had an earlier curfew than I did at the same age, and never once broke it. He went to college closer to home than I did, and came home nearly every weekend to do laundry and take bags full of food in Tupperware to his apartment. Granted, I was an hour and a half away at Stanford while he was twenty minutes away at my father's grad-school alma mater, UC-Berkeley, but he never stopped coming home weekly. And I rarely visited outside of school breaks. I got so sick of being in the Bay Area during my college years that I signed up to study in England for six months and spent nearly every summer out of state doing internships.

Mom letting me walk ahead was not just anachronistic parenting; it was recognition of my spirit.

And because she was always good at letting go, at giving me a long rein, there was always distance between us. Not a tense or unhappy one. A loving distance, where we grew businesslike with each other, admiring each other but often bonding in transactional ways. In Kelley's and my latch-key days, Mom's directives to me were like the apple, a task and a deadline: Before she came home from work, I had to feed Kelley and myself a snack, wash all the dishes without leaving bits of food or soap traces on them, portion out the one hour of TV we were allowed to watch, and get started on my homework. When she came home, I reported on the afternoon's activities like I was her business partner, not Kelley's sister.

Kelley and Mom had a different bond, one of kindred spirits. They were homebodies at heart, and they needed each other. In my Dad's volatile times, they were like anchors for each other, not necessarily speaking of his illness, but drawing closer to each other instinctively. I looked away, or escaped. Dad and I, before he became ill, had developed a deeper bond. "So much like me," he proudly said, if I was very determined at a task or displaying precocious intelligence—or even if I was being particularly stubborn, which was often.

That was how it was growing up: Kelley was a Momma's Boy and I was my father's daughter. Yes, as a child I was a little afraid of Dad, but I also longed for his praise, longed to be his reflection. I liked learning how to use tools, to ride a bike, to swim, and, later, about cars, from him. These things made me feel strong and capable. Like he once was.

æ

During my elementary school years, our family took roadtrips all the time. Mom, Dad, Kelley, and I traversed the western United States from Idaho to Yellowstone to San Diego/ Tijuana, took annual trips to Yosemite and Tahoe, visited national parks, all piled into a royal blue Oldsmobile with a white vinyl top. I can reconstruct my childhood from the backseat of that car, watching freeway signs fly by, the back of my Dad's Brylcreemed head in front of me, his hands steady on the wheel. Mom and Kelley asleep, their heads slumped over, leaning on padded blue interior.

Mom and Kelley seemed to have inherited the same brand of automotive narcolepsy; as soon as they got into a moving vehicle, they nodded off. I took it upon myself to stay awake for Dad's sake. The two of us were the vigilant ones, keeping watch over the world that was our family car.

Dad would use the hours on the road to sharpen my mind. Our favorite game was States and Capitals. Dad liked to stay at Ramada Inns, which were inexpensive and ubiquitous. The chain produced an advertisement of its various properties in the fifty states disguised as an educational guidebook listing the states, and giving a little bit of information about each. Dad took a couple of copies; at first he had me read it to him while he drove. Then, together, we recited all fifty states in alphabetical order. As an immigrant, this was also somewhat new to him. It intrigued him that New England had so many tiny states with odd names ("Why did they call Rhode Island that if it's not an island? Why even make it a state, it's so small?") while the West Coast had only three large states. The map and the country, as expansive as Taiwan was small, full of possibility and unknown.

By naming them, memorizing them, we performed our own minor conquest of the vast nation we were traversing, mile by highway mile. When I mastered the states, we started on the capitals.

"Tawl-eh-hawss . . . what kind of word is this?"

"Tallahassee," I said slowly. "I think it's French." (I was wrong, but I wanted to show Dad how knowledgeable I was.)

"What's it the capital of?" he said, raising an eyebrow at me in the backseat.

"Ummm." I frowned. His pronunciation was shaky on many of the words, but his memory was always a few steps ahead of mine.

"Florida!" he said, laughing. "Tall-a-hass-ee, Florida. How are you going to remember that?"

I giggled. "If Florida were turned upside down, it would be TALL-a-hass-ee-ER than the other states." Dad couldn't say "pneumonic devices" in

English, but he knew what they were.

"Not Idaho!" he said, chuckling with me. "What's the capital of Idaho?"

"Boise!" I said. That was easy; we had been there on an earlier roadtrip.

"Very good! My smart daughter," he said, grinning into the endless horizon.

The piece de resistance was a rapid recitation of states and capitals in the appropriate order: Alabama, Montgomery; Alaska, Juneau; Arizona, Phoenix; and so and so forth, all the way to Wisconsin, Madison, and Wyoming, Cheyenne. The game became our own private language. Sometimes, Mom or my brother Kelley would wake up in the middle of the M's—when Dad and I were muddling through Michigan, Mississippi, Missouri—and look at us with bewilderment.

During college, Dad had driven with me from California to the places where I did summer internships—Arizona my junior year, and Oregon my senior year. He was manic for the former, depressed for the latter. The family had stopped taking roadtrips after Dad's illness manifested. Once Kelley and I had our own cars to drive, the idea seemed antiquated, like a nostalgic television version of our family had once taken those journeys. But Mom insisted he drive with me to Phoenix and Portland. And once Dad and I were on the road each time, we managed to slide into our familiar patterns from those childhood roadtrips. Except that I'd do most of the driving. He'd watch my speed, chide me not to hang out in the passing lane. We took meal breaks at Denny's restaurants. He'd order coffee, drink several refills with lots of cream and sugar—and then offer me the last sip, full of sugar. The one I always begged for when I was a kid. The adult me would turn up my nose at the carnage of empty sugar packets on the table and shake my head, laughing.

In the middle of the Arizona desert or on a monotonous stretch of I-5, he would suggest we rehash the states and capitals game. That second summer, while we were crossing the Oregon-California border on my way home, we finished all 50 states but one—we could not for the life of us remember the capital of Vermont. We verbally kicked ourselves until the next gas stop and then we forgot about it. A few days later, my mom and I were in the kitchen when he walked upstairs from the bedroom, a surprise during his depressed days.

"Montpelier," was all he said.

"Yes!" I yelled.

"Mont-pel-i-er!" we shouted in unison, the way I had sounded it out for him those many years ago, when the word was new to both of us.

Mom rolled her eyes. And then he walked back downstairs, back to bed.

13.
Bitter, Sweet

"Xiao Fan (my Chinese nickname), where are you? You do not answer my call. I have five, maybe six, big boxes in the garage storage area that are yours. I can't keep them here. I need that space. When can you come and take them?"

To: Angie Chuang
From: Tien-Yuh Chuang
Subject: Re: Boxes in garage
XF,
Did you receive my phone message? You have six big boxes in my garage storage space that you need to take. I will throw them away if you do not want them, but I have hernia and Dr. says I should not move heavy things. When can you move them? It has been here too long and you do not return my calls.
Dad.

To: Angie Chuang
From: Tien-Yuh Chuang
Subject: RE: Re: Boxes in garage
XF,
Do not tell me the boxes have been there ten years. I am not stupid. I have a Ph.D. and I can count. This is my house and I am not Rent-A-Storage or Public Storage or those places you pay. And you do not pay me

a penny to put your stuff up there and now I have a hernia. HAVE SOME RESPECT! **GET YOUR BOXES ASAP!!** <u>**THIS IS NOT YOUR HOUSE.**</u>

Dad.

"Xiao Fan,

I am calling you again, returning your message. When did you call? I am up late and early and still your call goes to voicemail. Are you avoiding me? You say that Portland is too far away to get your boxes. So now they are my problem? You are just like your mom, you think my house is your own storage place and I am your employee. THIS IS NOT YOUR HOUSE AND I AM NOT YOUR EMPLOYEE.

"You know how to drive. I taught you. Come down here."

When Dad swung out of depression months after the divorce, he flew back into mania in his empty house. Mom, Kelley, and I had all left decades' worth of belongings in the home I had grown up in. Dad decided it was time to clean house, literally, and decided to expunge all traces of his ex-wife and family who had betrayed him.

Every day, sometimes multiple times a day, he dropped of bags and boxes of junk from the house that Mom "left behind." He knocked on the door of her new condo so many times, sometimes at the wee hours of the morning, to make these bitter deliveries, that when ordering him to stop was clearly futile, she begged him to just use his copy of her car key and leave the things inside the trunk of her parked car. Sometimes the delivery was just a bag of junk mail that had been sent there under her married name; she had now changed to her maiden name, Chen. I knew white kids from school who had also changed their last names to their mother's maiden names when they felt alienated from their fathers after a divorce. But I never thought for a moment that I would or could do so. Mom certainly never suggested it. I was a Chuang, for better or worse.

I was in Portland when Dad's calls about the boxes came, about the time my hopes for the Hong Kong job had faded. The week after I interviewed there, the newspaper had suffered a minor economic crisis in that bureau, and the job opening I had been considered for was used to absorb one of several laid-off employees. I'd check my email or voicemail obsessively, waiting to hear from the recruitment director, who had left me hanging with a weak, "We'll see if we can work something out for you stateside." Instead, my inboxes filled with messages from Dad, and his obsession with those boxes, which I had left behind when I graduated from college. It began to feel like my world was no bigger than those six, maybe five, boxes. And my father, who, after more nonsensical, shouting, phone calls, would not hear anything I had to say about illness, medication, the need for a psychiatric evaluation. It was hard enough for me to say these things to him, but I had to. This bout of mania was different than the ones that had preceded it. It had sharper edges, an undercurrent of rage, an ominous unhinged quality to it that could not possibly end well. But his vitriol, the well-worn but still stinging outbursts of, "Anyone who calls her father crazy is no daughter of mine!" followed by a dial tone, were still hard to take. At least, I'd tell myself, he'll be angry enough to leave me alone about the boxes for a while.

But the next day, he'd call again, as if nothing had happened, with the same refrain about the boxes. Mania had a short memory. Mom would call me, rehashing the number of times he had called her, dropped off useless items from the house, baited her into a shouting match over the terms of the divorce—he had never agreed to them, he was going to take her to court.

"What is he going to do?" she'd say to me, her voice a wire stretched near breaking. "I already gave him the house, his house, as he reminds us of all the time. What else does he want from me? I walked away with almost nothing. I wanted to owe him nothing. And now he will never let me have what I wanted most: peace."

It had been during our time in Taiwan, at *Wai Gong* and *Wai Po*'s house, that I had allowed myself to see the toll the divorce had taken on her. Every night, Wai Po would devise some new concoction, like a small, hard pillow filled with odiferous Chinese herbs, or a special tea from the Chinese medicine shop downstairs, to help Mom sleep better.

"She's not sleeping," *Wai Po* would say to me after she sent Mom to bed with the cure du jour. "She's so thin and so tired. You have to take care of her when you go back."

"I know," I'd reply, and clasp my hand over hers, soft and wrinkled like worn paper money. But did I? I didn't know how to explain to *Wai Po* that the distance between Portland and San Francisco was greater than the entire length of Taiwan. And that the emotional distance I had created between myself and my family was immeasurable.

But hearing *Wai Po*, a mother, say it, I could no longer deny it: Mom was in pain, and I did not know how to help her any better than I knew how to deal with Dad.

☙

After a month of the incessant emails and phone calls about the boxes, after Dad's behavior continued getting more irrational, I decided to go to California. He had sent the police to Mom's condo at three in the morning when she wasn't returning his calls. Family friends were starting to call Mom, wondering why Dad was calling them at odd hours and keeping them on the phone for as long as he could, rambling almost incoherently. I imagined terrible things: He'd burn the house down. Or destroy everything inside it. He'd run his car off the road. Or, unthinkable yet unavoidable, he'd end his life like his brother did, hanging himself in his own home, leaving his lifeless body for one of us to find.

The Ford Expedition I rented was so large and so heavy it felt nautical, like I should sound a foghorn. I had cruised down from Portland, leaving before dawn on Saturday, and had arrived by mid-afternoon at Mom's. She had dark circles under her eyes, her sleep even more elusive ever since the three a.m. visit from the police. She, Kelley, and I had a quiet dinner, didn't talk much about Dad except to say, "What else can we do?" He had exhausted us all. I decided to just get the boxes and go; what point would there be to bring up therapy, treatment, medication, psychiatry? Those words that we threw at him like feathers into a tornado.

When I arrived at the house Sunday morning, he was up, skulking about, his quick strides and abrupt motions dismissive of me but full of anger.

"I took them down for you," he said, pointing to the boxes on the floor of the garage. "I don't know why you want this crap anyway. It looks like all papers and some plastic horses. It's about time you came and got them."

"Dad, you shouldn't have taken them down," I said, weakly. "Your hernia."

"Oh, and you would have taken the ladder and gone up there?" he said, practically hissing.

"Well, yes," I said. I had done it before, with me up in the rafters, him passing boxes up to me from halfway up the ladder. It had been precarious, but I had done it. We had.

"Ha! Fat chance," he said. Actually what he said was *go pi*, which literally translated to "dog fart" in Mandarin. It had the same meaning as fat chance or bullshit, but was an ugly word, all but requiring the "P" sound of the second word to be spat out.

It stung. Not just because of the profanity, which was rare for him, even in mania. But because all of the ways he taught and nurtured me as a child—riding a bike, swimming, using tools, learning to drive stick shift— were about me being capable, being an unconventional Chinese daughter who could do things a son could. He had been proud of my adeptness, my independence, my physical strength.

And now, in two syllables, he had negated all of those.

My throat closed in on itself, swallowing the words with which I wanted to fight back, to tell him he needed help, to tell him not to destroy the house—or himself. I didn't look at him as I lifted the boxes into the back of the SUV. I felt him watching me, his anger burning into my bare arms, which I knew were tan, thick, and muscular in a way that most first-generation Chinese would find unfeminine, peasant-like. I threw the boxes in with exaggerated motions, as if to show him that this was easy for me, that I was strong, that he could not take away what he had cultivated in me.

I slammed the rear door shut and drove off without saying goodbye.

I drove through the flat, dry stretch of far Northern California, through the state's notorious early-fall heat (as a child we referred to them as "Indian Summers" before we realized the political incorrectness of the term), then climbed the mountains near snowcapped Shasta, and wound around the azure lake where Dad used to take us boating. I heard his voice in my head saying, "Don't sit in the left lane unless you're passing." And I'd ease over into the right lane, and recite more state capitals, talking out loud to myself.

As I left California, the "Welcome to Oregon" sign brought a pang of happiness. I pictured Dad and me in the old Chevy Malibu station wagon we drove to and from Portland that year, the Year of Montpelier, finishing our recitation at the exact same border.

The road flattened out. Welcome to Oregon was well behind me now. The landscape was incrementally growing greener by the mile, Northern California's signature golden hills a thing of the past. Medford lay ahead, the next major city on my way back home. Or was I coming from home? I didn't know.

All I knew was that I was closer to Portland, my home without Mom and Dad in my midst, than to the Bay Area, my home where Mom and Dad weighed on me, gravities each suffocating in its own way. It shouldn't have felt so good to drive away, to feel the powerful, gas-guzzling engine under my accelerator foot. The feeling of an automatic transmission was still foreign to me; from the day I learned to drive, for the past dozen years, I had only owned manual-transmission cars. My current steed was a five-speed Honda Civic. Automatic transmissions like this Expedition were all forward momentum without the possibility of rolling backward.

I had been through the states and capitals three times by now, and nailed every one. I eyed the six boxes in the rearview mirror. Before I had gotten on the road, I had pulled over in a supermarket parking lot, cut away the remainder of the yellowed, cracked packing tape with my pocketknife to see what was in them. One had all of my middle school and high school yearbooks. Another the letters my friends from Chinese School camp had written to me during my high school years, before we started using email. Edges of pink envelopes and Hello Kitty stationery peeked up. Two of the six were filled with Breyer model horses, frozen in mid-walk or trot, a youthful passion of mine, carefully wrapped in layers of newspapers. Other mementos: Award plaques I had won at high school graduation. A graduation cap and gown, in material that felt like a disposal picnic tablecloth. A Depeche Mode concert T-shirt. These were the last things I had in my childhood home. Dad had wanted them out of there, rejecting my place there as he felt we had rejected him in supporting Mom's decision to divorce him. Now, any tie I had to that house was in the back of this SUV.

I leaned back in the ridiculously large and padded driver's seat, one hand on the steering wheel, switched on the cruise control to seventy-five. I was driving the way Dad had taught me to, relaxed but alert, fast but within reasonable range of the speed limit, in the right lane, left used for passing only. My past and present, all inside this vehicle.

I opened the windows and took in the warm evening air. I wouldn't reach Portland until after midnight. But in this SUV, with this behemoth of a transmission, I was all forward without backward; present and future without past.

And for the first time all weekend, I felt like I could breathe.

Even after I took the boxes from the house, Dad kept shipping me more boxes, ones he packed with hastily scrawled shipping labels, the handwriting shaky. Back when I was his office assistant, I had learned how to forge his signature, the writing in formal cursive, loopy but symmetrical, an immigrant engineer's penmanship. The childlike block-printed letters on the packages looked like they belonged to a different person entirely. Inside, I'd find bizarre collections of detritus from the house: Junk mail still being sent under my name, a few stray cassette tapes from high school, old and yellowed family photos, gifts of on-sale knick knacks he bought from office-supply stores—once, he sent three different mini-staplers still with the "CLEARANCE $1" signs on them. Never a note. Yet the messages contained within were mixed and unsettling. He was trying to give me gifts, however bizarre, he was trying to evoke nostalgia, and he was trying to tell me that the house was no longer my domain. I wanted not to respond, putting the accumulating stash of cheap office supplies into a bag I'd donate to Goodwill. Not that non-response was much of a choice, with a manic person. Every day after Dad mailed a package, he would call and ask, "Did you receive the package? What did you think?" Until I was forced to acknowledge that I did receive it, and thanks, yes I liked it, but you don't need to send me the junk mail and I don't need office supplies. "Ungrateful, just like your mom," he'd grumble and I'd steel myself to ignore him, just let him get off the phone.

Meanwhile, Dad had taken on a tenant in the upstairs level of the house, an employee of a restaurant-owner client of his who was likely an undocumented Chinese immigrant. She was in her thirties, "about your age," Dad pointed out in his emails and phone calls. "Maybe you can be friends over email," he said, every time we talked. I had a bad feeling about it.

I tried to avoid talking about her in my obligatory return calls and emails to Dad. He had stopped shipping boxes to me when the tenant moved in, instead telling stories about how she brought food home from the restaurant for him or told him about her troubled relationship with her boyfriend, also an immigrant from China living in the area.

"Dad, remember what you used to tell me," I said, recalling my real-estate-office-assistant days. "Don't make friends your tenants and don't make tenants your friends."

He ignored me and asked if he could give her my email address. I said no. I knew Dad was lonely, and it pained me to think of it. But I also knew he was manic, and none of his relationships in this state ended well.

Things at work had slowed down. I felt stifled under the weight of Dad's mania, and frustrated by my thwarted attempt to both advance my career and put distance between me and my family by moving to Hong Kong, If I couldn't get out of the United States, at least I could get out of Portland for a while. I rented a cabin on the Oregon Coast for a long weekend. I sent a group email and invited any and all of my friends to join me out there for a getaway. It was November, and rentals were plentiful and cheap. I loved the coast at that time of year, blustery days, walking along the ocean as the ubiquitous Northwest drizzle and the spray of the ocean became indistinguishable against my Gore-Tex jacket. Curling up with a book by the fire, and writing with the backdrop of crashing waves.

A few co-workers came out for the first couple of days, and we cooked sumptuous meals, drank wine, played board games, and talked into the wee hours of the morning. I started to feel the weight of the last few months lift from my shoulders. I still thought about Rochina, Nazo, and Asad—by now a reflexive nostalgia for a time when I felt purposeful and embraced, when I was not waiting with dread for Mom's next phone call about how Dad was upsetting her.

And, on the next day, when the co-workers left, Laila called me on the cabin's landline I had included in the email, since cell reception was spotty there.

"Were you serious about coming out the cabin? Because Maiwand and I got your group email, and he wants to bring my aunt and Aisha for a night. Only if it's OK with you."

My heart lifted, even more so than when my co-workers had arrived with wine. Ever since we had returned from Afghanistan, I had been searching for clues that the Portland Shirzais's bond with me would continue, that the trip wasn't a kind of bookend to our relationship.

They came that evening, all in one car. They quickly took over the large, drafty cabin as if it were their own, Maiwand stoking a roaring fire, his wife Padama bringing a carload of Afghan food to cook, Aisha finding every secret hiding place, and Laila encouraging me to let them do their nesting while she and I chatted by the fire. I was overwhelmed, touched by the idea that their warmth and hospitality as a family was so portable. Expecting escape from family, I was suddenly ensconced in the company of my other family. Though I had offered to host them, now I was reveling in the sweetness of full-on, Afghan-style hospitality for the first time since I had left Kabul.

The next day, we all took a drive along the coast, and Maiwand proudly played cassette tapes of patriotic Pashtun songs that I had brought back from his nephew Ayub in Kabul. Laila rolled her eyes, "He always wants to play these in the car. We made him stop on the way here. Now he knows he can get away with it because you're here."

Maiwand grinned in the rearview mirror. I smiled back complicitly from the backseat, though the Pashto I had learned for my trip wasn't helping me understand the lyrics.

"*Watan*, see?" Maiwand said. "That's a word you know. They are singing about watan, the country. Our country."

I nodded. Padama admonished him. "Don't make Angie bored," she said in her accented English.

"I'm not bored," I said. "It's interesting."

"See?" he said and nudged Padama playfully across the front seat. She smiled.

Laila shook her head and mouthed, Don't encourage him. I just leaned against the window and watched the coastal highway fly by, the reflection of Aisha's head bobbing in time to songs about *watan* superimposed over the lapping waves of the Pacific.

I felt emotional, choked up almost, when the Shirzais packed up the car that evening after another homemade meal, and we hugged each other goodbye heartily. I had come here for some alone time, but after they had descended on the place and placed me seamlessly into the fifth seat of their car, I now dreaded the quiet—and what would follow when I got back into cellphone range.

That night, I read while watching the last embers of the fire fade. I could have added more logs, but it was a warm night and I liked the idea of letting the Shirzais's fire leave as they did. Spending my first night alone in the cabin, I noticed how loud the ocean was from the second-floor bedroom. All too soon, I'd have to rejoin my own family, see how many manic voice messages and emails from Dad had accumulated, hear Mom, in her bitter, sleep-deprived voice, talk about how Dad was depriving her of her longed-for peace.

I drove back the next morning, stopping in a town on Highway 26 for gas. My cellphone had come back in range and there were six voicemail messages from the night before. Five missed calls from Mom, and one from Kelley.

My stomach dropped to my feet. Dad. What was it? Rather than listen to them, I just called Mom directly.

"Xiao Fan," she said, her voice raw and hoarse. "Where have you been? It's Dad. He's been arrested. Something about the tenant. It looks like he may have attacked her boyfriend. He resisted arrest. He's in jail."

⁊

I returned to the Bay Area for the holidays. Dad mentioned multiple times I could stay at his house, in my old room, but I always changed the subject. When I finally told him I was staying at Mom's, he said he would pick me up from the airport and take me there. When we all lived in the same house, he had always given us rides to and from the airport. I told him I could take public transportation, but he insisted.

I dreaded the conversation we might have in the car, what fights he might pick. He had been released from jail the day Mom had called me. A court hearing had been scheduled for a disorderly conduct charge; the police dropped the initial charges of threatening and resisting arrest. The tenant had fled the day of the arrest and never been seen again. Her boss' wife had come to get her things, and ignored Dad the entire time.

Mom, Kelley, and I never did get the whole story about what happened. The police report described officers arriving after the tenant's boyfriend called 911 and claimed my father was threatening him. The boyfriend, the tenant, and my father were in the garage, with the door open. Dad was shouting, belligerent, and did not respond to the officers' attempts to question him, and then to calm him down. When they arrested him, he resisted.

"Did they hurt you?" I asked Dad in our first phone conversation after he had returned home from jail.

"No," he said. "They broke my glasses. I asked them to pay for them, but they wouldn't. I'm going to ask again in court."

"What happened?" I said.

"Nothing," Dad said. He switched to Mandarin, calling the tenant and the boyfriend epithets that people from Taiwan used for mainland Chinese, implying that they were both primitive and manipulative. "They made the whole thing up because she didn't want to pay her rent."

"What? They called the police because she didn't want to pay rent?" I said, incredulous. "That's not what the police report said. Why didn't you just cooperate with the police?"

"They made that up too," he said, getting angry. "They just said that because I tried to close the garage door on them."

"Well, you shouldn't do that to police officers," I said, feeling trapped into his manic delusion.

"It's my property!" he said. "Whose side are you on anyway?"

I took a deep breath and decided I would wait until I arrived in the Bay Area to confront him about the usual issues: a psychiatrist, perhaps a therapist, medication. Maybe the arrest, the humiliation of spending a night in jail, being pushed to the ground by police officers and having his glasses broken, the threat of a criminal record, were enough to convince him that it was time to change the status quo.

"Was it bad in jail? I would have looked for a bail bondsman but I was out of cellphone range when Mom called," I said. I learned later Kelley had found one, but Dad was released before it was necessary to post bail.

"It was fine. Free meals," he said, indignant. "I was bored so I did pushups."

Pushups? I tried to imagine Dad, almost blind without his glasses, his body now weakened and twisted by his inactivity when depressed and his lack of sleep when manic, reverting to old Taiwanese-army exercises.

Trying to feel powerful when made powerless. Maybe imagining a jailbreak, action-hero style. It was absurd and awful. I was having a harder time coping with the idea of Dad in jail than he was.

When Dad picked me up from the airport, he was in a good mood. He hugged me, awkwardly, with one arm and offered to help with my luggage. I shook my head, mumbling about his hernia, and threw my suitcase into the backseat. The trunk was far too full of tools, papers, on-sale knick knacks—the detritus of his mania—to use. I took a deep breath before I slid into the passenger seat.

"How's work?" he asked. "How is your car?" "How many miles do you have on it?" (He still related best over cars.) "Are you thinking of buying in Portland?" (Ever the real-estate broker.) I asked him about the court case. He said he had appeared on the appointed day, and neither his former tenant nor her boyfriend was there. In fact, neither of them had been seen, not even at the restaurant where she worked, since the day of the arrest. They apparently had fled, fearing immigration enforcement. The judge dismissed the case. Dad was free. I was grateful, but part of me had wanted him to suffer greater repercussions, to help make him see that his behavior was out of control. I had fantasized that the judge would mandate counseling, maybe require visits to a psychiatrist.

Maybe this is rock bottom. That was something people said after a troubled family member's arrest, a jail stint, a brush with the law. I wanted to think it, to say it to Mom and Kelley, maybe even to Dad. But it would have no meaning to any of us. I wondered how anyone ever really knew where "rock bottom" was, how they knew things weren't actually going to get even worse—or get better and then get worse. That was the thing with bipolar disorder: It defied trajectory. It was not a reverse bell curve; it was a fever chart with ever-lower lows and higher highs. And whether the lows or highs were the "bottom," no one could say. My father in bed, depressed, neglecting to bathe or changed clothes was certainly a low. But my father manic, high, getting arrested in an irrational rage, doing pushups in a suburban jail cell, felt like it should be the bottom.

Yet Mom, Kelley, and I knew by now, that as long as Dad continued to deny doctors or treatment, there would be no bottom—because we could never expect things to get better. And we had grown to count on the fact that he would always refuse those. So he did get better—or calmer, at least—after the arrest, but I understood that as part of an ebb and flow that defined our existence with Dad's illness. With it, there was no bottom, and there was no rock—nothing that solid. It was like watching the tide come in and go out on one of those islands that scientists predicted would someday be swallowed up completely by the rising ocean levels. Only we didn't know if the island was Dad—or if it was us.

When Dad and I arrived at Mom's condo from the airport, Dad lingered in the entryway for an awkward moment. Then, he was gone, I put down my luggage, and Mom and I went for a walk.

She had rented a place next to the meeting point of two of the suburban East Bay Area's largest trail systems, the Contra Costa Canal and Iron Horse trails. And she had walked. Rain or shine, for miles and miles, she wore out her sneakers, and then bought another pair on sale at TJ Maxx. She had an umbrella for rainy days, a big floppy hat for sunny days. She had always liked to walk, but her fervor had reached a new level. It was as if all the energy she had channeled into living with and worrying about my father had been reborn in her feet. It calmed her, and I was more than happy to join her. With me as her walking companion, she turned to another outlet: talking.

"You know, once, when I was living with your father and you had moved out of the house, I couldn't stand it anymore," she said, her voice shaking at the memory. "He was manic, yelling nonstop, just nonsense, and I kept telling myself, 'Keep quiet. Just keep quiet. You'll only make it worse.'

"So I got into the car, drove away, with nowhere to go. I just drove down to the end of the block, turned into the dead-end at the bottom of the hill, stopped the car and screamed at the top of my lungs. It must have been a minute, or more. Then I just cried and cried."

I had known this. Or did I? The revelation, the unrestrained emotion, so new to me, to us after more than a decade of looking the other way, of never using words like "manic" or "depressed," I wasn't even sure what I knew and what I had absorbed by being in that house, steeped in that awful silence.

I said nothing, just nodded, and kept on walking alongside her. She continued, one story after another, barely pausing to take a breath: more about the pain and frustration she endured, others about her continuing worries about my father ("Who will take care of him now? I don't want you and Kelley to be burdened by him."), and then, when those were out of her system, updates or gossip about people in the Chinese American community. I listened, sometimes interjecting with stories from my work and life in Portland, sometimes just absorbing her words.

Kelley was returning from medical school on the East Coast in a couple days. Our first holidays, the three of us at Mom's small condo. On Christmas Day, I'd make us a simple Italian meal with the finest ingredients from an authentic Sicilian deli I'd discovered near the condo. It seemed right, in our new normal, to have neither Chinese food nor traditional American Christmas fare.

Kelley was gaining the medical knowledge to try to make sense of Dad's mood swings and his psychological state (and concluded, as we had suspected, that his long cycles didn't fit any textbook description of bipolar disorder although he had all the symptoms). Now, with the arrest, we thought it was time for another confrontation about diagnosis and treatment. Kelley and I each called him to wish him a good Christmas, and promised each other we'd bring up those topics with Dad before the New Year.

Dad called me a couple days later, asked me when I wanted to meet for lunch or come by the house. I took a deep breath and said what I had rehearsed in my head.

"Dad, I know you think the arrest was some mainland-Chinese-immigrant conspiracy against you, but these kind of things don't happen to other people we know," I said, conscious not to say "normal people," a phrase that would set him off. "Have you thought maybe it's finally time to see a doctor? Maybe think about medication or therapy?"

"Again! This again," he said, fuming. "I am not having this conversation again."

"That's the thing, Dad," I said, trying desperately to take deep breaths, talk slowly. "It's never a conversation. You never want to talk about this. But we're all worried about you. We don't want these things, or worse, to happen to you. You're not acting rationally. It's not your fault. It's an illness. If you had pneumonia, you would go to the doctor to get antibiotics, wouldn't you?"

"I'm . . . NOT . . . TALKING . . . ABOUT . . . THIS!" he shouted. "End of conversation."

"OK then," I said, moving on to my next rehearsed move. "I feel so strongly that you need to do this for your own health and safety, that I'm not going to talk to you until you're ready to have this conversation. We need to have it."

"No daughter of mine calls her dad crazy and talks to him so disrespectfully!" he yelled and hung up the phone. My heart was pounding. The conversation had gone exactly as I had expected, and I was certain absolutely nothing would change. Even his angry exit lines had not altered in more than a decade.

His extremes between mania and depression were staggering, and Mom, Kelley, and I would still sometimes go through the perverse exercise of wondering which one we preferred—as if it were even a choice. As I started telling my high school and college friends who had known him about his illness, I noticed a pattern: All of my high school friends, who had known him during his first major depression after he quit his engineering job, said, "I hardly knew your dad. He was always so quiet, like he wasn't even there." My college friends, on the other hand, would say, "Wow, is that why he could never stop talking? Your dad was always so energetic, so gregarious."

Kelley's attempt didn't go any better. And Dad stayed quiet for a few days. Then, in classic manic fashion, he called me to ask when we could have lunch or when I was stopping by the house, as if nothing had happened. I didn't return the call.

As my time in the Bay Area wound down, Dad started calling about taking me to the airport. We could have breakfast on the way, like we used to, he said on my voicemail, meaning when we all lived and stayed in the same house. When I ignored that call, he called Mom to get my flight information. Weary of conflict with him, Mom gave it to him, and he called me back and left a message on my voicemail telling me he would pick me up two and a half hours before my late-morning flight, so we would have time for breakfast. He sounded cheerful, almost, on my voicemails. I was starting to feel guilty for not seeing him during my entire time at home.

He would call Mom and repeat every message he left on my voicemail. Finally, Mom said, "Just let him take you to the airport. Your ignoring him isn't going to change a thing."

She was right. I had known this when giving him my ultimatum.

Dad had proven me right. There was a certain peace that came with the acceptance that things with my father would always stay on their unhappy trajectory, regardless of what we did or didn't do.

The early morning of my outgoing flight to Portland, he picked me up at Mom's and we went to a Denny's near the Oakland Airport. As if to prevent me from bringing up the arrest, and the usual taboo topics, Dad talked nonstop. He reminisced about our old family roadtrips, as he liked to do, while stirring four packets of sugar and a whole thimble-like container of creamer into his coffee. Like many bipolar people, my father had a near-photographic, obsessive memory for certain events—even if they were decades old, he could recreate them down to the last detail, and would talk about them constantly. For others, particularly anything that happened during his depressive periods, or the details of that possibly fateful flight from Florida that still eluded me, I might as well have been talking to an amnesiac.

He started telling the story of how I put my head between the bars of a chair at the fast-food restaurant. "And you were crying and screaming, and your head was swelling, and no one could get you out. Do you remember?"

"No, I really don't," I said. "But I've heard the story from you and Mom."

"And then the manager of the restaurant came out and said he was going to call the fire department, that they would saw the chair off of you," Dad said, a glint in his eye. "And what did you do?"

"What did I do?" I said, giving him the punch line.

"You heard him say 'fireman' and 'saw' and all of the sudden, pop! Out came your head," he said, grinning. "And everyone in the restaurant applauded."

He had told me the story in painstaking detail so many times, I could almost feel the constricting bars around my neck. Still, it was good to see him happy, non-combative, this morning.

"*Tiao pi*," my father said, shaking his head. Mischievous. "You were always sticking your head where it didn't belong. Maybe that's why you became a reporter."

I laughed. "I think there's some truth to that," I said.

He gulped most of his coffee. He pushed the mug my way.

"Here," he said. "Remember?"

He seemed to have forgotten I had rebuffed his over-sugared coffee on those roadtrips, when I was in college. Long before that, when I was in elementary school, Dad used to take me to the bank with him. He always drank the free coffee there, and I would watch, fascinated as he dropped sugar cubes and stirred creamer into the Styrofoam cups. Sometimes, when he wasn't paying attention, I'd sneak one of those perfect white cubes and pop it into my mouth, tasting and feeling the crystalline sweetness as it dissolved. But always, back then, he would save the last sip of coffee, the sweetest one, for me. It had tasted like candy, but also had made me feel grown-up.

"Yes," I said. "The last sip."

This time, I took the mug and drank from it. It was sweet. It was a taste of my childhood, a time when Dad was larger than life and could do no wrong. It was what we had left.

14.
Transgressions

Daoud left a fractious Afghanistan, its disparate population unable to get behind the "Gucci Afghan" Karzai and come together, especially across the fiercely tribal rural areas. After his stint at the Ministry was done, Daoud worried his work was not effective. His efforts were getting mired in the corruption and inefficiency of the Afghan government, compounded by the incompetence of the American military, agencies, and NGOS. It was early 2005, and things were getting more dangerous across the country, even in Kabul, for Americans and Afghan Americans. An Afghan expat was kidnapped, dismembered, and dropped off in a burlap sack with the message: "Welcome Home." Improvised Explosive Devices and suicide bombings, once relegated to the War in Iraq, became commonplace in Kabul and the countryside. Daoud said he would not have allowed Stephanie and me to go as we did seven months earlier with the current situation in Kabul. It made me sad that we likely could not schedule a return trip, as I had hoped to do someday, keeping my promise to Rochina and Nazo.

Daoud returned to Portland, exhausted and disillusioned, to find that his family, the one that had felt so united after September 11, was fraying at the seams as well. The nieces and nephews, now all college graduates, were coming into their own. But not in the way he had envisioned for them. Whispers of Laila's continuing relationship with Tim were starting to filter through the family grapevine, though Laila had kept mum about it to her uncles. Tim was neither Afghan nor Muslim, so she had little hope he could be acceptable in any way. Yet she could not let go either. Daoud's niece Sarasa, Mohammed's middle daughter, was still not speaking to any of the uncles, and vice versa, their long-held grudge calcifying over the years.

But the main problem? Mohib, Sarasa's older brother and the eldest of the six. Mohammed's firstborn and only son. He was now thirty-one, the same age as me. The family's attempts to ensure he carried on his father's legacy and culture had backfired miserably.

Mohib—or "Mo," as his non-Afghan friends called him—had not been particularly discreet about dating in and after college, preferring women who were drastically un-Afghan: provocative dressers, often blond, always irreverent. Sarasa resented bitterly that the uncles silently tolerated these girlfriends, sometimes looking the other way and being polite but tight-lipped as he brought a conspicuous "friend" to family functions. Meanwhile, she had been driven out of Maiwand's house years ago because she was dating a non-Afghan she hadn't even dared bring near the house. Laila, as was her way, took the double standard in stride, telling me she knew her relationship with Tim would be nearly impossible because Pashtun culture was so protective of its daughters.

When Mamoy had arrived a year and a half ago, Mohib seemed to calm down for a while. The most recent "friend" disappeared suddenly, and he was spending more time with his mother and sisters in their new shared home. That was when I learned of a surprising plan for Mohib's future that had been put into motion years ago. When Mohib was eighteen, settled in the United States for barely a year, the uncles—perhaps in an effort to remain traditional, or perhaps sensing that his restless spirit might need some anchoring—suggested he consider an engagement to a woman close to his age in Pakistan that the family there had identified as suitable for him. As Maiwand had done when he met and married Padama, they could arrange a chaperoned meeting in Peshawar. If Mohib agreed, they would start her immigration paperwork, which would give him time to finish college before she arrived and the marriage made official.

Knowing "Mo" as I did, the fact that anyone would even suggest this—or that he might agree to such an arrangement—seemed ludicrous. But here was where the versions of the story diverged, and this divergence lay at the root of the deepening family conflict: The uncles said Mohib was very different then, and he was even enthusiastic about the marriage after he corresponded and met with his intended. They put the wheels in motion, and Mohib went to college—and never completed the immigration paperwork. Then he denied ever agreeing to the engagement, and the fights with the uncles that ensued sent Mohib off on his ever-more-rebellious sprees. Even Mohib's female "friends" flouted his unwillingness to be engaged. The uncles were distraught that the family's honor—and a young woman and her family's lives—were hanging in the balance of Mohib's callous capriciousness.

Mohib and his sister's accounts were quite different. They maintained that Mohib was not truly consulted, that the seriousness of the transaction was not conveyed to him. Yes, he met with the young woman in Pakistan, and yes, he told them he liked her. But they lived in America now, for goodness sake, where one does not get railroaded into a binding lifetime commitment because of a teenager's offhanded compliment. Worse yet, Mohib and his sisters said later, when it was clear Mohib was balking, Daoud and Maiwand strong-armed Mamoy into moving the engagement forward from Peshawar, scaring her with hints of his American exploits and rumors of his drinking alcohol, a sin that, more than anything else, Mamoy was certain would condemn him to hell. A wife would give him responsibility, the uncles told Mamoy, a reason to respect their culture and the Qur'an.

The uncles wrote to the fiancée and told her to prepare to come to the United States, that they could marry her by proxy in Pakistan (another long-held practice in a country where brides and grooms were often unable to get to each other), and start the immigration paperwork for a spousal visa, which was faster than the fiancée visa they had originally intended to obtain.

Mohib was infuriated. Overnight, a young woman in Peshawar's expectations had become leverage for the uncles, without his knowledge or agreement. Now, her hopes were riding on his acquiescence, but the marriage was the last thing he wanted. Maiwand and Yusuf told him they had felt the same trepidation about their arranged marriages to Afghan women, that they, too, had dated American women in and after college, but that they were happy with their wives. Traditional marriage was the only way to become a true Pashtun man, and ensure that culture and language were preserved for the next generation, they said.

His father, Mohammed, would have wanted it that way.

"How dare they use my father against me that way?" Mohib seethed. We had gotten into the habit of having regular workday lunches, since our offices were close to each other. They became venting sessions for him; I was someone who knew well what he was talking about, things that would be unfathomable for most other non-Afghans. I was also safe—I promised I would not share anything he told me with the uncles, or even Laila (whom he viewed as too acquiescent to them), and I kept my word.

"They're playing with this woman in Pakistan's life, lying to her and making her think she has a life here with me. Afghan women kill themselves over things like this, don't they realize?"

I couldn't disagree with him, but I resisted this interpretation of his uncle's intentions. Surely, the Daoud I had come to know and understand, the one who told his family he wanted to "save" three girls as well as three boys, the one who shook women's and men's hands, would not treat a young Afghan woman this way. Particularly one who had not had the opportunities that he had given his nieces Laila, Sarasa, and Mina.

"Maybe the uncles didn't really tell her these things. Maybe they're just trying to pressure you with a bluff," I said. "You should sit down and talk to them reasonably, tell them this is not equivalent to Maiwand and Yusuf's former reluctance to marry. That you really don't want this. They wouldn't want to hurt her."

Mohib scoffed. "You don't really know my uncles," he said bitterly.

Like a cornered animal, Mohib made a break for it and ran wild. He abruptly moved out of the house with his sisters and Mamoy, into his own apartment downtown. Mamoy was baffled and distraught, often tearful when she talked about her son. In time, Mohib's lunchtime venting to me turned into confessions: Heavy drinking, blacking out, sometimes waking up in strange women's apartments. He juggled multiple girlfriends at once, relishing his own skill at keeping them secret from each other. But every time, his stories of debauchery were interspersed with examples of his uncles' scathing disapproval, how they belittled him with a stare or an offhanded comment. It all boiled down to: "You are not becoming the man your father would have wanted."

He wasn't. But he was determined to fail in spectacular fashion.

Beneath it all, for Mohib and for his uncles, was Mohammed. Mohib didn't need to say so; he rarely mentioned his late father. In Shinzmaray and in Kabul, Mohammed's absence had resided in Grandma's photo room and in the abandoned sitting room for which Amina was caretaker. In Portland, I came to realize, it was harder to locate because it was everywhere: in Mamoy's tears, in Daoud's nightmares—and in the unwelcome weight of expectations thrust upon Mohib. To the uncles, Mohib was the bearer of a legacy. To Mohib, his uncles were abusing that legacy to exert control over him.

I wasn't sure what to make of Mohib's confessions. The drinking and random trysts worried me—not because of the moral implications or the state of his soul, but because he was indulging with such recklessness, anger even, that it seemed inevitable he would get hurt somehow. I still had trouble reconciling that the rational, seemingly progressive Daoud was taking such an ill-conceived course. Had the time in Afghanistan embittered him somehow, made him want to rein in the chaos that he *could* control, among his own adopted children? Perhaps living among the outlines of Mohammed's absence had galvanized Daoud's determination to ensure his late brother had a male heir who was truly Afghan, truly Pashtun.

"I know you're angry at the uncles," I'd say. "But don't run yourself off a cliff."

"Oh, what are you now, my mother?" Mohib would glare at me, his amber-brown eyes narrowing, head shaking: *Not you as well.* "You wouldn't understand what it's like. They never judge you. You're all smiles and rainbows with them, just the good journalist. You don't know what it's like to be a member of this family. To be a *Shirzai*."

He spat out the last word with vitriol, sarcasm. It stung.

I was a friend by now, not just a journalist, I wanted to argue. *I'm practically family*, I said to myself. Why was that important to me? But he was right, I got to bask in the orbit of the Shirzai family without having to conform totally, to subject myself to scrutiny. I wasn't one of them, as much as I wanted to see myself that way. It was a romanticized construct, the honorary family member, the immersion journalist so deeply immersed I was no longer a reporter but a member of the tribe. Gone native— that had negative connotations, I reminded myself. There was a certain condescension and delusion about that phrase, though many a researcher or observer had succumbed to its allure. Was I that cliché, that gullible?

I wondered sometimes if I should say something to Daoud, but I couldn't imagine doing so. I still had the kind of regard for him, and the upbringing in a Chinese family, that made it difficult for me to break generational protocol. My attempted confrontations with my father had generated only anger or withdrawal. Why would Daoud be any different? And who was I to get involved with another family's conflict? As Mohib said, I didn't really know what it was like to be a Shirzai.

My better instincts told me to withdraw myself, to leave Mohib to his self-destructive behavior, but I didn't. Each time he called or texted the next lunch invite, I found myself saying yes, feeling more sympathetic to him as he spiraled more deeply out of control.

৵

"Do you want a beer?"

Mohib asked the question casually. But as I heard the muffled touch of socks against kitchen tile and the soft suction of the refrigerator door, the word beer hung in the air.

"Well?" he said.

"No," I said, too insistently. I looked at the hand-me-down loveseat, hesitated, and sat down, surprised when its softness swallowed me.

His face was hidden behind the refrigerator door, and now a hum filled the small apartment. A brisk waft of cold breezed past me.

"It's OK, you know. We're not with my family. We don't have to pretend we don't drink," he said. But *I* don't have to pretend, I wanted to say. Yet in four years of knowing the Shirzais, I had never even sipped from a glass of wine in front of any of them.

The clinking of bottles, followed by more steps, a drawer opening— looking for a bottle opener. "Are you sure?" he said, drawing out the "sure."

"Yes."

"Water?"

"No, thanks, I'm fine. I can't stay long."

He sauntered out with the amber bottle with the label of some boutique microbrew I didn't recognize, took a swig, and leaned his meaty shoulder on the doorframe of the living room. He crossed and cocked a socked toe against the hardwood, and gave a close-mouthed smile. He was playing the role of the confident American bachelor. This was the "Mo" his hard-partying non-Afghan friends knew. Daoud and Maiwand hated that he tried to Americanize his name.

He pulled up a chair in front of the couch. I was relieved he didn't try to plunk down on the loveseat with me. It was November 2005, now a year and half since I had gone to Afghanistan. Earlier this evening, we had both been at the family's Thanksgiving dinner. My second year in a row spending the holiday with the Shirzais. Though my own family had never made a big deal of the holiday, since the divorce and my father's ensuing mental decline, I was eager to have alternate plans.

Mohib rested his elbows on his khaki-clad knees, cradling his beer. He glanced down at my feet.

"Thanks for taking off your shoes. People always forget to take off their shoes even though there's a place right there," he said, motioning to a row of his expensive Italian leather dress shoes lined up near the door.

"I'm from a no-shoes-in-the-house culture too, remember?" I said. I pictured my mother's small condo, with neat rows of shoes in the entryway. I pictured her falling asleep on the couch tonight to a made-for-TV movie, a happy white family on the screen carving turkey as she dozed off, alone.

"Right. Got to love the Chinese," Mohib said.

He must not have many Muslims visit the house, I thought, unable to stop staring at a painting of a giant wineglass.

This was my first time seeing the inside of his apartment, the subject of much strife among the Shirzais. I had gasped audibly when I first walked in and saw the art he had picked out: Three matching vertical canvases extended from ceiling to the tops of the furniture, all with photo-realistic oil paintings of wine—glistening deep-green wine bottles, detailed corks and corkscrews, a wine glass with a swirl of ruddy Pinot Noir in it. In most bachelor pads, they would be a wine aficionado's way to proclaim his passion and good taste. In Mohib's apartment, they were defiance against religion and culture.

I had been curious about this place. I had imagined him renting a loft in the trendy warehouse district with lots of brushed steel and glass, black leather sofas. But the scuffed, rippled hardwood floors, and chipped crown molding of this building spoke to a thrifty impulse in him, and an appreciation for tradition—just not his own family's. The apartment was typical of this unassuming corner of downtown that had changed little since the early twentieth century.

"My mother hates these paintings," he said. "This place makes her cry. Everything makes her cry."

Mamoy had a way of tearing up that made her round, dark eyes look magnified by the film of salt water, stark against the white headscarves that she wore. When the tears began to flow down her soft cheeks, she'd pick up a corner of her scarf and wipe at them. Thinking of Mohammed's loss, of Mamoy sending food and clothes to the prison in hopes that he would come out alive, I wanted so much for Mohib to be a comfort for her, not the source of more grief. Ironically, Mohib looked just like his mother, the same broad face and pronounced cheekbones, the same expressive brows and round eyes, only hers were jet-dark, and his golden-hued. Though Mohammed's features had found their way onto his youngest daughter, Mina, it was still Mohib who was seen as his father's inheritor. Now, he was the prodigal son, throwing away his father's cultural capital and good Pashtun name on hedonistic American pursuits.

I pictured Mamoy dabbing at her eyes as she surveyed her wayward only son in this drafty World War I-era building, surrounded by paintings of wine and a refrigerator full of craft beers. She had holy water from the sacred Zamzam Well, collected on her pilgrimage to Mecca, stashed in rinsed-out Pace Picante Sauce jars in her refrigerator. She had been so pleased when I had learned to wrap the *chador* she had loaned me. Now I was in her son's apartment, alone with him, watching him drink.

Mohib changed the subject. "How do you get people to take off their shoes before they go into your place?"

"I just ask them."

"I was thinking about putting up a sign."

"That's not a bad idea."

"I was thinking it could say, 'Please remove your shoes—and pants.'" White teeth. Sparkling chocolate eyes. Then, a downward glance, heavy lids and thick black lashes, at my thighs on the couch. I was wearing a light gray sweater and brown velvety pants, chosen for their comfort and forgiving waistband. Suddenly they felt too tight, and not because I had just eaten Thanksgiving dinner.

I laughed, too hard. He had once implied I was just a journalist. Now, alone in his apartment, I suddenly realized that we were almost the exact same age. We were both single—or at least he appeared to be between girlfriends. With any other single man my age, I would have been on my guard. But because this was Mohib, a Shirzai, I had entered into this space without thinking, with my guard down. He knew my closeness to his uncles and mother meant I should have been off-limits for his flirtations. He honored that, most of the time.

He changed the subject again, to something innocuous, something about his family. Our comfortable conversational space was his family. He vented and confessed. I tried to encourage him, as always, to give his uncles the benefit of the doubt. That conversation was familiar, comfortable.

Then he went kitchen to get another beer. As the refrigerator door shut, there was a long silence. No bottle opener. No footsteps. Just silence.

"Angie," the voice had changed. It had a touch of gravel—less certain, less playful. "Come here for a second."

೭

Earlier that day, Mohib had called me in morning, as I was leaving the gym.

"You're going to Uncle Maiwand's tonight, right?" he said, without saying hello or identifying himself. That's what he did when he wanted something from me.

"Yeah," I said. "What do you want?"

"I need a ride. I don't have a car now and I don't want to ask anyone else because they're all mad at me now."

About the same time he had moved into the apartment, Mohib gave up his beloved convertible BMW—to help make rent, he said. I suspected DUIs, a suspended license, might have had something to do with it.

Mohib hadn't even known that Uncle Maiwand had invited me to Thanksgiving dinner this year; I had been the year before, so Mohib assumed I'd be there again.

I thought for a moment that it might not be a good idea to show up with him at his family's Thanksgiving. "Why are they mad at you?"

"Duh. The usual reasons. Because I moved out. Because I'm a bad son. A bad nephew."

"And you still want to have Thanksgiving with them?"

"Whatever," he said, sighing. "Why not? Free food."

His cavalier attitude wasn't convincing, and I felt a pang of sympathy. There was a longing beneath his dismissiveness. I went to the Shirzais's Thanksgiving because it was an occasion of warmth, an affirmation of acceptance.

My own family had never embraced the holiday, proclaiming that "Chinese people hate turkey" (not untrue—for a culture that perfected the art of baking fatty duck to a delectable crisp, a turkey was alarmingly large and dry), so I loved the idea of immigrants taking on this very American ritual. Whom you spend Thanksgiving with means something. I wanted to be that meaningful to the Shirzais. Why was Mohib going?

Thanksgiving dinner proceeded as expected in most ways, the now-familiar rituals: Maiwand carving the turkey and walking around in an apron to receive compliments, the many family members and guests staking out corners of the family room or sitting on the carpet for lack of chairs, Daoud making his usual late entrance and early departure.

Mamoy, and her daughters Sarasa and Mina, had decided to stay at their own house and eat there—this surprised me. The showdown with Mohib had become a sore topic between the three of them and the uncles. Mamoy, though upset by Mohib's behavior, refused to openly express disapproval or denounce him. Daoud and Maiwand thought she was being too soft with him. Mamoy, Sarasa, and Mina were all close to the woman whom had been picked to be Mohib's intended. They were unhappy that the uncles had misled her, getting her hopes up.

No one mentioned Mamoy and her daughters' absence. I wondered if they had just wanted to avoid a scene with Mohib in front of the uncles.

Throughout dinner, Mohib didn't speak much to his uncles. Maiwand tried to bring up the topics of his apartment—"Are you getting lots of 'peace and quiet' in your new place?"—and his mother—"You should call her more. She's upset you're not living with her." Instead of answering, Mohib immediately and silently skulked to the kitchen to get another helping of food.

After dinner, I helped with the dishes, as the women congregated in the kitchen. Then I migrated to the living room, where the men were discussing world affairs over tea. As I walked in, I noticed that Mohib was not with the men. Curious, I kept walking around to the family room, where he was playing with four-year-old Aisha, Maiwand's daughter—and the only member of the family who wasn't riding him about his decision to move out.

"Let's go," he said.

"What?" I said. "It's too early."

"No it's not. This is boring. Let's go."

Aisha left. She must have recognized there could only be one person acting like a four-year-old per room.

"It's rude to leave this early," I said. "And I'm not bored."

He glared at me.

"It's my car!" I said, louder than I had planned.

Without missing a beat, he yelled back, "Well, it's my family!"

As I drove him home, we wound out of the fir-lined cul-de-sac in which his uncles lived, and rolled down a dimly lit boulevard alongside the Willamette River, the waters dark and roiling after a week of nonstop rain. My Honda Civic was the only car on the road. As the latticework of Portland's bridges came into view, I veered onto side streets, through the concrete anonymity of an industrial district, down Southwest Broadway to his downtown apartment. Illuminated by energy-efficient street lamps, the brick building looked more charming than worn-down.

The farther we got from Uncle Maiwand's house, the lighter Mohib's mood became. He started smiling again. "Why do you like my family so much more than I do?" he teased. "I guess they can be nice enough when they're not judging you."

Again, with the judging. He was right. It was one major thing that rendered me distinct from family members.

"I guess they don't have anything to judge me on," I said, not knowing what else to say.

"I could change that," he said.

What did he mean, *I could change that?* What a strange thing to say. I was just glad he was no longer combative.

But I should have asked. Like so many things when it came to Mohib, I let it slide.

৵

So was that what he was thinking about when, at his apartment, he called me into the kitchen with that oddly raw voice?

"Angie—come here for a second."

I was curious about, drawn to, the changed quality of his voice.

I found him standing in the doorway to the kitchen. His wide frame filled the space. The hallway felt tiny, as if its walls and ceiling were pressing me toward Mohib. There was no beer in his hand.

I stepped forward. He did too and I was stumbling into his broad chest, nowhere else to go. I steadied myself by hooking my arm around his back and grabbing his shoulder from behind. His warm hand nestled in the small of my back.

He was not much taller than me, and our faces were now millimeters apart. My head filled with the musky citrus scent of his cologne, followed by the coolness of his breath. It smelled like peppermint, not beer. He had gotten a breath mint in the kitchen. This was not an accident.

I pictured myself doing sensible things: giving him a gentle but decisive push, or a cinematic slap in the face. But I was still there, not moving against the solid warmth of the embrace that was now sliding up on me, his hot, surprisingly soft palms on the back of my sweater-clad arms —tentative at first, then more forceful when I didn't object or move away. I felt pressure on my arms, those hands pulling me in ever so slightly. I studied the whorls in the worn hardwood floor, black on tan. I knew what happened when you looked men in the eye in situations like these.

Do something. Pull away. Or just let him kiss you.

Then he exhaled gently, let go of my arms, and pulled me in for a bear hug, allowing my face to find his shoulder. I sighed. This felt familiar. We had done this before—when we hugged hello or goodbye, though I had pushed him away once when he tried to do it in front of Mamoy.

So nothing had happened tonight except that we hugged in the hallway.

I let myself fall a bit into his arms. His cashmere sweater invited me to press my cheek a bit more into his shoulder. Mohib pulled me closer, harder, his hands stroking my back, his minty breath in my hair, which was loose around my shoulders.

"Oh, Angie," he said, his voice catching on the back of his throat. Was he going to cry? He was shaking his head, his face in my hair. "I'm so fucked up."

He was actually admitting this. Or was he trying to make me feel sorry for him? Because it was working.

"No, no you're not," was all I could think of to say.

Then, gently, he caught the base of my skull, lacing his fingers in my hair with one hand, and looked at me in the eye.

"Please," he said. I liked his voice when he wasn't being cocky. His baritone was a touch throaty, with that barely detectable accent. "Let me kiss you. Just once."

I imagined saying the word no, tongue touching the roof of my mouth, lips parting. Nothing happened. Don't look at him, I commanded myself.

"Just once," he repeated. "And I'll never do it again. I swear."

This is the last moment I can stop this from happening. His heavy-lidded eyes looked beautiful—an amber glow escaping from behind dark brown. The last four years of my knowing the family seemed contained in that light. I felt loved, not necessarily by Mohib himself, but by him as an extension of the whole family—because I was included, because I was trusted.

In Afghanistan, I had realized what was theirs not mine: the secrets, the grief, and even the men, like Asad. Now, something of theirs—Mohammed's only son—was offering to be mine, if only for a moment. For all that my attraction to Asad had been mired and mediated in cultural subtleties and family politics, Mohib's desire was blind and urgent. It existed completely outside of culture and family. Asad was the Shirzais's good son; Mohib was the bad son. For the former, America was a long hoped-for threshold of opportunity; for the latter, it was a playground of forbidden indulgences and paths to rebellion. I had been drawn to both of these first cousins, for different reasons—though the one thing they had in common, as far as I was concerned, was that my attraction to either of them could jeopardize my relationship with the whole family.

But in this moment in the hallway, Mohib was handsome, and his ardor a force field around him, like his cologne—sweet but insistent. He was fucked up; I somehow wanted to take part in and prevent his self-destruction at the same time. This felt perverse, which made me a bit fucked up too, which made me just want to stop thinking so much.

Then the softness and fullness of his lips on mine felt as inevitable as everything else—meeting the family, becoming intertwined into their lives, going to Afghanistan, sharing Thanksgiving with them, and, eventually, trespassing against them. I melted into all of it, into the sweet belonging, into the weight of the secrets shared with me, and into the sting of betraying the family. The kiss was all of these things: belonging, betrayal, and now, another secret. And it was everything a single kiss that is promised to never happen again should be: lingering, not too assertive, sensual without being fall-into-bed sexual, riddled with unspoken guilt, and utterly forbidden.

I pulled away and looked at in his eyes again. The light in them had changed. Gratitude or apology? The hallway around me was askew. From where I was, I could see one of the wine paintings—the one with the bulbous red-wine glass and a splash of scarlet liquid in it.

The opposite of *halal*—the Muslim term for permissible, kosher—was *haram*—forbidden. Now I, like the wine, become another one of Mohib's transgressions, one more way in which he lashed out against his family. And as for me, what had I done, if not lashed out at them too, bitten the hand that literally had fed me tonight? *No. You did it to be closer to them,* that perverse part of me said. It whispered lines from Rumi to me: *Don't look away. Keep your gaze on the bandaged place. That's where light enters you.*

Something would change now with the Shirzais. Or would it? I suddenly felt paranoid, like the world as I knew it, everything I had built with all of the Shirzais, would fall apart tomorrow. *I could change that*—a threat on Mohib's part? Had he planted a trap, just waiting to tell his uncles I was not who they thought I was? I would be blamed, and shamed, as an immoral saboteur, an unwelcome interloper. My thoughts spiraled to worst-case scenarios, as if I were on Lariam. But I hadn't had a milligram of it in my body for a year and a half now. My breath was shallow, my chest tight. I wrested myself away from Mohib's arms and blindly, clumsily headed for the door.

"You don't have to go," he said, his voice a whimper.

He extended an arm to hug goodbye, like he always did, his face sheepish. We're still pals, see? No harm done.

I leaned over to give him a quick one-armed hug and as I pulled away, he turned his head and kissed me again. I hesitated for a moment, then leaned into his mouth, hoping for what was good about the first one. His right hand slid under my sweater. I inhaled sharply, breath returning to me now. I did not pull away. The pads of his fingers were barely touching my side; his palm hovered over my ribs, heat radiating onto my skin. I pictured the molecules of myself in contact with the molecules of him. His hesitation was strangely endearing; yet those five points of contact felt as if they were on fire. *Just put your hand on me, damnit.* But then the wine glass swam into my vision.

I guess they don't have anything to judge me on.

I could change that.

"I can't," I said, pulling away and looking him straight in the eye. "This can't happen again."

"I'm sorry," he said, like a child. "I just don't want you to go right now. Please stay. I won't . . . "

I shook my head.

As I turned, he reached for my shoulder. *Don't stop,* I told myself. *Leave.* From behind me, he gently slipped a thick arm over my shoulder and dropped his face into it.

"I need you," he whispered into my neck. It sounded neither romantic nor sexual. He was the Shirzai family's bandaged place. *Don't look away,* Rumi had said.

Cold sweat beaded on my face, and my legs were shaky. I slipped out from under his arm, as if he were asleep and I didn't want to wake him. *Do not look back at him.* I fumbled around for my purse and coat, zipped on my boots, and walked out the door, letting it slam shut, solid and heavy. Alone in the musty hallway, I felt bad. Had I overreacted? Was it unkind to leave him when he clearly was feeling vulnerable? I didn't have a right to storm out in a huff when I had not exactly resisted. I had been as guilty as he was—maybe more, since I was supposed to be the one who was less "fucked up." The one who sympathized with his family's pain at his secrets, his indiscretions—which now included me.

When the cool air hit me, it felt sharp, not refreshing. Why had I gone out in late November without a heavier coat? I drove on the empty streets, on the slight incline up seedy Burnside Boulevard, just cops and taxicabs still on the streets, to my neighborhood. All the quaint coffee shops and boutiques were dark inside, closed for the holiday. I couldn't shake the feeling that something had been damaged.

That painted wineglass, how unbalanced it seemed on its fragile stem, how ready to tip and shatter it was. One sip of wine left in it. And then I started thinking of Mohib, of that brief golden light in his eyes, how good his lips had felt, his fingertips burning into my bare side as I ached to lean into his touch . . .

No. He was just a spoiled child who had seen me as an accessory to rebellion. He resented my uncomplicated closeness to his family. And he had found the ultimate slap in the face to his family.

The worry that somehow the uncles, especially Daoud, would find out about this, gnawed at me. But it was unlikely Mohib would say anything to them. What would he have to gain from that? And he was hardly talking to them as it was. What had changed, what had been damaged, was in my own mind: I could no longer see my connection to the Shirzais as unmarred and pure, if it had ever been. They were as flawed and messy as my own family was, and I had just stepped over the barrier that would allow me to remain uninvolved with the mess. I was, in some twisted way, taking sides.

That's where light enters you, the Rumi poem whispered.

Mohib had pleaded for me to stay with that boy's voice, a wounded voice. What was he doing now, alone and sad in his apartment on Thanksgiving night? Drinking? Crying? Calling one of his girlfriends?

As I drove on the empty streets, my cell phone pinged—he had sent me a text message. He's going to ask me not to say anything to his family, I thought.

Yr lips so soft. Happy Thksgiving!

"Huh!" I said out loud, alone in my car. But, in my rearview mirror, I caught myself smiling.

15.
Departures

I almost told Laila about my encounter with Mohib, about the kiss, about how I slipped out before anything else happened. In that winter of 2005, she and I had become even closer, drawn together by the growing weight of her own secret: Tim. My confession about Mohib had been on the tip of my tongue more than once, but Laila's own conundrum had become urgent and all-consuming. More than once she had told me she had stopped talking to Tim, who had moved back to Colorado for law school. Laila said she had seen the fruitlessness of their relationship and it was just too painful to keep talking to him, knowing he was impatient and needed to move on with his own life as well. Then the mutually enforced silence would take hold and Laila would be restless and miserable for weeks, months even. Then one day, she'd casually drop into our conversation that Tim had told her this, or Tim had joked about that—and I'd raise an eyebrow and she'd smile back at me guiltily. Laila wasn't capricious, quite the opposite. Unlike some women, she found no enjoyment in the ups and downs of their relationship, particularly because they were not based on lovers' quarrels or other romantic dramas.

For Laila, the dilemma was as impassable as a compound wall in Afghanistan: If she wanted her family's love and approval, she had to cut Tim out of her life. If she wanted the only life partner with whom she had ever been able to envision herself, she would lose her family. Had someone asked whether she would like to have either her heart or her lungs removed—would she rather live without blood in her veins, or without air to breathe?—the choice would not have been any easier.

"Look," she said to me once, in a coffeeshop between our offices where we liked to meet in the afternoons. "It's not like I'm playing out some kind of romantic fantasy for kicks or out of infatuation." She pled her case as if I were one of the uncles.

"The thing is, they would tell me that I was taught that you only get this close to one person in your life, the person you're going to marry, the person you know is right for you to have a life with," she said, gripping her steaming paper cup of black tea. She had oversteeped the tea bag and the liquid was murky, opaque. "And I would tell them, 'You're right. This *is* that person. I didn't ask for him not to be Afghan or Muslim. I didn't choose that.'"

We were both silent after that. She looked away, but I knew without seeing that her eyes were wet behind her glasses. She put her tea down, undrunk, and said she had to get back to work. It landed with a loud thunk in the garbage can on her way out.

On his part, Tim seemed to be stepping up his own campaign; though he was in Colorado, he found excuses to be in Portland more often. I never really knew how they managed to keep up their long-distance, sometimes intermittent, relationship over the years. Laila talked about it in a perpetual present tense: We're talking on the phone every day. He is in town for a while, checking out clerking jobs for the summer, and we are meeting for lunch. Then, a month or two later: I am no longer talking to him. I just don't see a way. I can't tell my uncles. He's upset with me. He wants me to just tell them.

Not wanting to outright lie to Maiwand, but scared to tell him, Laila would make little effort to hide her phone conversations, or casually drop a mention about meeting her college "friend" Tim for lunch when he happened to be in town. Maiwand stated to pry more, about Laila's long late-night phone conversations, about how distracted she seemed lately. And he dropped hints about some nice husband candidates in the Afghan American community.

The more I was drawn into Laila's conundrum, the more frustrated I felt on her behalf. Yet I couldn't see a way out, either. Like a good girlfriend, I vented some frustration at Tim, whom I did not know: "How can he insist that you just tell your uncles? Does he know your uncles? It's not that simple."

During one of his visits, Laila suggested that Tim and I meet. We agreed to have lunch downtown. I was nervous all of the sudden. I had gotten used to Tim being an abstract concept, Laila's secret. I had been at Maiwand's house when he ribbed Laila about her always being on the phone, or dropped a mention of a new Afghan family in town that had a son her age. Strangely, for all that the idea of Tim had become ever-present, I had never imagined actually interacting with Tim the real man. None of the uncles had, obviously. I had already shown my support of Laila's wishes, as impossible as they might have seemed, by being her confidante. But meeting with the two of them felt oddly conspiratorial, yet another one of the growing number of secrets I had to keep from the uncles.

Then I wondered if Tim and I would have anything to talk about, if he might wonder why I was so close to Laila's uncles—they were his nemeses, in a way. I met Laila and Tim in the waiting area of a Chinese restaurant Laila had chosen. Laila was in her workday uniform of slacks and a button-up shirt; Tim echoed her with khakis and a striped button-up shirt of his own. In my mind, as Laila's preoccupation with the relationship grew, so had my mental picture of Tim's proportions. By then, I had imagined him as a tall, hulking man, taking up as much physical space as he did psychic space. So it was shock to see that he was compactly built and a bit bookish, wearing glasses in a way that made them seem integral to his appearance—like Laila. For being so different on the surface—American vs. Afghan, fair vs. dark, lapsed Catholic vs. faithful Muslim—they were surprisingly alike, a matched set. Salt and pepper shakers.

As we took our seats, Tim leaned forward, chopsticks poised, and began asking questions. "So," he said, blue eyes wide with anxious energy behind his wire-rimmed glasses. "What is Daoud really like? I mean, is he really scary one-on-one? Was he really different in Afghanistan than he was in Portland?"

I gave him my best descriptions and anecdotes. I told him about that first car ride with Daoud, how fast he drove, how the tires squealed as he whipped into the church parking lot. Then how he commanded the audience's full attention at the speech. And how he softened, became more vulnerable, in Kabul. Tim soaked this all in, rapt. Laila looked on, quiet, giving Tim his moment.

As our soup arrived, Tim continued: "What about Maiwand? He's a really interesting guy, huh? Sort of western and Afghan at the same time." Then he asked about Yusuf.

As the main courses came out, accompanied by steaming bowls of rice, Tim asked about Shinzmaray, about Amina, Jumagul, Fahima. Laila sat next to him, a small smile on her face. Sometimes, when I said something funny or when Tim gasped in surprise, the two of them exchanged a glance like a private joke was passing between them. They sat close to each other, but not too close—a holdover from Laila's habitual wariness of an accidental sighting by Uncle Daoud when they were classmates and secret sweethearts at Mt. Tabor College. She occasionally chimed in, agreeing with my observations, but was content to sit back and let Tim satiate his curiosity.

Then it occurred to me. To me, all of these people were flesh and blood, as real as—lately, even real more than—my own family members. To Tim, they were character sketches, figments of his and Laila's collective constructions through their many conversations. He longed to know them because he loved Laila; but he could not even meet them precisely because he loved Laila. He knew Mina, Sarasa, and Mohib, as well as Laila's brothers, at least in passing, because they had all gone to college together. But other than Mina, who had there for the start of Laila and Tim's relationship in a survey class for underclassmen, Laila kept the others arm's length from Tim. She did not want them to slip and tell the uncles. My presence here was not just another secret; it was a sign of Laila's trust.

"Wow, sometimes I feel like I know these people because Laila talks about them so much," Tim said, sitting back out of his forward lean for the first time. "But you're so close to all of them."

Envy? How easy it had been for me to befriend the Shirzais, to earn their trust, to gain such insight into Laila's family and life. By the time our fortune cookies arrived and Tim chivalrously grabbed the bill, there was an uncanny solidarity between us. Tim didn't resent my closeness to Laila's family, as I had feared; he started talking about "we," as in he and I, the interlopers who wanted an "in" to the Shirzais. I was possibly the only outsider who could give him nearly as much insight into the family as Laila could. I made the Shirzais more real, three-dimensional, to him. For Laila, I affirmed the things she had been telling Tim for all these years about her family.

But now what? Laila clearly loved Tim, but she had yet to tell her uncles, despite their suspicions and hints.

Tim handed the small plate of fortune cookies to Laila, and then me. He broke open his own. "Good things come to those who wait," he read from his, "But great things come to those who act."

He raised his eyebrows at Laila. She read hers: "Three people can keep a secret if two of them are dead."

We laughed, looking at each other.

"That's not even a real fortune," she said. "It's a saying. I hate it when they don't actually tell you anything about your future."

"But maybe it *is* telling you about your future," Tim said. She narrowed her eyes at him. She didn't want to be reminded that she should *just tell her uncles*. Not now.

By the time we said goodbye on the sidewalk outside, any residual tension was gone. We were joking about an approaching pack of aggressively hipster Portlanders, complete with tattoos, piercings, and unwashed, ironically corporate T-shirts: "Have a Coke and a Smile." "WalMart: Always Low Prices." "Dow: Better Living Through Chemistry."

"Let me guess," Tim said loudly to them. "You're law school students? Future corporate litigators?"

They looked at him incredulously, and then turned away, mumbling and scoffing.

Tim grinned, then turned to me and hugged me, his wiry frame slight but strong.

"Thank you," he said, softly. "Laila feels alone in all this sometimes. I'm glad you're here."

Laila chuckled, like we were scheming teenagers who had gotten away with something.

"It's nothing," I said, sharing the laugh. A crisp breeze ruffled the branches of the trees above us, the air alive with vibration. Tim was not laughing, though.

"No," Tim said, turning to look me in the eye. "It's everything."

Unprepared for the weight of his gratitude, I looked away, at Laila. For the first time during that lunch, she touched him, her fingertips barely resting on his upper arm. She barely caught my eye as she swept her gaze downward, the way I had seen the family's younger women express gratitude to Amina or Mamoy.

So I'd become complicit to Laila's deepening, forbidden relationship. I *had* taken sides.

Just as with Mohib, I had been reluctant to think of Daoud and Maiwand's stance on their nieces and nephews' relationships as anything but well intentioned, maybe misunderstood. But as time went on, and I saw the toll their rigidity took on Mohib and on Laila, whose life stalled in an agonizing holding pattern as she wavered between her love for Tim and her fear of losing her uncles—her de-facto parents. My actions were speaking louder than my thoughts.

Laila had never asked me to take her side. I just did. I wanted her to be happy, to be independent—like I was raised to be.

I knew then that I was doing far more than just listening to Laila, just meeting Tim for lunch. I was intrinsically involved in something profound, another sort of transgression far deeper than kissing Mohib—something that could change the Shirzai family forever.

As Laila's dilemma over her uncles and Tim became more pressing, she became more intrigued by Daoud's past, speculations about his own relationships. The nieces and nephews held him in such high regard, they only spoke of them in whispers. Or, in the case of Mohib, with vague bitterness that suggested Daoud was hypocritical. They mentioned his "girlfriends," but offered few specifics and didn't seem confident that the women were indeed romantic interests. Even back in Kabul, Nazo had asked me—looking around the corner to make sure neither her uncle nor any of the English speakers in the house were in earshot—"Do you know anything about *Ustad*'s wife?"

"Wife?" I said, skeptical. I wasn't even sure I believed the whisperings about girlfriends.

"*Ustad* was married once, I heard. A long, long time ago. Our grandfather arranged the marriage with a girl from the village while he was away at school," Nazo said, delighted at my shock. In my first interview with Daoud, he had told me he was not married. He didn't tell me he had *never* married.

"They never met. They had the ceremony," Nazo said, meaning that they married by proxy, with a stand-in for Daoud, "and then she died before he came home."

I kept quiet, taking it all in, waiting to see what else Nazo would reveal.

"I heard," she whispered, leaning so close to me I could feel a stray curl brushing my face, "she saw a picture of Daoud at school, with another woman, and she died of a broken heart."

"What?" I said. "How do you know this?"

"Everyone in the family talks about it," Nazo said. "But not in front of *Ustad*. But you, you should ask him. When you . . . how do you call it? Interview."

I shook my head. Nazo had, with this whispered revelation, brought me into the circle of "everyone in the family." Suddenly I wasn't sure I wanted to know everything. Why had the nieces and nephews chosen to remain somewhat in the dark about Daoud's past relationships? Surely they could have found out if they had really wanted. I had written in my stories that he was unmarried, with no children of his own, working for his country and adopted family. I had written that he was "monastic," thinking back to his volunteer work as a janitor in the church homeless shelter. I wasn't ready to let go of that word and revise the story, even in my own head. I needed Daoud to be on a pedestal, the same way the nieces and nephews did.

"Ask him," Laila said, back in Portland, after I had told her what Nazo revealed to me. It did not surprise Laila, but she said no one really knew the whole story because they were afraid to ask. "And ask about the girlfriends," she said, playful. But I could tell she wanted to know. "It's so much easier for you to ask him things than it is for us. Just bring a notebook and tell him it's for a story."

"I can't," I said. "Where would I even begin with that? And what kind of story would I say I was writing?"

"Surely, the *National Enquirer* is looking for some fresh material," Laila said, grinning. "I think I met some of his 'girlfriends,' though he would never introduce them that way.

"And they were definitely not Afghan."

I had picked up on this as the nieces and nephews made insinuations. But to hear Laila confirm this, I wondered: How could Daoud object to

Laila's relationship with Tim if he had also had relationships with non-Afghan women?

Unlike Mohib, who resented what he saw as Daoud's double standard, Laila had always made it clear she harbored no bitterness about any of the uncles' choices. She was simply curious—and perhaps hopeful that if Daoud had had non-Afghan girlfriends, he just might be a bit more empathetic about her relationship with Tim.

I did have a chance to ask Daoud, about his brief marriage at least, a couple months later when I was fact-checking a magazine article I had finished long ago, but was just coming up for publication. It had been about his work in Afghanistan. I had written in the draft version that he was "not married, without children of his own"—though I had stopped using "monastic" as a descriptor. As we sat in our usual spots in his narrow Mt. Tabor office, I read the first phrase out loud to him, to which he nodded his agreement.

"But not 'never married'?" I said, sounding as casual as I could.

"No, no, not 'never,' " he said, almost lightly. "You can say I didn't have children and that I'm not married now."

I looked over my notebook at him, waiting, hoping, for him to elaborate.

"You probably heard I was married once, only briefly," he said.

I nodded, just barely.

"I never knew her," he said. "She died before I had a chance to return to Shinzmaray."

Then he told the story, much as Nazo had told it—his father had arranged the marriage while he was away at college. He wrote back, telling his father he wasn't ready. But the next letter came, telling him the marriage ceremony had happened by proxy. A photo of his wife, and a letter from her—she was one of the few women in the village who could write—was enclosed.

"I wanted nothing to do with it," Daoud said. And, with the guilt and pride of a truant student: "So I didn't go home. I went to Europe that summer and hitchhiked all over with my friends. We were all international students—an Arab, a Nigerian, and me." He smiled slightly, the smile of a younger man, and said that they had stayed in Switzerland a while, after befriending some young women. "I stayed in one of their homes. It was a very nice family," he recalled.

I imagined him—the movie-star-handsome version of him from that graduation portrait in Shinzmaray. I imagined the young Daoud and his male friends, standing on the side of a road in the Alps. The idea was so alluringly out of sync with the man before me that the storyteller in me couldn't resist the contradiction. The woman in me was thrilled by the image of those three men, rucksacks at their feet, laughing, confident, and darkly exotic to passersby. The Swiss girls never stood a chance.

Did Mohib know about this? Did he realize that he and Daoud were more alike than he imagined? Mohib, running away from an arranged marriage that felt forced on him—hadn't Daoud done the same? *Do as I say and not as I did.*

After young Daoud returned to school, he received a letter from his father. His wife, it said, had fallen ill. "I don't know what it was. We didn't really know anything back then. People got suddenly sick and died all the time," he said. "I do recall she had jaundice. They said she turned yellow before she died.

"I didn't know her. I had met her once, I think, when we were younger, just in passing. My impression was that she was nice," Daoud said.

"Did you feel sad?" I said.

"Of course," he said. "I felt sad the way I do when anyone dies young and unnecessarily, which happened too often there. I'm sure had she been here, they could have saved her."

He paused. I pointed out the obvious: His life would have been different had he married.

He nodded. Of course. He did think about marrying after that, at times.

"There were relationships," he said, carefully but without hesitation. "I don't know—what else do you want to know?"

Suddenly, a world of possibility opened up. All of the questions that surely Nazo, Laila, and the others would have wanted me to ask. All the things I wanted to know—who were these women? What were they like? What did they look like? What made him *think* of marriage, and why did he not marry again? Did he ever want children of his own? Did he ever feel lonely?

He glanced over at the copy of my story draft and my notebook. I hadn't made a mark on either of them.

"Umm," I said, suddenly mute. I didn't need to know, not for the story. But did I want to know? Maybe not.

"I guess I have what I need for the story," I said. "I'll stick with 'not married.'"

Silence settled in. Daoud appeared to be studying some book titles on a shelf over my shoulder. But he knew every book in that office like the back of his hand. Was he disappointed that I didn't ask?

"You know," he said, "there are so many things I've done—the career, the Fulbrights, the speaking, the work in Afghanistan—the kind of life I've led, that would have been impossible if I had married. Marriage changes everything. Look at my brothers. I look at myself when I was in relationships. It's difficult."

I nodded, not wanting to break the spell of this uncharacteristic openness.

He sighed deeply, shook his head and smiled a close-lipped smile. His face suddenly lost its characteristic furrows and his eyes had a surprising glint to them. I saw the man in the graduation portrait in Shinzmaray.

He raised his eyebrows, looked me straight in the eye.

"Women," he said, with a sigh, "are demanding."

A sharp laugh escaped from me. I couldn't help it.

"Well, men are no picnic either," I threw back, surprising myself.

His eyebrows went higher. Now, he was speechless.

࿇

"What else do you want to know?" Laila practically yelled at me. "He asked you what else you wanted to know?"

She couldn't believe I hadn't gotten Daoud to divulge more. "How he met them? Why they broke up? Whether he told *his* parents and uncles? What about some names and email addresses?"

But I knew that, like me, Laila would not have asked Daoud for more, and certainly would not have emailed anyone even if he had given the addresses. The truth was, Daoud rarely even talked to Laila about anything remotely concerning Tim or her marital future. That responsibility fell to Maiwand, who had started prying about Laila's phone conversations:

"Another two-hour conversation, huh?" "You were up awfully late last night, talking on the phone, weren't you?" "Why do you always close the door and whisper when you talk on the phone? Are you making drug deals or something?" Maiwand would crack a smile, like he was joking, when he made these queries. But there was an edge to his voice, and he never asked whom she was talking to. It was like he didn't want to know the answer—or he already knew the answer, and wished he didn't.

Laila knew the situation as it was could not continue—she would either have to come clean about Tim, soon, or break up with him. It had been seven years since they first met, nearly six since they first became romantically involved. He was ready to face the family and tell them he wanted to marry her. She thought he had no idea what he was up against. And she didn't know what she would do if her family, as predicted, forbade her from marrying him—then she would be forced to choose. At least by keeping him secret, she could imagine a future time when her family would become more understanding, when they might see a way for her to be with Tim.

Despite Laila's professed curiosity, I didn't expect Daoud to give me another chance to ask him about women. But Portland was the kind of place where if someone had seen her ex in a magazine article, she probably knew someone who knew the journalist who had written that article. And that was how I came to be introduced to Julia, not long after that conversation with Daoud, and the publication of the story. Of course, she had no way of knowing he and I had just talked about his past relationships—she hadn't spoken to him in years. It was just a coincidence.

Julia sent word through our mutual friend that she wanted to meet with me. She didn't have any bad feelings, she wanted me to know; she just thought it would be interesting to reflect on a long-past part of her life. I wondered if I should. I didn't tell Laila, or anyone else, about the offer. But ultimately, my curiosity got the better of me.

Neither Julia nor I ever acknowledged it, but we met with each other for the same reason: Daoud. We both wanted to know more about him, things about him that we, for entirely different reasons, could not easily find out. I wanted to know more about his past, and she about his present. We were both trying to understand something about ourselves by better understanding him. In different ways, Daoud had been an elusive center of gravity in each of our lives.

I met Julia at a restaurant in a recently gentrified North Portland neighborhood where none of the Shirzais ever hung out. She was sitting at the bar, a slim hand wrapped around a vodka tonic, when I arrived. My pulse pounded in my ears. How would we begin this conversation? What would she think of me? Would she tell me something I didn't want to know?

She appeared to be a few years, not much, younger than Daoud. She was small and trim, her short, straight hair in a lemony shade that framed her small face. She wore little makeup, but the tailored cut of her black pantsuit let on that she paid attention to her appearance. Her large pale-blue eyes studied me. We scrutinized each other, unabashedly.

I proceeded with the niceties of a first-meeting conversation. I told her about my journalism career; she told me she worked as an office manager for an architecture firm, using the income and fairly regular hours to feed her other passions—travel, reading, learning. She still took classes on topics that interested her whenever possible.

"That's how I met him, you know," she said, her robin's-egg eyes startling me with their directness. "I had to count to figure it out—it was almost thirteen years ago."

A local left-leaning community center had been hosting classes on international issues with local academics. She had taken Daoud's class on Middle East policy. She was impressed by—in awe of, really—his capacious mind, how easily he drew upon facts and theory, weaving dates and statistics with Noam Chomsky and Edward Said, in free association. The passion with which he conveyed information, as if somehow his words and thoughts could alter the course of world events. They started meeting outside of class, and then the relationship started. I should have asked her how: How did you know? Who made the first move? Did the transition to intimacy happen in a matter-of-fact conversation over coffee, or in a frantic, fumbling trail of clothing between an apartment door and a bed? But these questions were beyond my courage to ask, the answers beyond my willingness to know.

He had told her from the beginning—like that voice that reads the drug warnings on pharmaceutical commercials —that he was not interested in marriage or a permanent relationship. *Those with pre-existing hopes for a husband or commitment should not take this man.* She went in eyes wide open. He gave what he could, which was not a lot by conventional-relationship standards. "But it *felt* even," Julia said. He was honest, he was good to her when he could be, and she admired him greatly. He just couldn't be hers.

"I knew it was going to be that way from the beginning," she said. "And it was OK. But ... "

She poked at her half-eaten steak. "Well, you're a woman. You know."

I did, and I didn't—that is, I understood what she was talking about, that innate need to be loved wholly despite all caveats to the contrary. But I, like Daoud, had also put up barriers in my own relationships.

Ultimately, though, I had no context to apply these ideas about womanhood and love to Daoud, to imagine him as her lover, or as anyone's. I began to hope that she would change the subject.

So I did, sort of. "Did you meet the nieces and nephews?" I said.

"Meet? I saw them all the time," she said, her cool eyes becoming warm. "How are they? They must be so—adult by now."

She winced and brought a hand to her brow. "The nieces, they were so sweet, so beautiful—what were their names? I can't believe I've forgotten them."

I reminded her, and gave her a brief update—college, graduate school, and jobs—on Sarasa, Mina, and Laila.

"And the oldest boy? The older brother to the two girls?"

I told her Mohib was working and in law school now.

"I taught him to drive, you know," she said. "I spent a lot of time with those kids. To them, I was a 'friend' of their uncle's, but I think they knew."

"They did, pretty much," I said.

I teased her about Mohib's driving. "He's a bit of a crazy driver nowadays. I'm not sure what you taught him."

"That boy," she said, shaking her head, "from the moment I met him I knew he wanted—what—to be American."

She recalled taking him on the freeway for the first time in her compact four-cylinder Ford, and Mohib immediately floored the accelerator, like he was speeding away from the expectations placed upon him.

"Daoud really, really cared about those kids," she said, her tone shifting. "They meant everything to him. I sometimes think he used his responsibility to them to prevent me from getting too close."

"But he allowed you to get close to them," I said.

"I was close to them. Especially the girls," she said. Sarasa, Mina, and Laila had arrived in the United States at the cusp of their teenage years, she explained. They were so eager, hungry, for some idea of how to become a woman in this strange new environment. Julia let them try on, and sometimes keep, dresses she had made for herself; she was careful only to offer them longer ones that would pass the uncles' "modesty test." The girls soaked up her attention. Julia had never had or wanted children, but this role came naturally to her.

This, I realized later, was also how the uncles ensured the girls could navigate the tricky terrain of their teenage years. Between Daoud and Maiwand, a handful of non-Afghan female "friends" came in and out of their lives during that time. Since there was no way either uncle could help the girls buy their first bras or show them what to do when they started menstruating, the women took on these tasks. The nieces never asked questions; they accepted the "friend" narrative, and were relieved not to have to share these intimate rites of passage with their uncles.

"We were together a year and half," Julia continued. "Then I decided I needed more. We didn't part on bad terms at all. He understood."

But did you? I wondered.

She told me she had been living with a man for the last few years, and it was good relationship. She kept up with Daoud in the news, set up a Google Alert for his name—which was how she learned about me. She knew she could have contacted him, or even situated herself to run into him, but she never did. It was only after I had hugged her goodbye and our meeting had ended that it occurred to me she never asked me if I would tell Daoud about it. Maybe she already knew I wouldn't.

"Wow," Laila said when I confessed to her. "I remember her. She was around a lot, right after we arrived in America. She was really nice."

And, just like that, silence fell upon us. I waited for her questions, her admonitions that I should have gotten even more information. I wanted to hear Laila confirm that Julia had taken her bra shopping, had taught her about her period—I wanted the women "friends" to be given proper credit for this. But Laila said nothing, and I couldn't think of anything to offer her unsolicited. Between us, we were not ready to let go of Daoud as we needed him to be, as somehow more than a mere man. Above the selfish, rutting urges of the human world, be they the lusts for women or for war. Monastic.

⤞

When the six nieces and nephews first arrived in 1991, Daoud was living in a small white two-story house with Maiwand near Mt. Tabor. None of the uncles had any experience with childrearing. He sent Yusuf to pick them up at the Seattle Airport when they first arrived.

How must it have been, in those first days, with six tired, confused teenagers suddenly overtaking his small space? From bachelor academic to provider of shelter, food, clothes, education, and adaptation to a radically different culture for half a dozen twelve-to-seventeen-year-olds, overnight. They were intimidated by their uncle, one they had never known well, whom had been talked about like he was a legend. Surely they started out on their best behavior, but they were culture-shocked, hormonal, and unquestionably needy. American high school would be a minefield of bullying, ostracization, and temptations for new-immigrant students that Daoud wanted them to avoid. He had learned to read the Qur'an at age five, crossed the threshold out of Shinzmaray, gotten scholarships at top American universities, and become a full professor. But what in his experience had prepared him for this?

Like the parents of newborns, he and Maiwand went into survival mode for the next few months, triaging needs as they arose. Uncle Daoud was a terrible cook, the nieces and nephews recalled, but Maiwand got better over time, and took over the cooking, shopping, and domestic duties. Meanwhile, Daoud hired the after-school tutor, established strict rules, checked homework, and sat them down in front of Peter Jennings' nightly newscasts. Tired of explaining their unusual family situation to teachers and school administrators, when the nieces and nephews filled out school forms, they listed "Daoud Shirzai" under "father," and "Maiwand Shirzai" under "mother."

"Were you scared?" I asked Daoud once, about the arrival of the six.

He paused, thought about it. "No, not scared," he said. "Serious. I knew I had a serious responsibility to fulfill."

But he must have been scared, if only in spells. Maybe not in the chaos and activity of the days in that little white bungalow, when there were always tasks to be done, young minds to be shaped. But at night, when the house was quiet save the soft snores and breathing of six teenagers, when he fought exhaustion to prep a class or write an article, things for which he once had endless time. He must have thought about Mohammed, wondering if he could see traces of his late brother in his three children. Surely, he noticed Mina's long, straight nose and her habit of half-smiling with closed lips, a mirror image of her father. Maybe he had hoped to see more of Mohammed in Mohib, noticed the boy's restless nature, feared what might come. And it could not have escaped him that the three girls were on the verge of puberty. *That* must have terrified him.

He must have felt, most of all, lonely. Who in the world could know what it felt like to be in that house at night, so full of life, but so devoid of confidantes? Only mouths to feed, legacies to nurture, responsibilities to shoulder. Maiwand was there, but he was nearly twenty years younger than Daoud. They hadn't even grown up together. Daoud never would have admitted vulnerability to his much-younger brother. The two men bore their parental duties with stoicism, not acknowledging fear, weakness, or exhaustion, for the same reasons Kelley and I didn't acknowledge what was happening to our parents—to share in these admissions would be to make them real. By denying them, it was easier to soldier on.

I understood then why Julia must have been a welcome refuge for Daoud. A single, childless intellectual, as he had once been, she not only represented the life that he missed, but also a kindred spirit. Her closeness to, and appreciation for, the nieces and nephews, softened Daoud, helped him see what she did: That Mohib's rebellious kick could be charming, natural for a seventeen-year-old boy. That the girls were indeed transforming into women—self-possessed, interesting women. That what he was doing was not only important, but also beautiful and admirable. And what every parent wanted to know: that he was doing a good job.

಄

Soon, Daoud was preparing for another stint in Kabul. Laila threw herself into her final year of grad school, studying to get her Master's in

Education, Daoud's program at Mt. Tabor. Things with Tim cooled off a bit as they continued to disagree about whether Laila should tell her uncles about him. She just couldn't see a way to have both him and her family. There was a new sadness and hardness to her; it pained me to see it. At Maiwand's suggestion, she started going to coffee with an Afghan American friend of her brother's, a Pashtun. "He's OK," she said, shrugging her shoulders.

I dropped by Daoud's Mt. Tabor office with some gifts for him to deliver to Rochina and Nazo. Rochina was pregnant with her second child and I had wrapped up some baby clothes for her.

"Oh, good, these aren't heavy," he had said, testing the weight of the wrapped packages as he sat at his desk. "The family thinks I'm their pack mule or something, with all the gifts back and forth."

Things in Afghanistan were even worse, he said. Suicide bombings happened all the time. He had stopped working for the Afghan government, exhausted by the rampant corruption and ineffectualness. Now, his employer in Kabul was a non-profit center based out of an East Coast university. They insisted that he stay in Shar-e-Naw, Kabul's New City district where expats flocked. He would live in the center's compound just for American-based employees, instead of at his sister's, in the house he had purchased. He probably wouldn't see much of Amina, her family, or Grandma this time around.

"That's too bad that you can't stay in the Kabul house," I said, thinking of Daoud listening to the radio in the courtyard, Daoud stirring his instant coffee in the kitchen in the morning, Daoud shouting in Grandma's good ear.

"It's for the best, I think. This family is changing too," Daoud said. "I used to bring vitamins, medications, and blankets. Now my nephew is asking for a two-hundred-dollar baby monitor and designer shampoo."

He was referring to Rochina's husband. I laughed, but Daoud did not.

"And it's not just over there," he continued. "This family here is not what it once was."

He had not acknowledged this to me before. I thought of Mohib's anger, his apartment with the wine paintings; Mamoy's pain, how she and her daughters had stopped showing up at family events; Laila and Tim's uncertain future. And where was Yusuf? I hadn't seen him around the family in months. I had heard that his wife and Maiwand's wife weren't getting along with each other. And Daoud—he had sort of checked out. His appearances at family gatherings were briefer than ever, if they could even be called family gatherings anymore; usually there was just a subset of Shirzais who were still speaking to each other.

Lately, I had been so busy bouncing from household to household—Maiwand's, Mamoy's, Yusuf and his wife's—somehow keeping the Shirzais together in my head, that I hadn't noticed they were rarely together in the flesh anymore.

"This family," Daoud said, "is splitting into three parts."

I nodded. The rifts were clear. But where did that leave Daoud?

"And I—I have outlived my usefulness here," he said.

I began to protest, and Daoud lifted his hand slightly from the armrest of his chair to stop me. *But they do need you,* I wanted to say. *They ache for your approval.*

I had gone to that first Sunday dinner in order to see, as Maiwand said, "how family happens." I had been entranced by the family rituals, the ways in which Daoud, Maiwand, and the others sacrificed—their commitment to family above all else. I had wanted to be more like them, even fantasized that I could make my family more like theirs. Maiwand was right. It had taken four-plus years, not an evening, but I had seen how family happens, because of—and in spite of—the great love and unity of purpose I felt at that first dinner.

They were becoming more like my family. Maybe our two families were more alike from the start than I had wanted to admit. I wanted Daoud and the nieces and nephews to talk to each other, to realize how much they still mattered to each other. But the walls between them that could not be penetrated, how were these any different than those within my own family? I thought back to that afternoon in my father's garage, my plans to talk to him about his illness as I picked up those boxes. And how they all faded in the anaerobic air of my father's bitterness and my own fear of confronting him. My family's walls existed because of culture, habit, and because we knew tearing them down would hurt more than keeping them up. Were the Shirzais's any different?

Could I reconcile the Daoud I admired, with whom I had chats in this office, with the Daoud who was contributing to Mohib's nihilistic behavior, the intended fiancée's false hopes, Laila's seven years of conflicted limbo with Tim, and the Daoud who had never given Julia as much as she had given him? And could I reconcile the contradictions within myself, that I could admire Daoud, chat with him in this office, and kiss Mohib, support Laila in her secret relationship with Tim? Daoud seemed too preoccupied with other things to care whether I had gotten involved, taken a side; then again, maybe he assumed I was on his.

It had been easy for me to overlook Daoud's, and all of the Shirzais's, fault lines, to see them as I wanted them to be.

"I said I would adopt them until they turned eighteen, and then they were on their own," Daoud said. "Their lives are their own to lead now, for better or worse."

You know and they know that's not true. Why couldn't I bring myself to argue with him? After all these years, I still felt like he was the professor and I was the student. Or maybe, that he was like my father and I, his daughter. Even though my own father and I could not communicate these days, he *had* given me the gift of independence and self-sufficiency. Daoud was granted his own freedom—the freedom not to marry—through a combination of circumstance and willful self-determination. Didn't he want Laila to have the same ability to choose for herself, I wanted to ask? But of course I didn't. In any case, Daoud had made up his mind. Now, his project was Afghanistan instead of family.

Was he like me, detaching himself from the painful realities of a fractured family by getting on an airplane, taking on an assignment?

May cause emotional detachment.

"My brothers have their own families to worry about now," Daoud added. "And there are things—just things that can't be overcome. People are wounded and will not recover."

Was he referring to Mohib's choices? The arranged marriage? Or to Mohammed's death? Was Mamoy the wounded one? Or was Daoud referring to himself?

"So now I go to where I am needed—"

I was about to nod in agreement.

"—as a pack mule to bring two-hundred-dollar baby monitors and expensive shampoo for balding nephews."

He smiled. Just barely. But it was a relief, and I laughed.

"You know you're needed for more than that," I said.

"Perhaps," he said. "But in a country where the president needs American security just to stay alive, where I can't even go to my birthplace and see my own mother, live in my own house, where I have to live under lock-down to avoid getting kidnapped or blown to bits—what can I do?"

"You'll find out," I said.

"Yes. We shall see," he said with an air of finality.

He stood up, and I stood up. "Good luck," I said, shaking his extended hand. My throat felt tight all of the sudden. I was afraid I might cry. Did his resignation about the family's splintering, or the state of Afghanistan, sadden me?

Or was I afraid this was the last time I'd see him?

"I will see you back here in Oregon," he said, his voice catching on a slight chuckle, "or I will see you in heaven."

Part Five:
Jia / **Home and Family**

A poem, like a home, is a honeysweet burden
Where love desire pain sadness are housed, sameness and difference
accommodated

—Chen Li, "In the Out-of-the-Way Corners of Our Lives"

16.
Tribe

When I arrive in Taoyuan, I take a taxi from the airport to Grandma and Grandpa's high-rise apartment, chat with the doorman and remind him whose granddaughter I am, then ride the rickety elevator to the twelfth floor. I always find them staying up, waiting for me, no matter how late it is. Mom is always there before me, but it is *Wai Po* and *Wai Gong* who take over, who follow the same routine to greet me every time.

After that 2004 visit to Taiwan, the one following my Hong Kong job interview, Mom and I started planning annual, sometimes twice-yearly, trips there. After being estranged from my mother's birthplace for more than a decade, returning was like becoming reacquainted with a part of myself I didn't know was there. There was something about Taiwan: Chinese but not really mainland-Chinese; cities of glass and neon amid rain-stained tile-covered concrete buildings from an earlier era, grids of new and old; surrounded by water and with impassable mountains at its heart; tropical yet temperate; exotic yet familiar; its people a little pushy and a little friendly; Confucian, Buddhist, and yet secular. A nation founded on flight, on the dream of starting over—but at the expense of a long-marginalized aboriginal population. All of these dichotomies creating a precariously balanced tension that explained so much about me, my family, and the first- and second-generation American immigrants among whom I grew up. Our fluctuating, uneasy relationships with extroversion versus introversion, with spirituality and religion, with identifying with pre-Mao mainland Chinese culture but rejecting China's perception of Taiwan as a "Renegade Province."

Most of all, modern Taiwan was at ease with not knowing who or what it was. It was, by nature, a contradiction. Taiwan borrowed and improved by imitating, China, Japan, and most of all, the United States, both a paragon and a foil. There was pride, not shame, in near-copies, a tongue-in-cheek sense of humor in the close-but-not-copyright-infringing: The Gap became Net, with the same navy blue-and-white logo, with the same font, and even cheaper fashionable basics. KFC became KLC, in bold red and white, with fried-chicken buckets and a nudge-wink hope that maybe locals wouldn't know the difference between the middle letters. Starbucks became 85 C, named for the ideal temperature at which coffee should be served. In being like, and yet unlike, so many things, Taiwan became itself.

Sometimes, I felt inexplicable in America; returning here, I understood why.

The first minutes at *Wai Po* and *Wai Gong*'s always go like this: First, they want to feed me. "Have you eaten?" *Wai Po* asks after she enfolds me into her soft embrace. "Did they feed you on the plane? Are you hungry?" Every possible way she can ask about the state of my nourishment. Then she offers me an entire meal no matter what time it is. Pan-fried whole fish with garlic and ginger. Lightly sautéed Chinese greens, bearing the touch of her burnished, slightly dented wok which she refused to replace with a newer model. Rice, always rice—white, long grain, pillowy and slightly sticky out of a barrel-shaped rice cooker. In fact, the word "rice" and "meal" are synonymous in Mandarin and the Taiwanese dialect. "Have you eaten?" is asked, "Have you eaten rice / a meal?" *Wai Po* and *Wai Gong* speak to me in both dialects, alternating, though I only really understand Mandarin. Over time, I've learned their most-used phrases in Taiwanese, more than half of them having to do with food.

Then the fruit. Even if I steadfastly refuse dinner at, say, midnight, I must have some fruit. It is said that mainland Chinese make trips to Taiwan simply to eat the fresh tropical fruits: Guava, passionfruit, mangos, starfruit, the sweetest pineapples, custard apples, dragonfruit, lychees, bananas in shapes and sizes unseen in the United States. Fruits that don't even have English names, but whose flavors and textures spark flashbacks to my childhood visits as soon as they make contact with my tongue and palate. We never stop eating fruit in Taiwan, *Wai Po* slicing it for us, always sliding something in front of me and saying, "They don't have this in America, right?" Then, when we're out, Mom and I buy cut-up fruit from street vendors, walking and spearing it out of plastic bags with the long toothpicks provided—until we reach *Wai Po* and *Wai Gong's* house, only to be served more fruit.

As soon as the eating is done, Wai Gong wants to make tea from his perch in front of the television, where he stays up until the wee hours watching U.S. professional basketball games via satellite. He knows the stats of every team (translated literally into Chinese, the names become puzzling to me—The Lakers are "Lake People," the Heat "Hot Fire," the Spurs "Prick Horse") and all the star players. *Wai Gong's* Tea Shop, he calls it, in his booming voice. An elaborate tray with hot plates and liquid receptacles among multiple containers of fine Oolong teas, much higher-quality and more expensive than I ever drink in the United States. He brews the tea in traditional ceramic pots, waits just the right amount of steeping time, then transfers into a small jug just for pouring, and then into small glasses from which he also occasionally drinks Johnny Walker Black Label or Chivas Regal. The tea is redolent, so deeply amber and thick with flavor that I sometimes think I am drinking warm whiskey or scotch.

Wai Gong used to drink copious amounts of both, and was a committed smoker. Hours of Tai Chi in the morning after walking on a nearby mountain trail kept him healthy beyond credulity, his hair still black with a few streaks of silver, his complexion tan and unlined. In fact, on a much earlier visit, in college, my welcome was not tea, but a glass of Chivas with Grandpa, the alcohol hot and burning my throat as the taste, sweet and heavy, like tobacco, lingered. I flushed and felt slightly dizzy; *Wai Gong* poured himself another, slinging it down in a single gulp and a deep-throated grunt. "One more?" he'd say, teasing. Keeping up was not an option.

But now in his nineties, grayer and with more furrows in his face, Grandpa gave up smoking a long time ago, now does his daily Tai Chi in his room, and the last few bottles of his whiskey-and-scotch stockpile lay stashed around the house, to be used as gifts or for special occasions. He makes and serves tea with the same gusto that he used to pour liquor, enjoying the process, swirling the teapot to aid the steeping, the passing the glasses, and accepting everyone's admiration for the fine taste. I down cup and after cup of tea, *Wai Gong* proclaiming the Mandarin equivalent of Jumagul's welcome to Shinzmaray: "We drink a lot of tea here. I hope you can keep up."

Rice and tea. Cardamom-infused or leafy Oolong, moist and mounded in a ricebowl or fluffy and spread out as *pilau* across a platter—these two elements at the hearts of homes in Afghanistan and Taiwan. I had gone to Afghanistan, gotten close to the Shirzais, in part to escape my own family. But had I just been traveling the circumference of a circle, coming ever closer back to myself and my own roots?

In Taoyuan, after the tea, or the scotch, after the meal or fruit, Grandma would gently lay her hands on my forearms and point me in the direction of their Confucian shrine, made of solid polished rosewood, occupying an entire wall of the apartment, the altar constantly occupied with whatever fruit we were eating later that day or, when I arrived, whatever fancily boxed snacks I had bought on my layover at Hong Kong or Narita, not wanting to show up empty-handed. Eventually, everything on there would get eaten after doing time as offering. Food was never wasted.

The shrine had only two images: Guanyin, the bodhisattva of compassion, female, serenely beautiful, and of *Wai Gong's* mother, my devoutly Buddhist great grandmother whom I remembered from visits here before her death in 1995, in her late nineties from dementia. I face them, palms pressed together in front of me, and bow three times. "Make a wish," Grandma would whisper in my ear, with a smile, as she did when I was a child to make the act feel less alien, knowing that Mom and Dad did not raise us with these traditions.

In the act of prayer, I fill myself with thoughts of Guanyin, of my great-grandmother, whom I called *Ah Co* when she was still alive, as well as of Wai Po and Wai Gong's well-being, and Mom's healing. I lose the self-consciousness that I usually associate with organized religion. In the States, I even squirm a bit when saying "Amen" at the end of ecumenical prayers at public ceremonies or weddings. But here, I pray, even as Grandma looks on while I bow, scrutinizing me in the way she always does for the first forty-eight hours. Looking for traces of familiar Chineseness amid my American mannerisms, observing (out loud, always) if I had gained or lost weight, if I had gotten more or less tan (paleness was a fiercely guarded quality among Chinese women, with parasols, face masks, and bleaching creams with actual bleach). My tan, my willingness to seek out the sun, instantly branded me as American no matter how well I spoke Mandarin or how enthusiastically I ate entire small squids, steamed and oozing with their deep black ink sacs; stinky tofu, smelling like a deep-fried locker room; or other delicacies at which Westerners blanched. When I did *bai bai*, as praying was called, in front of the shrine, I forgot *Wai Po* and *Wai Gong* were watching their alien but beloved oldest granddaughter and immersed myself in the idea of those who came before me, their legacy in my genes, their watchful presence here, held close by the offerings of oranges and passionfruits and bananas. As I rose from my third bow, I'd look into the black-and-white photo of *Ah Co*, so young I had never even as a child seen her like that. Her all black hair pulled back in a severe bun, those dark round eyes, warm and searing at the same time, looking out at me. Could I see traces of myself in her face?

Ah Co, whose devoutness I witnessed when she was alive. She would climb the stairs to a special rooftop shrine, inaccessible by the building's elevator, twice a day, to meditate and pray for hours with a single long strand of wooden beads, worn to a soft polish by endless repetitions through the channel created by her thumb and forefinger. She climbed the stairs even after she broke her hip, badly, in her late eighties, the walk up as laborious as the hours of vigil with the beads. The doctors had said she would never walk, let alone climb stairs, again. One step, one bead, at a time.

On nice days in Taoyuan, Mom, Grandma, and I set out, down the high-rise's rickety elevator. Grandma steps over the uneven pavement in the courtyard, and Mom and I, each on opposite side of her, instinctively reach out and cradle her arms. We walk on like this, taking up too much room on the narrow sidewalk as people veer around us. Truth is, she doesn't really need our help so much—at most, only one of us. But she smiles quietly to herself, happy to have a reason to have daughter and granddaughter so close, doting. We are linked, physically and genetically, three generations of women, our lives spanning the early twentieth century to the twenty-first. We walk this way, taking a loop around the two-block-square park next to the apartment building.

On other days, I venture into Taipei and see my cousin there, sometimes stay until the night markets, where we stuff ourselves with treats like oyster pancakes, all manner of deep-fried foodstuffs on skewers, fresh fruit juices, pressed sugarcane nectar, and, of course, stinky tofu. I learn the newish subway system, the MTA, ride the elevator to the top of the Taipei 101 tower, and window-shop at high-end stores I can't afford. All the while, the pitched hums of mopeds, seas of mopeds, sing in unison Taiwan's constant aural backdrop, the whole country vibrating at a higher frequency than the United States and its sedate thrumming sedans and SUVs. After the first few days, I notice it less, until I return to America and am struck by a stark absence of sound. Mom and I travel to eastern and southern Taiwan, where the soaring marble faces of the Taroko Gorge and balmy beaches of Kenting gamely resist the tourist incursions while Taipei transforms itself into a modern metropolis. Rain falls harder and wetter here, typhoons blow through, and the humid air is so present it has its own smell, at once heavy and green. But every possible opportunity, when we're in Taoyuan, we take our walks with *Wai Po*.

Somehow, the second *bai bai*, performed right before I leave, makes the departure a little easier, when the time has to come. *Wai Po* and *Wai Gong* focus on the ritual, not the goodbye, so I do as well. Though when I hug *Wai Po* goodbye, her body shorter and softer with each passing visit, my heart breaks, knowing I might not be able to do so again. Still, Grandma always is tender and casual about parting. Clear-eyed and grateful, unconcerned about the future in that moment.

"Take some fruit," she says, pressing a plastic bag of oranges and cut-up guava spears into my hands. "Will they feed you on the plane? Hurry now, don't miss your flight. Come back and see us soon.

"Come home again soon."

In the spring of 2006, I traveled to Los Angeles to conduct some interviews for a story, and managed to stay through the weekend to visit my Second Uncle—my mom's younger brother; like in many Chinese families, we identified all of our extended family by their birth order. My maternal "Big Uncle" was the oldest of six siblings, and my Mom was next—Big Sister to her siblings and Big Aunt to my cousins. Second Uncle Mike, his wife Angela, and one of their daughters, Karen, asked me over for a barbecue. They also invited my Fourth Uncle and his wife, who had just recently emigrated from Taiwan to Los Angeles, over to the house as well.

Fourth Uncle and his new wife had met each other a few years ago in the Taipei suburbs, through a new Taiwanese dating service for single-parent divorcees. When they married, it was Brady Bunch-style, each of them bringing two preteen boys to the relationship. The four boys, now newly enrolled in American high schools and colleges, would all be there. As the weekend approached, Second Uncle Mike emailed everyone to let them know that my cousin Aaron from Singapore, son of my mother's youngest sister (Little Aunt), was in town, checking out American colleges. He would join us too.

I arrived early at Second Uncle Mike's palatial two-story house in the coastal South Bay area, just outside of Los Angeles. My cousin Karen, now in her mid-twenties, squealed when she hugged me and immediately recruited me to help cook in the newly remodeled kitchen. Leaning into the granite-topped island with a view of the ocean, we fell easily into the routine of chopping vegetables and catching up on each other's lives. It had been so long since I had seen my relatives, I feared we might have trouble settling into familiarity. But we didn't. Uncle Mike and his wife, Aunt Angela, came to the kitchen to greet me, and then Fourth Uncle, his wife, and their boys arrived, and then Aaron, shockingly full grown from the last time I had seen him as a toddler. We talked over each other in a mixture of Mandarin and English, obsessed about the food—the women over the salads and side dishes in the kitchen, the men over the meat on the patio grill—and shared news about all of the family members who weren't there. They inquired delicately about my mother and father; they knew the details of the divorce and his illness already, so I told them that Mom was doing better on her own, and Dad was "improving, more stable." They nodded vigorously.

There was a time, in grade school, when most of my mom's siblings lived in Northern California, the Bay Area, when I saw most of my uncles, aunts, and cousins regularly. Kelley and I had lived with Second Uncle Mike and Second Aunt Angela for weeks as my parents traveled in Europe when we were young, before cousin Karen and her sister were born. Aaron's mother, my Little Aunt Wendy, the baby of the my mom's family, had lived with us while she was attending high school and college in the

United States; she and I used to pretend, much to my mother's chagrin, that we were sisters. Fourth Uncle had also lived with us while he had attended college in the United States. Cousin Karen and I had played together as children; I remembered chasing her around her family's house when she was a toddler. I had held cousin Aaron in my arms right after he was born.

I had come to think in my teenage and adult years that a certain loneliness surrounded my nuclear family—that, unlike the Shirzais, we did not have a network of extended family around us. But in Uncle Mike's house, surrounded by generations of black-haired, brown-eyed, average-heighted, tan-skinned people who had the same roundish Asian eyes and flat noses as me—as Ah Co in that photo on the Taoyuan shrine—I realized I had one all along.

Just as Mom had stopped encouraging us to go to Taiwan as a family, she had kept her siblings at arm's length for the years between my father's descent into illness and their divorce. There were so many good reasons to: Dad tended to pick fights with and alienate them when he was manic; he was impossible to explain when he was depressed, in bed and unable to greet them if they visited. Mom just didn't want their befuddlement, their judgment, or even their pity. The psychic and practical distance she created also prevented me from thinking of them. I felt our family was alone, not because we could not access our kin, but because Dad's illness and the shadow it cast on us could not be understood by or shared with anyone, not even the aunts, uncles, and cousins in this room. But since the divorce, Mom had called them one by one, paid visits to them by herself, and explained everything. Now, I didn't have to say much more.

After everyone had stuffed themselves, Uncle Mike brought his laptop into the kitchen and called cousin Karen's older sister Erica, who now lived in New York, on Skype. Her familiar smiling face, the laughing half-moon eyes, appeared on the screen, and Uncle Mike slowly swept the webcam over all of us to show her who was in the room. We had formed a semi-circle around the island without thinking about it; the image Erica saw from her small East Village apartment looked like a posed family portrait.

"Ohmygosh!" cousin Erica said over the computer's speakers, not having lost her Southern California affectations on the East Coast. "Angie, I haven't seen you in sooo long."

Next up on the Skype queue was Mom. Uncle Mike called his big sister and perched his laptop on his shoulder, walking through the kitchen, which opened out into the family room, where the boys had started playing video games. Mom exchanged hellos with everyone in the room. Then he came to me. She looked exuberant, sitting at her desk in her small condo, with the slightly startled expression of someone still unaccustomed to using a webcam.

"Angie, I am so glad you are there," she said in Mandarin. "It's so good that you're with family."

"Family" in Mandarin, *jia ren*, literally "home people."

As opposed to with you or Dad? I wanted to ask. But I understood: this crowded room, with food, laughter, warmth, *felt* like family.

Then Uncle Mike checked his watch. It was morning in Taiwan. He dialed Grandma, *Wai Po*, on Skype. Mom's and his oldest brother, Big Uncle, who lived part of the year in Taiwan with Grandma and Grandpa, answered. After he got passed around, *Wai Po* got onto the phone.

"*Waaaah,*" she kept saying as Uncle Mike walked around with the webcam, her dark, round eyes wide. Wow. Behind her, I could see the familiar Taoyuan family room, Chinese landscape paintings and a lunar calendar on the wall, the polished rosewood furniture, the shrine with Guanyin and *Ah Co*, pyramids of oranges stacked up as offerings. "*Da jia lai la,*" she said. Everyone has come. Or, literally translated, The big family has come—or the big home has arrived. We yelled out greetings to her, knowing her hearing wasn't good.

As we all shouted and laughed, the voices, in two languages, in Californian, Chinese, and Singporean accents, washed over me like the waves crashing into the beach below. As we leaned in together around the kitchen island, focused on the laptop computer, I was immersed in warm water, womblike and comforting, the buoyant embrace of salt water carrying me along.

But as soon as Uncle Mike got off the webcam with Wai Po and hurried outside to check on the meat, everyone in the room dispersed. The boys went back to their video games, the women to their own conversation, and just Karen and I were in the kitchen. She busied herself with the salad, and I found myself alone at the counter, like the tide had just washed out. Suddenly, inexplicably, I felt as if an undertow was pulling my feet out from under me, salt water stinging my eyes, my breath as if underwater. I gripped the polished edge of the granite countertop, fearful I might faint. Or burst out weeping.

My cousin Karen sidled up to me, brow furrowed. "Are you OK?" she said. "Maybe you're dehydrated. Too much wine and not enough water?"

I nodded.

She handed me a glass of water, put her hand on my arm, and steered me toward the sliding glass door.

"Some fresh air will help," she said. I had a flashback to an image of Karen as a chubby toddler, me at age nine pushing teacups away from the edge of a coffee table as she attempted to grab them. Now, she was a self-assured young woman heading to law school, cooking elaborate meals for dozens of people—and taking care of me.

I stepped outside onto the back patio overlooking the Pacific Ocean. The cool air was a shock to my overheated system, like an ice bath. My skin tingled and my breathing deepened, saturating my lungs with oxygen. Cousin Karen was right. I felt like myself again. I found a lawn chair and sat, by myself, hearing the hum of conversation around the grill but not listening to it. I tuned into the distant sound of the ocean instead, letting it soothe me and take my thoughts where they wanted to go.

I remembered Tamim Ansary's memoir, the book that had been published as I was getting to know the Shirzais. Ansary had described the Afghan compound, the separation of public and private naturally built into Afghan home design. Within the walls, he writes, there was no concept of nuclear family, and certainly not of solitude. "In the compounds, people spent all their time with the group. As far as I can tell, none of my Afghan relatives was ever alone or ever wanted to be," Ansary said. "Namely, our group self was just as real as our individual selves, perhaps more so."

He goes on, trying to define that group: "*Family* doesn't cover it. Even *extended family* feels too small. *Tribe*, however, is too big."

But I liked the word, tribe. It was one that Daoud employed a lot, not just to describe a larger family group, but to describe a concept, a way of being, a loyalty that was particular to Afghans, particularly Pashtuns. U.S. military officials and pundits increasingly spoke of "tribalism" in rural Afghanistan as an obstacle to their goals, but to Daoud, it was a virtue. "They don't understand that tribe comes before national government," he said of the Americans.

Amid the constant shift of conquerors, rulers, governments, invaders, and occupiers, Afghans had remained faithful to their tribes. Leaders could be assassinated, governments overthrown, allegiances renounced— but tribe was blood; it was immutable.

What I had yearned for when I met the Shirzais was not just about my parents, nor the intactness of my nuclear family. In Afghanistan, the nuclear family fades in importance, subsumed by a much larger entity: The extended family. The tribe. The Shirzais had literally broken up nuclear families—Laila's, Mamoy and her children—for the sake of the extended family. Within this house overlooking the Pacific Ocean, I had been reunited with my own tribe. I wanted to feel the way I had, the moment before tears and that unnamable undertow overwhelmed me, forever.

A cold breeze came in from the ocean, making me shiver. I thought of the Shirzais, and a different kind of sadness washed over me, quiet and cool. My bond with them, as a family, had to be finite. I had come into their lives because of outside forces, the unforeseen collision of September 11 and my profession and their homeland. For a while, they—and I—were united by a collective project, summed up by Daoud's question, "And how do you plan to help the country?"

But now, the War in Afghanistan had been going on five years without a resolution in sight. The country was splitting into factions; the U.S. public was wearying of the mission. And so, too, were the Shirzais, their own post-9/11 idealism losing momentum, running out of fuel. Real life, American life, had gotten in the way. Maiwand and his wife now had two daughters, Yusuf and his wife one, and both of those nuclear families were consumed with the new-parent frenzy of feedings and diapers. Mohib's rebellion and Laila's relationship with Tim thrust an immovable wedge between the older and younger generations. The younger ones were moving on: Tim and Laila drew together again, bolstered by her promise to make her big revelation to the family soon. They were talking—fantasizing at first, but the discussions were starting to feel more real – about starting over together somewhere, far away from Oregon. Even Mohib had finally squelched his uncles' arranged-marriage talk and now had a steady girlfriend whom he had introduced to Mamoy and his sisters. The girlfriend had convinced him to drink less and he had earned back his driver's license. I heard Sarasa and Mina had their own non-Afghan boyfriends, and sensed that even the uncles might not be able to withstand the coming tide of—of what? —of what happened when immigrant children grew up in multicultural America.

So it was I, not Daoud, who had outlived my usefulness to the Shirzais. I had been trying to bridge their fault lines the way I could not with my own family's—an impossible task. I wanted to remain friends with some of the Shirzais, especially with Laila, with whom I had forged a unique closeness. But they could not be my surrogate family forever. I was looking to move out of Oregon, for different professional opportunities on the East Coast, maybe even a teaching job. And, as I was learning on my visits to Taiwan, as well as on that night at Second Uncle Mike's house, it was time for me to discover my own tribe, to find what my own definition of family was —whether it was praying at *Wai Po* and *Wai Gong*'s shrine, being nestled here among extended family, taking long walks with my mother, or having airport Denny's breakfasts with my father. Imperfect and fragmented, just like the Shirzais.

ॐ

Before I had met the Shirzais, I had been an excellent reporter, my expertise the human-interest story: I knew how to approach strangers, earn their trust little by little, share just enough of myself to get them to reveal their innermost secrets so I could tell their stories in print. Then I made a graceful exit when the article was done.

I had enjoyed the initial reporter's detachment I had from the Shirzais, even as I was longing to be closer to them. Then, when I did not exit because, for the first time, I found myself not wanting to, our ties to each other became tangled. I had run out of Mohib's apartment when he tried to get too close. But I was more threatened by my own confused desire, my own receptiveness when my guard was down. Mohib was right: I couldn't remain the good journalist and not subject myself to judgment, not risk getting hurt. Any more with the Shirzais than I could with my own family.

Now in the midst of this confusion, I didn't feel like a journalist anymore. I had wanted my connections to the Shirzais, however complicated, more than I had wanted to be a model of objectivity. I had wanted those moments of closeness—Thanksgiving dinner, driving down the Oregon Coast to Maiwand's patriotic Pashtun music, having Laila's trust and Tim's gratitude—even more than I had wanted the foreign-correspondent job in Hong Kong.

I was the one my father raised to be tough and capable, who hated crying and kept holding back tears, until saying goodbye to Nazo drew them out of me. Because she was not my family, because she was a twenty-two-year-old Afghan woman whom I'd probably never see again—because she posed no threat to my own walls.

For the past five years, I had been fixated on emotional walls. The Shirzais's, each step bringing me closer to the inner sanctum of their lives and their story, even into the rooms that symbolized their most closely held loss: Mohammed. And my own family's, as Mom, Kelley, and I desperately bricked over the dark and messy rooms of my father's illness, just as we ignored the unfinished renovations in our house. We were finally, tentatively, just starting to remove these barriers, one brick at a time.

But what about my own walls? The ones that were mine and mine alone? In Daoud, I saw myself: using his work in Afghanistan to remove himself from the painful realities of the family he had raised, from relationships with women when they got too demanding, as he would say. How had I used journalism to build my buffer zone, using work as an excuse to avoid family, and prevent relationships with men from progressing.

The Shirzais had become a stand-in for all those I could not allow myself to let in past my walls. I had fallen in love with them. But now, I had to find a way to do the same with others in my life, maybe someday with a man. If I took a hard look at myself, I had to acknowledge that even the failed or incomplete relationships I had hesitated to tell Rochina and Nazo about in Kabul had tapered off in the last couple years, as I got more involved with the Shirzais's emotional life.

Not only had the Shirzais replaced my own family for me, they had become my primary—and only—love affair. The walls of their homes had become a bubble inside which I experienced emotion and connection, negating the need to relinquish my walls in other areas of my life. As a collective unit, they provided all the archetypes I needed: The patriarch. The strong matriarchs, ready to guide me. A female confidante and co-conspirator. A "good" boy, and a "bad" boy, to fall for.

Did I need to pull back from them—not for their sake, but for my own?

Sometimes, when I flew back from Portland to the Bay Area to visit, Mom, Kelley, and I existed in her condo like she was a widow and Dad was not there. Both ends of his illness made it impossible to do anything else: In mania, he was so bitter at my mother, so confrontational, that to have them in the same space was throwing a match into a room with a gas leak, the sulfurous and invisible accumulation engulfing everyone in flames. It would burn out, eventually, Mom heaving with sobs, Dad still ranting on his way out, tires squealing on the pavement. Depression was no better. He had to be coaxed out of the house, and conversation was like trying to traverse a room flooded waist-deep in molasses. Reaching the other side was exhausting for all parties.

There simply was no family of four left. We had become a toxic combination. We had to subdivide: Dad with each one of us children alone, and then Mom and the two of us, staying in the condo. Sometimes, in his better times between mood swings, Dad and Mom could be civil for a time, as long as Kelley and I were not there to be his audience. Meanwhile, each of us gradually grew more emboldened about confrontation, and took turns bringing up his illness, offering to take him to a psychiatrist, espousing the virtues of medication and therapy. Accordingly, each of us was subject to his rage, his claiming he was cutting us off, disowning us, through with us (while manic). Or we would just be ignored by him, the suggestions sinking into the dark, opaque molasses (when depressed).

When Dad was depressed, he was simply nonresponsive, making just enough effort so that we wouldn't panic and take up even more time or energy than his placating us required. He could disappear when depressed —as he worsened, he sometimes nearly did, allowing his phone lines and email accounts to get cut off, so that we'd be forced to go back to the house, that drive to my childhood hometown becoming one that brought dread, a sinking feeling, to all of us. It bled every scrap of nostalgia from the house in which I grew up, for the house in which we spent so many years. My most significant milestones had happened here: Receiving my acceptance to Stanford, the thick envelope curled up in our yellow metal mailbox shaped like a shotgun house with a peaked roof and hinged flag on the side. Now the mailbox was rusted, cobwebbed, and defunct, the Post Office opting not to deliver after a long period during his most recent depression when he didn't empty it, ever. My first kiss, in the kitchen, in the vicinity of the sink and dishwasher, while my parents were out of town. The awkward pre-prom corsage and boutonniere exchange in the vestibule area, where the upright piano on which I practiced for years sat. Nothing from those memories was recognizable in the bombed-out shell of a house that my father inhabited now, deteriorating from neglect during his depressions, becoming pathologically cluttered with useless purchases from his manic periods—random office supplies, completely unnecessary and multiple items (at one point, we saw three unopened fax machines strewn across that vestibule with the piano, even though his office fax was functioning fine). And of course, the upstairs bathrooms were still unfinished, still cluttered with tools, spare tiles, and sheet rock.

No wonder we could hardly bring ourselves to visit the house. We did what we could to keep things from completely falling apart, discreetly sending Dad checks or paying for a landscaper to tidy up the front yard. But how he managed to survive, keep the power on, and not get evicted, remained a mystery to us. When Dad was up to talking, I made a point to meet Dad at restaurants, and he was more than happy to oblige—he knew on some level the house was in a shape he was not proud of, that it disappointed and frightened us. I tried on different demeanors with each meal we had: forceful about treatment, understanding about his resistance, blithely ignoring the illness and letting him ramble or stew quietly, matching his loquaciousness with nonstop talking of my own. Nothing changed anything.

My most peaceful times together with my mother and brother were also our most bittersweet, as a family of three. Having a quiet Thanksgiving in my mom's two-bedroom condo, watching a movie together on her couch, and, more often as time went on, meeting to try to make plans to find a comfortable situation for Dad as he worsened and continued refusing treatment or medication. They were hard conversations, but we were having them—something which would have been unimaginable a decade ago. As the walls between us three finally eroded with the passage of time, with the unspoken complicity that we were the only ones who knew, the only ones who understood what the other two endured, we found a kind of love. It was a feeling that over time became sweet even, at least among the three of us, as we let go of our bitterness and accepted what was.

I was seeing, finally, how family happened. It was my own this time.

17.
The Familiar Hearts of Strangers

The day Laila received her Master's in Education from Mt. Tabor College started out gray, a June morning that couldn't quite make up its mind. And then, after I had left the house in a summery cotton shirt and linen skirt, with no jacket, it poured. Not the light, drizzly Oregon rain that hardly merits the opening of an umbrella, but a pounding rainfall worthy of an Eastern-seaboard summer thunderstorm. Thick rivulets of water rolled across my windshield as I drove through the packed parking lot.

I sat in my car, hoping the rain would pass and I could make a break for the building. The pelting persisted. The ceremony would start soon. The Shirzais were waiting for me, saving a seat in the bleachers. Equally unprepared families darted past me with newspapers and garbage bags over their heads. Oregonians prided themselves on not carrying umbrellas, fancying themselves like their Gore-Tex® jackets—as if the state's seven months of constant drizzle should just bead up on their skin and roll off. A couple marched past me with a huge golf umbrella, smug. Out-of-towners.

It was June 2006, exactly four years since I had joined the Shirzais to celebrate Laila receiving her bachelor's degree—the whole family at Maiwand's house, Daoud asking her, as he had asked all the others, how she planned to help the country. Now, so much had changed. The family had scattered, geographically across the Portland area and emotionally, divided by generational and cultural battles. But surely Laila's accomplishment would bring them together, if only for a day. All six nieces and nephews had received their bachelor's degrees from Mt. Tabor College, a testament to Daoud's influence. But for Laila, the youngest, to receive a Master's from the Graduate School of Education, where Daoud had taught for his entire career, completed a circle. The first and the last.

Daoud rarely went to commencement ceremonies, even when his nieces and nephews were graduating, even though they were at his university. Occasionally, he'd sit in the audience, incognito and apart from his own family and the other faculty in their colorful regalia. He derided the ceremonies as pompous and long, and mocked the robes and multi-colored draped hoods as "monkey suits." For him the most important ritual was showing up at the family celebrations afterwards, at Maiwand's house, and to shake the graduate's hand in front of everyone else. "So," he'd say, "now that you have this degree, how do you plan to become rich and famous?" And of course, "And how to plan to help the country?" Few had followed through yet with their plans to teach English, design new infrastructure, build schools or medical clinics in Afghanistan, but it had still been an important exercise.

Only a few minutes remained before the start of the ceremony and rainwater was still cascading over my car. Quick, rummage around, find anything: a hidden umbrella, a plastic bag, anything to shield myself. Nothing. A deep breath, flinging myself out of the car, running as fast as my heels would allow me. I had chosen a long linen skirt, with a long-sleeved top, ever mindful to wear things that would pass muster culturally with the Shirzais. The family always arrived early to claim seats for everyone, which would have meant they had missed the downpour. This was not the way I had wanted to arrive to Laila's graduation, clothes soaked and damp hair clinging to my neck.

I shook myself off and entered the gymnasium. Immediately, I saw Maiwand's wife, Padama, with a stroller and their new baby daughter. She embraced me and then jumped back a bit. "Wow," she said. "You're so cold." She pointed up at the bleachers, to where the rest of the family was sitting.

They were easy to pick out in the crowd, a row of black-haired people punctuated by women in brightly colored *shalwar kameez*. Aisha, now five, sat happily sandwiched between Mina and Mohib. I waved. A dozen arms waved back. I forgot about being cold and wet, and jogged up the bleachers, as the women—some family members, some friends—jostled about and found a place for me in their midst. Wedged between them, our hips and shoulders touching each other, I settled, warmed against the damp chill.

Laila had asked me to go shopping with her a week earlier, to find an outfit to wear under her cap and gown, for the school's reception afterwards. We went to the mall together, browsing the trendy women's clothing stores. She had chosen a silk red-orange ombre below-the-knee wrap skirt; anything higher than ankle-length was a risky move before her uncles and more traditional family members, especially during the summer when knee-high boots couldn't keep her calves from being exposed. The truth was, it suited her perfectly, the brightness of the fabric playing off her dark hair, the petite cut of the A-line skirt hitting at just the right spot to accentuate her slender but muscular calves. She told me she planned to wear her favorite platform sandals.

"What do you think, with a short-sleeved black shirt?" she said in the fitting room. She was asking, but she'd made up her mind.

"It looks great," I said. "What will your uncles say?"

"They won't like it, but they won't say anything," she said. Lately, she had been pushing more boundaries. She now talked on the phone with Tim right in front of Maiwand, baiting him to ask her the obvious questions. She had mentioned him obliquely to Daoud before he left for his most recent stint in Kabul, inviting him to ask, "Who's Tim?" Neither of the uncles said anything. A sleeveless shirt here; a trip to Colorado with a female college friend, where they stayed with Tim's family; joining her brothers and their friends when the young men smoked flavored tobacco in a hookah at Maiwand's house. She was testing the uncles, trying to get them to say something.

"I don't even think Uncle Daoud will be there," she said of her commencement.

Daoud had been scheduled to return from Afghanistan two days before graduation. He never allowed any family members to pick him up from the airport, preferring instead to take light rail and spend his first night in Portland alone in his downtown condo. His occasional emailed dispatches from Kabul had painted a grim picture—more suicide bombings, less progress—and hinted at his ever-growing discouragement. No one had asked Daoud if he was coming to the ceremony.

Laila really wants him to be there, I thought, as we left the mall with her skirt.

The ceremony started as the band played the plodding notes of "Pomp and Circumstance" and the faculty, in their colorful regalia, marched in. I craned my neck. "Where's Daoud?" I asked Mina. She shrugged. I began to scan the audience, seeing if he had taken a seat in plainclothes. No sign of him there either. How could he not show up for Laila?

Then two long lines of graduates, wearing black caps and gowns, marched in on either side of the gymnasium. I was still looking for Daoud when the women around me began to wave madly and yell, "Laila! Laila!"

Laila waved back at us. Even with her platforms, she was a slight figure amid her taller, bigger cohorts. She had worn her contacts, and her face was aglow. Her hair flowed loose and sleek under her cap. I caught a peek of bare calves and ankles as she walked in, and wondered if the others noticed.

As the usual formalities proceeded, I kept scanning the faculty and crowd for Daoud, wondering if I might catch the familiar white-and-cardinal-red-trimmed robe and hood from Stanford, his alma mater and mine. I didn't.

The Mt. Tabor Graduate School of Education's commencement speaker was William Schulz, then the executive director of Amnesty International. He spoke of the global community, and the graduates' responsibility to it. He quoted from one of my favorite essays, Cynthia Ozick's "The Moral Necessity of Metaphor."

In it, Ozick invoked *Leviticus*: "The stranger that sojourneth with you shall be unto you as the home-born among you and you shall love him as yourself because you too were once strangers in the land of Egypt." And, Schulz said, though we had never been victims of the Rwandan genocide; though Abu Ghraib, Bagram, and Guantanamo Bay might feel like just names to us, we could make the metaphorical leap that Ozick described—because we, too, were once strangers.

"Through metaphor, the past has the capacity to imagine us, and we it," Ozick wrote. "Those at the center can imagine what it is to be outside. The strong can imagine what it is to be weak. Illuminated lives can imagine the dark. Poets in their twilight can imagine the borders of stellar fire.

"We strangers can imagine the familiar hearts of strangers."

I had read these words before. But to hear them, with members of the Shirzai family pressing in on both sides of me, on the day of Laila's graduation, they took on new meaning. It had been nearly five years since September 11, since I first called Daoud, looking for my editor's "human face of the country we're about to bomb." Of course, I had formed a bond far beyond face value with the Shirzais—I had shared rituals, holidays, secrets with them. I had gone to Afghanistan and lived in their home there. They had trusted me, and I them, on that perilous journey to Shinzmaray. I had gotten involved, overly involved, as the recipient of Mohib's angst and supporter of Laila's romance with Tim. And I still treasured my long-distance sisterhood with Rochina and Nazo, as well as the ways in which Grandma, Fahima, and Amina—each in their own way—had given me gifts of insight, perspective, and connection. That first glimpse of Shinzmaray, the taste of Afghan ice cream, stolen glances at Asad, Rochina biting down on her pinky knuckle, Nazo's tears on my scarf, and mine on hers. These were inseparable from my relationship with the family entire—and, I realized, with my own family, in California and Taiwan. Inseparable from myself.

Hearing Ozick's words, what lay at the heart of it all: metaphor, or, more precisely, story. The Shirzais had welcomed me because they were hospitable, because they wanted others to know the truth about Afghanistan at a critical time—and because they wanted a witness to their story. And I had been looking for story (and not just one for my editor), looking for family, as if they were one and the same. When I searched for that amorphous void left by the loss of Mohammed, I was trying to find metaphors for his story. And one by one, the Shirzais, consciously and subconsciously, led me to them—Yusuf's snapshot, Mamoy's ring, Grandma's photo room, the view from the sitting room, even Mohib's misguided desire. They entrusted me to take it in and to tell it back to them.

Ozick, again: "Without the metaphor of memory and history, we cannot imagine the life of the Other."

When Laila Shirzai was finally called to step up and receive her diploma, we all erupted into cheers. She looked up at us in the bleachers and grinned as she walked across the stage. As the ceremony ended, we met her on the gymnasium floor. Her two brothers hugged her. Her cousin Mohib shook her hand briskly, and then darted out of the way to avoid talking to Maiwand, still upset about the dissolution of the arranged marriage and Mohib's new non-Afghan girlfriend. Things were a bit cool between Mina and her uncle too. Yusuf and his family were not even there. Mamoy had not come, and Sarasa had slipped off to Afghanistan months ago, though not to visit family. She had been cagey about her work there, saying it had to do with the U.S. military ("But not the combat part, of course," she had said quickly). I wondered if she had just finally gotten worn down by the freeze between her and her uncles, and wanted to get away. In any case, I had a feeling her uncles would not be happy about the true nature of her work there, whatever it was. Yet, ultimately, it was only she and Daoud who had made it back to Afghanistan to work—whether to help or not was in the eye of the beholder.

Daoud was right. The family was not what it once was. Even the graduation of Laila, the youngest of all the nieces and nephews, from Daoud's own department, could not bring everyone together, nor erase the tensions between those that did come. Then Laila stepped away from her family, in a familiar stance: cell phone pressing against her ear, sly smile on her face. Tim. He couldn't be here—too conspicuous—but he had called to congratulate her. She paced in her platform sandals, bare calves exposed. I noticed Maiwand noticing her on the phone.

We intercepted Padama and the stroller, and the group walked outside together, toward the graduate school's reception across the campus. Aisha, who had been with us in the bleachers, joined her mother and baby sister. The rain had stopped and a sliver of sun tried to find its way through the clouds. Laila came, her mortarboard in hand, trying to comb out her hat hair with her fingers. We walked on the brick path to the reception building.

Suddenly, a black, red, and white robed figure sauntered up on another path, meeting us at the crossroads. He stopped in front of Laila and turned up his palms, revealing voluminous velvet-trimmed sleeves, as if to say, Here I am. You happy?

"Uncle Daoud!" Laila said.

"Ustad," her brother said, eyes wide. "Nice duds."

Laila laughed heartily and Daoud reached to shake her hand, and swung his left arm around to pat her shoulder in a sort of half-hug. She was buoyant. I couldn't stop smiling. Had he been at the ceremony all along, and we had missed him? Had he marched in with the rest of the faculty, in regalia? If he had, surely one of us would have spotted him. That meant he had put on his robe, the "monkey suit"—something he had never done for any of the other Mt. Tabor commencements of the nieces and nephews —and arrived just as the ceremony was ending to meet us. He had even donned his doctoral headgear, the velvet, gold-tasseled tam parked slightly askew on his head. I was so flabbergasted by this moment, this meeting at the crossroads, that I never asked. To this day, I don't know if he actually attended the ceremony.

But that didn't matter to Laila, who was basking in his presence as everyone else clamored to greet him with hearty handshakes. This was the first time anyone had seen him since he left for Afghanistan.

"How's Kabul?" Maiwand asked him, the brothers clasping hands.

"Worse," Daoud said. "But they sure fixed up that new five-star hotel fast after anti-American bombers blew out all the windows."

Maiwand shook his head. Then he looked his older brother up and down, surveying the robe and its cardinal red and white trim, and smiled. "Is this what the Kabulis are wearing nowadays?"

Laila looked at her two uncles, happy. Here were the two men who raised her in the United States, who had stood in for her parents since she was twelve.

Daoud then turned to me. *"Salaam aleikum. Tsenga ye?"* he said, shaking my hand.

"Welcome back," I said, thinking of our last conversation. "So we meet in Oregon after all."

He motioned at his regalia. "This should look familiar too you."

I wanted to tell him how much it meant that he wore it for this occasion and how I knew that, though he looked terribly self-conscious, this was his way of telling Laila that her graduation was special to him. I could have even told him that it meant a lot to me that he enjoyed pointing out that we had both graduated from the same university.

"It does," I said.

"I got mine on eBay," he said, deadpan, but with a raised eyebrow. "It was a steal."

He turned back to Laila, and they chatted, as I watched Aisha skip up and down the brick path in her favorite red and white Gap Kids outfit. Padama eyed her ruefully and said, "I got in a big fight with her this morning. She didn't want to wear Afghan clothes today. I tried and tried to get her to wear *shalwar kameez.*"

And so it started now. What other battles would follow?

Splat. A splash of cold on my arm. Then on my head. Another on my other shoulder—large, wet drops. One by one, the people around me looked up. Padama threw a baby blanket over the stroller. The sky paused, then shifted from gray to almost opaque white. Heavy with moisture, it had stooped down, pressing on us, seemingly lower than the gymnasium ceiling.

And then, cold sheets of water, falling so loudly around us that everyone's yelling was unintelligible as we scattered. Laila headed in one direction, her brothers in another. Mohib and Mina in yet another. I ran with Padama and the stroller, grabbing Aisha's hand as she shrieked with joy. Daoud disappeared, his seamless entrance and exit making me wonder if Mt. Tabor had secret faculty trapdoors and tunnels. Padama and I joined a family taking cover under an arched stone entryway of a late 19th century building. There was about a three-foot space between it and the actual door of the building. I yanked on the door. It was locked. Maiwand at first had run off in another direction, but then came barreling across the walkway toward us, giddy.

Padama moved the stroller to make room for him. He was in the throes of a high-pitched giggling fit as he squeezed in, soaked, with us. His laughing fit, apropos of nothing, reminded me of moments during that first Sunday dinner at his house, when he cracked himself up with puns about "whirled peas" in the midst of talk about war. This side of the normally stoic Maiwand, rarely seen of late, had always delighted me. He was clearly enjoying his own unabashed cackling more than anyone, certainly more than Padama who was rolling her eyes at him. "What is so funny?" she asked in her accented English, trying to sound exasperated.

The wind shifted and began to blow the rain into the doorway, soaking us even more. Maiwand could barely catch his breath to speak. "The rain," he gasped, eyes crinkling and body convulsing with laughter. "Everyone was standing around . . . and then they all ran . . . and now all the women are worried . . . that their makeup is going to run."

Padama guffawed. But her big eyes were shining, bemused. "You are not making one bit of sense," she scolded, suppressing a smile.

Maiwand just shook his head and giggled some more. Aisha joined him, for the sheer delight of laughter. Padama pretended to ignore them, and lifted the blanket over the stroller to find the baby sleeping through it all. I peered in, marveling at how tiny she still was, those long black lashes fringing the half-moons of her closed eyes, her miniature mouth working away at a dream-nipple. Maiwand and Aisha's laughter was drowned out by the rain slapping the ground even harder.

I was overcome by the random beauty of the moment: The surreal downpour, the likes of which I had rarely seen in Oregon. The light in Laila's eyes when she had spotted Daoud on the path, in his regalia. The palpable surge of energy I felt among the family members in his presence. The sky opening on all of us a moment later, and the frenzied running that followed. The begrudging affection in Padama's voice as she scoffed at her husband. The fragility of an infant's sleep amid all this chaos. And a father and daughter giving in to a spell of silliness, laughing for the joy of it, because everything on this day was so unlikely, so imperfect—but perfect.

It was as if the coming together of the Shirzai family at the crossing of two paths, with Daoud in his "monkey suit," had been too much for the universe to sustain. And so the rain came.

As Maiwand began to catch his breath, Padama began to look impatient, and the baby began to stir, the rain slowed down to a steady shower.

Drenched people emerged from under overhangs and began to jog toward the reception hall. Some shook themselves out like wet dogs, others patted themselves dry with sweaters or wraps. Padama and I looked at each other and, as she draped the blanket back over the stroller, we began walking.

The hall was packed, and I soon was separated from Padama and Maiwand. I found Daoud, still in his robe and tam, near the cake table trying to talk to some colleagues over the noise of the crowd. He nodded hello at me. "Do you know where everyone is?" I shouted over the din. He shook his head. "Are you going to Maiwand's house after this?" He looked at me quizzically. He hadn't heard me. Then a student, in cap and gown, approached. "Professor Shirzai! I didn't know you would be here." And I moved on.

I found Laila just outside the building, with Maiwand and her brothers. She had already returned her rented cap and gown and was in her new outfit, the silk skirt nice and dry after being covered by the polyester gown. Padama had taken Aisha and the baby home to dry off. Mohib and Mina were nowhere to be found. Maiwand handed me a camera and I took some pictures of the four of them, then the brothers swapped out so I could be in a photo. Maiwand was back to his usual demeanor and stood serious and still for the photos, though Laila gave a cursory smile. Smiling for pictures was not a very Afghan thing to do. They were standing against a plain cement wall, and there was something austere—sad, even—about this moment. I wanted everyone to be here, for Daoud and Maiwand to stand with Laila. For Laila to have a picture of herself in her cap and gown, next to Daoud in regalia. The first and the last. I wanted the camera to capture the moment when Daoud and everyone else came together, as well as the ecstatic spontaneity of the downpour.

I wanted to write this story the way I had seen and felt it a moment ago, to create the metaphor of memory and history through which I would imagine the Shirzais. But now, it had passed, and the point-and-shoot digital camera was preserving another story entirely—a fragment of the family awkwardly lined up against a bare wall. Which one was real?

The men were standing impatiently, looking at each other without speaking. And Laila slumped a bit, worn out by the day.

"Are people coming over?" Maiwand asked.

"I asked a couple people from my cohort to come by," Laila said.

"He means family," I blurted out. Realizing what I had done, I blushed. Unfazed, Laila looked over at her brothers. "Well?"

They shrugged. "Maybe later," the eldest said.

"Does anyone need a ride?" I said.

The brothers shook their heads. Laila said she didn't know whether Mina came with Mohib or Padama, and that maybe I should make sure she didn't get left behind.

Then Laila, her brothers, and Maiwand all set off toward different parking lots. Now what? What if I couldn't find Mina? Wasn't Daoud going to go to the family gathering? Where was he?

I walked through the hall, looking for Mina or Daoud, and found the latter just outside the other door, heading out. He had taken off his tam and tucked it under his arm. I waved him down.

"Are you heading to Maiwand's house?"

"I don't know," he said. "I just got back the day before yesterday. I'm exhausted. It was really hard this time. Things are not going well there, for anyone. It's not the same as when you were there. People have given up."

But you really need to be there for Laila. You can't give up.

"That's terrible to hear," I said. "I had hoped it would be different."

"We all did," he said. "But life goes on. It always does. Afghans survive. We always do."

I scanned the crowds of families headed to their cars. "Have you seen Mina? Does she need a ride?"

"No, I haven't. I think she went home with her brother," Daoud said. I wondered if he deliberately avoided saying Mohib's name. At the very least, he ignored the fact that Mohib's "home" was no longer hers.

In the silence that followed, I wanted to shake Daoud: *I know you see what's happening. You told me so yourself. You can stop it. Let's round everybody up and take them to Maiwand's house. You'll shake Laila's hand in front of everybody and ask her how she plans to help the country. And we'll all believe that the country can be helped.*

And you will all be together, united, like you were in the fall of 2001.

"OK," Daoud said, extending his hand. *"Khudai paaman."* Goodbye.

I grasped it, and watched him walk away, his black robe swaying as he strode toward the faculty parking lot.

I was alone. Should I try to find Mina? Still damp from the downpour, I felt chilled all of the sudden. I remembered that night looking out at the Pacific at Uncle Mike's house, that cool sadness. I had sensed that something with the Shirzais was coming to an end, as all stories do. But I wasn't ready for it to end now, not like this.

I walked around the building, heart pounding, feeling aimless, wishing I would see Mina and she would ask me for a ride to Maiwand's. Wishing I could do something, be of use to them. But the crowds were thinning out, and everyone was heading home.

Epilogue:
Two Weddings

When Laila married Tim two years later, the only one of the three uncles who attended was Maiwand. I had moved to Washington, D.C., a year before, to teach journalism at American University. On my last night in Portland, I had stopped by Maiwand's house as he, Laila, his wife Padama, and daughter Aisha were watching videos from our 2004 Afghanistan trip. Mamoy and Mina had come over too; I was as happy to see them over at Maiwand's for a change as I was that they had come to say goodbye to me. Everyone had laughed as Laila showed a video she had shot of me and Grandma in the women's sitting room. Grandma was talking and talking in Pashto, unaware that I didn't speak it. And I, not wanting to shatter the illusion, was periodically shouting in her good ear, "Wo . . . wo . . . xa . . . wo." Then she looked into the camera and said something, which made everyone shriek with more laughter. She said, "This one, she speaks such good Pashto," Laila explained to me.

After that, I lost touch with most of the Shirzais, except for Laila, who had called me regularly to report on things with Tim—how she had told her uncles and her parents in Pakistan about him, how they had objected as vehemently as she had expected, and how she had repeated to them a rehearsed mantra, "I would very much like your support, I'm sorry if I don't have it, but I'm not going to change my mind. I hope you do someday." Then, how he had converted to Islam (and now abstained from alcohol and pork, a significant sacrifice in his mind given his prior affection for beer and bacon), and how the two of them had started secretly planning their wedding for the fall.

One day, six months later, Laila had called me with the news that she and Tim had announced to the entire Shirzai family that they were getting married—only a month before the ceremony that they had been planning for the past half-year. "With my family," Laila said, world-weary, "it's best not to give them time to think. I made it clear we were *telling* them what we were doing, not *asking* for permission."

Hearing the strength and certainty in Laila's voice over the phone, I was elated. I had been wrong to think that my quiet support of her and Tim would change the Shirzai family forever. Laila herself had changed the family, courageously emerged from strife and naysaying to show everyone a different way to do things. She was writing her own definitions of Afghan, Pashtun, and Muslim. Her insistence on Tim's conversion showed how serious she was about religion, but as she told me about her wedding dress for the western ceremony—white and sleeveless—I knew she was ready to push boundaries.

The last, not the first, will be the one who carries the past and writes the future.

I had flown in to attend the western-style ceremony in the sunlit garden of a tony Colorado country club to which Tim's parents belonged. Laila and Tim had signed the *nikah*, the Muslim marital contract, a couple weeks before in Portland, in a small ceremony with her brothers and cousin Mina, who were here in Colorado as well. Laila had worn a long-sleeved Pashtun bride's dress and veil for that event, in multiple jewel tones and heavily beaded.

Here, dramatic red rock formations provided a backdrop for the manicured gardens and manmade pond. A sudden downpour, not unlike the one that had fallen on Laila's graduation ceremony, had forced them to relocate the wedding at the last minute to under an overhang with a view of the gardens. Daoud and Yusuf's absence amounted to a protest. Laila's narrow shoulders were defiantly exposed, her gown cascading elegantly from a fitted V-neck bodice with wide straps. "Hey, at least I have a veil on," she had said before the ceremony, motioning to the fine, sheer silk tulle cascading from her impeccably styled hair. "That should keep the traditionalists happy."

Tears streamed down Laila's face as she choked out her vows. Tim's voice kept breaking as well. I, who had claimed I never cried at weddings, cried at this one. I made eye contact with one of Laila's college friends whom I recognized, also wiping at her eyes. She smiled at me and mouthed, "Nine years." That was how long Laila and Tim had been together before this day.

ॐ

Within a year, I would be at another wedding, in Southern California not far from Uncle Mike's beachfront house. Kelley married Christine Luu, the daughter of wartime Vietnamese immigrants from Orange County, California, on a spring day in 2010. Both Mom and Dad attended, though Dad's manic behavior at the time pretty much guaranteed that there would be an embarrassing scene by the end of the evening. There was, with Mom's siblings, but before that, he and Mom were ushered separately down the grassy aisle of the outdoor ceremony, and nearly all of Mom's siblings and the in-laws—Big Uncle and his wife, Second Uncle Mike and Aunt Angela, Fourth Uncle and his wife, Third Uncle and Third Aunt—and several of the cousins were present, bearing witness.

Playing off a viral YouTube video of an alternative to a traditional recessional, Kelley, Christine, and the wedding party danced back down the aisle as the R&B beats of Chris Brown's "Forever" blasted, much to the delight and laughter of the guests. The reception took place in a palatial banquet hall, where hundreds of Christine's parents' business associates from their Little Saigon jewelry business came to toast the newlyweds and drop off red envelopes with cash. When the emcee announced the parents of the groom, Mom and Dad walked in together, awkwardly, Dad's posture and gait wrecked by his years of inactivity during his depressions, Mom erect and slim in a simple black-and-white striped A-line dress with a shiny, wide designer belt I had insisted on lending her as a nod to Michelle Obama's much-regaled fashion sense. Mom had regained her color, filled out a bit, after her insomnia and anxiety finally subsided years after the divorce. Dad bent his elbow and invited Mom to take his arm. Such a gesture had been unimaginable for the past six years. She hesitated, just a beat, unnoticeable to anyone but me, and then draped a thin arm over his black-suited one. They reached the other end of the dance floor, and separated to the two different tables they had been assigned.

My heart was in my throat for the entire seven-course Chinese banquet. When the meal was over, I'd have to give a toast that I had hastily pounded out on my laptop on my flight from Washington, D.C., and printed out at my hotel. Transforming myself into an teacher and an academic had been an exhilarating but all-consuming challenge. I hadn't had the time, between papers to grade and journal articles to write, to construct a carefully thought-out speech. I had given many wedding toasts before, and university teaching had even cured me of most of my public-speaking anxieties. But this was Kelley's wedding, there were more than three hundred people in the room, and a video crew would immortalize my speech. The best man and maid of honor each stumbled a bit when the videographers aimed their bright spotlight at them mid-toast. Then it was my turn. The dance floor felt vast, my high-heeled sandals precariously spindly.

I described that photograph of Kelley and me as kids in the snow, me in red and him in green, me covered and soaked, him dry and pristine. I told funny childhood stories that mentioned both Mom and Dad, wanting to be inclusive. I described my first meeting with Christine, over a high-end restaurant meal, how I knew Kelley was in love with her because he was willing to enjoy food with her that cost more than ninety-nine cents and didn't come in a paper wrapper.

I concluded the toast with the only words I had been sure I wanted to say at Kelley and Christine's wedding long before my last-minute toast-writing on the plane. They were lines from Rumi I had found nearly a decade ago, while immersing myself in Afghan books and culture after I had first met the Shirzais. Like all Afghans, they had told me that though the Persians liked to claim Rumi as their own, in the thirteenth century he actually lived and traveled in Khorasan, most of which is now modern-day Afghanistan. When I first came upon these lines, I had thought they were so beautifully evocative that, in an uncharacteristically romantic impulse, I saved them in a computer file, thinking I could use them if I ever got married. Since so much time had passed, and since I was still single, my career and the fierce independence Dad had cultivated in me still stymieing my attempts at relationship, I wanted to give them to Kelley and Christine:

Those tender words we said to one another
Are stored in the secret heart of heaven.
One day, like the rain they will fall and spread
And their mystery grow green over the world.

My voice was clear, resonant. Kelley and Christine smiled from their sweetheart table; she wiped tears from her eyes. Coos and awws escaped from the audience and I walked off the dance floor to loud applause.

I wanted to give them something achingly beautiful on their wedding day. I wanted Kelley to imagine the idea that all of the love that had transpired within our nuclear family, despite the pain and illness, would someday come back to us in ways we could not envision – like a sudden downpour. Maybe these words would begin to make up for my looking away that night nearly three decades ago in the restaurant, and how I continued to do so for so long. And, unbeknownst to anyone there but me, I wanted Kelley and Christine to have something from Afghanistan, something that reminded me of the Shirzais. Like rice and tea, like the street vendors who echoed each other's chants, these words were a bridge for me. Once I crossed it, I knew it would disappear, and the world in which Kelley and Christine were beginning a new life would be the side on which I would remain. And the Shirzais would be a part of my past.

Back at Laila and Tim's reception in the shadow of the red-rock formations, the groom's mother, father, and brother each gave heartfelt toasts, welcoming Laila to their family. Then, it was the Shirzais's turn. Maiwand, in lieu of a toast, raised a water glass and read a Pashto poem. I was impressed that he, of all the uncles, had come. I had thought of Laila as Daoud's favorite—and perhaps she still was, but his avoidance of the Tim question had put immeasurable distance between them. Maiwand, on the other hand, had been the one who had witnessed Laila clandestinely fall in love as she lived in his house, the one to whom Laila introduced Tim after she made her announcement to the family, the one who had been there, seeing Laila transform from a shy teenager to a woman who had just made the bravest decision of her life. He may not have completely agreed with it, but he understood Laila better than any of the uncles, even better than her own father. And he was the one who was here, on her wedding day.

"I know most of you will not understand this, but these are my words to Laila," he said. His voice halted and trembled a couple of times as he read the poem from a small, worn leather-bound book that he pulled out of his suit pocket. I'd never heard him on the verge of tears before. Laila's eyes welled up. With my limited Pashto vocabulary—rendered even more paltry by the time that had passed without hearing the language—I recognized the words for daughter, khor, and home, kor, rhyming with each other.

Then, in the second stanza, I heard kor, again, cycling with the other words I knew also meant home: watan, country; mena, birthplace; tatobay, homeland or native land—and again, kor, house. How fitting that the language, this poem, distinguished between these subtleties of home, acknowledged that one's house and country might not be in, or synonymous with, one's homeland. Laila dabbed at her eyes with a cloth napkin and nodded at her uncle across the reception space. I gave up on trying to decipher the poem from the few words I knew. I had learned from five years with the Shirzais that some things were theirs and theirs alone. This moment between Maiwand and Laila was one of them. Instead, I closed my eyes to take in Maiwand's voice, deep and gravelly with emotion, spinning out the lyrical verses, enunciating the four words for home, the softly guttural consonants and fluid vowels at once familiar and foreign to me, as they had always been.

Acknowledgments

I hope you will forgive the length of this section, as I have worked on this project for nearly a decade and have racked up a debt burden beyond word-count and page limits.

Thank you to Aquarius Press / Willow Books, Publisher Heather Buchanan and Editor Randall Horton, and the prose judges of the 2013 Willow Books Literature Awards—Pauline Kaldas, Latha Viswanathan, and Ana-Maurine Lara—for believing in this book.

I was never formally trained as a literary writer, but was wildly fortunate enough to encounter great teachers as a working adult, especially Martha Gies, Richard McCann, and Barbara Esstman.

David Biespiel was the first person to tell me to write this book. Héctor Tobar was the second. They have both provided invaluable encouragement and advice over the years.

A writer is no one without good readers, and Amani Elkassabany and Vanessa Hua, in particular, have been unfailing and always revelatory with their readings of draft after draft. Michael Harris Cohen had a sharp eye when I needed it, and the congratulations or commiseration of a comrade in words when I needed those. Ami Sands Brodoff gave me the ingenious idea, among many other invaluable suggestions, to name each section of the book for a word for "home."

I started this project as a newspaper reporter in Portland, but finished it as a tenure-track assistant professor at American University in Washington, D.C. My AU colleagues have everything to do with the fact that I actually finished the book, and remained employed with a roof over my head while doing so. I owe more than I can find the words to express to Rodger Streitmatter and Amy Eisman. Larry Kirkman, Rose Ann Robertson, and Wendell Cochran, along with Rodger, made my unlikely second career a reality; Jill Olmsted and my School of Communication colleagues supported me as I remade myself from ink-stained hack into a teacher, scholar, and an author.

Back at the news organization formerly known as The Oregonian, Dee Lane and Michael Arrieta-Walden, each edited and supported me on the stories that laid the groundwork for this book, and taught me a great deal about reporting and writing, as did Joany Carlin. I owe George Rede a debt of gratitude for bringing me to The O. and Portland in the first place.

Lynne Perri donated her design skills and created the beautiful cover from Stephanie Yao Long's photography. Stephanie, in addition to gifting the image, was at my side through this entire story and was the journalistic collaborator and travel companion every reporter should get to have at least once in a lifetime. Corrine Duchesne generously gave me my author photo, shot while we were both in residency at Ragdale. Mary Bowerman made the invaluable Shirzai family tree.

Excerpts of this book appeared previously in the following journals: *Adanna, The Asian American Literary Review, Blue Earth Review, Consequence, Creative Nonfiction, The Lindenwood Review, Little Patuxent Review, Vela,* and *Waccamaw.* I thank the editors at these journals. Excerpts of this book have also appeared in the *Travelers' Tales* anthologies, the 2011, 2012, and 2013 editions of *Best Women's Travel Writing,* all edited by the wonderful Lavinia Spalding, *Best Travel Writing Vol. 9* (2012), and Lonely Planet Publishing's *Tales from Nowhere* (2006), edited by Don George.

I could not have completed this book without fellowships and residencies at the Corporation of Yaddo, Hedgebrook Writers in Residence, Virginia Center for the Creative Arts, Jentel Artist Residency, Ragdale, and Caldera. The Oregon Literary Fellowship and Soapstone provided vital early support for this project. And Thousand-Acres-wide appreciation to Mary Jane Edwards and Neltje at Jentel, for their extra-residency support of this book (and for playing a mean game of Scrabble, in the latter's case). A hug to Linda Williams for feeding me so well at Ragdale.

This manuscript was the second place winner in the 2011 Santa Fe Writers Project Literary Awards. I thank SFWP's Andrew Gifford and judge Alan Cheuse for the invaluable support at a critical juncture in my writing process.

I relied on countless articles and books on Afghanistan on my reporting and book-writing journey. Among the most influential were Larry P. Goodson's *Afghanistan's Endless War*, Artyom Borovik's *The Hidden War*, Ahmed Rashid's *Taliban*, and Bijan Omrani and Matthew Leeming's *Afghanistan: A Companion and Guide*. Edward Girardet and Jonathan Walter's *Afghanistan: Crosslines Essential Field Guides to Humanitarian and Conflict Zones* was not only an invaluable reference for travel in Afghanistan, but also an endlessly reliable source of facts, history, and figures. Tamim Ansary's *West of Kabul, East of New York*, Debra Denker's *Sisters on the Bridge of Fire*, Said Hyder Akbar and Susan Burton's *Come Back to Afghanistan*, Ruqaiyah Abdullah's *The Importance of Sisterhood in Islam*, and the poetry of Rumi, Rahman Baba, and Chen Li of Taiwan, as well as Edward Yang's film *Yi Yi* provided important cultural inspiration and insight. The newspaper reporting of *The New York Times*'s Carlotta Gall and T*he Washington Post*'s Pamela Constable, and the radio reporting of Sarah Chayes, formerly of NPR, in the earlier days of the War in Afghanistan, provided excellent source material, as did multiple articles from BBC, National Geographic, and other news media. Hedgebrook Research Librarian Evie Wilson-Lingbloom tracked down the invaluable geological history of the Hindu Kush for me. My father, Tien-Yuh Chuang, self-published a book, *T.Y.'s Journey*, that provided essential details and filled in gaps in his and our family's history.

To the real-life Shirzais, my enduring gratitude for letting me in and telling me your stories. Perhaps the final outcome—of my writing, and of all of our lives—is not what you had imagined, but everything I have written about you since 2001 was to this end: To tell a real story of a real family that resisted simple conclusions about Afghanistan, Afghans, Afghan Americans. It is only in complexity that those three will begin to be understood by those who would dismiss, occupy, or reduce to a caricature your country, homeland, and culture. Fellow writers who provided necessary critiques and cheerleading along the way include Valerie Miner, Robin Beth Schaer, Sandra Beasley, Gillian Gaynair, Ronault "Polo" Catalani, Gosia Wosniacka, Theresa Tate, the Portland ITHeWBeT writing group (Luciana Lopez, Vanessa Nix Anthony, Denise Renner, Laura Oppenheimer Odom, the originals, and those who followed), as well as Linda Friedlieb, who did more cheerleading than non-legal (as opposed to illegal) writing, but I know slings a mean pen herself when she's not pounding out briefs or retrieving binkies. Tracy Jan, Janie Har, and Emily Tsao, the former Portland Asian-girl squad, have kept me sane and laughing since 2000.

Finally, to my family, immediate and extended, especially my maternal grandparents Hsiu Mei Chung and Hsiu Chin Chen, this book is in many ways an appreciation and love poem to all of you. I wish my father the peace to understand how much he has shaped who I am in the most positive ways. I thank my sister-in-law Christine Luu for joining our imperfect family and making my brother happy—and a slightly better dresser. And to my mom, Ling-shin Chen, and my brother, Kelley Chuang, despite the fact that there is an Asian American memoir appropriately titled *I Love Yous Are for White People*, I have written every word in this book as an expression of love for both of you—through the bitter and the sweet.

About the Author

Angie Chuang is a writer and educator based in Washington, D.C. Her work has appeared in *Creative Nonfiction*, *The Asian American Literary Review*, and multiple editions of *The Best Women's Travel Writing*. She has received fellowships and residencies from Yaddo, Hedgebrook, Virginia Center for the Creative Arts, Ragdale, Jentel, and others. She is an Associate Professor of Journalism at American University's School of Communication.